The Collected Oz

Volume Two

Richard Neville et al

Edited by Ronnie Rooster
Typeset by Wally the Comedy Rhinoceros
Cover and Internal Layout by Hennis for Gonzo Multimedia
Using Microsoft Word 2000, Microsoft , Publisher 2000, Adobe Photoshop.

First edition published 2016 by Gonzo Multimedia

c/o Brooks City,
6th Floor New Baltic House
65 Fenchurch Street,
London EC3M 4BE
Fax: +44 (0)191 5121104
Tel: +44 (0) 191 5849144
International Numbers:
Germany: Freephone 08000 825 699
USA: Freephone 18666 747 289

ISBN: 978-1-908728-63-0

For Richard, Felix and Jim

OZ Obscenity Trial · Old Bailey London 1971

Trial begins 22 June
Any information contact Friends of Oz,
39a Pottery Lane, London W11. 01-229 5887.

Introduction

Back in the day, and this particular day was about twenty years ago, I was friendly with a notorious Irish Republican musical ensemble known as *Athenrye*, and particularly with their guitarist, a guy called Terry Manton. I was very angry about a lot of things at the time, and quite how drinking with various groups of slightly dodgy Hibernians actually made me feel any better I am not sure, but it seemed to have the desired effect.

On one of their albums there is a song about Éamon de Valera. For those of you not in the know, over to those jolly nice people at Wikipedia.

"Éamon de Valera first registered as George de Valero; changed some time before 1901 to Edward de Valera; 14 October 1882 – 29 August 1975) was a prominent politician and statesman in twentieth-century Ireland. His political career spanned over half a century, from 1917 to 1973; he served several terms as head of government and head of state. He also led the introduction of the Constitution of Ireland.

De Valera was a leader in the War of Independence and of the anti-Treaty opposition in the ensuing Irish Civil War (1922–1923). After leaving Sinn Féin in 1926 due to its policy of abstentionism, he founded Fianna Fáil, and was head of government (President of the Executive Council, later Taoiseach) from 1932 to 1948, 1951 to 1954, and 1957 to 1959, when he resigned after being elected as President of Ireland. His political creed evolved from militant republicanism to social and cultural conservatism.

Assessments of de Valera's career have varied; he has often been characterised as

Lucky man of our times

<u>Chorus</u>
He was loved he was hated he was cherished despised
There were rivers of tears when the chieftain he died
But love him or hate him I cannot decide
What to make of old Dev this man of our times."

And it ended up:

"Now Spain had it's Franco and France it's De Gaulle
We had our Dev and god rest his soul"

It has been many years since I bounced up and down in a weird Gaelic moshpit shouting "Tiocfaidh ár lá" and I strongly doubt whether I shall ever do so again. My foray into such things had more to do with my reaction to the way that I perceived that I had been treated by my family over my particularly scabrous divorce, than any genuine political fervour, although I thought then (and think now) that the British history in Ireland has not been our greatest or most honourable hour. However, today I have had that song going round and around my head, ever since I read an email from Tony Palmer telling me that Richard Neville had died at the age of 74, in Byron Bay, New South Wales, the Australian hippy enclave where Gilli Smyth breathed her last only a few days before.

Now I never met Neville. Our acquaintanceship was confined to two emails about five years ago when I was working on the new edition of Tony Palmer's *The Trials of Oz*. I exchanged a few more emails with Jim Anderson, and had no contact whatsoever with Felix Dennis, so I cannot really be called an insider of the *Oz* scene. But Neville came out with one of my favourite quotes from the counterculture: "There is some corner of a foreign field that is forever Woodstock", and was an undeniably major figure in that much maligned social movement.

He seemed to be someone who brought out strong reactions in people. Whilst I was working on *The Trials of Oz* I discovered that people were either terribly fond of the man or disliked him intensely. I never found anyone who was ambivalent towards him. Even after his death, as I sent emails around the usual suspects asking for their memories of him, most people refused to be drawn one way or the other, with those who had been friends with him at various periods of their lives being totally devastated that they had woken up this morning to a planet on which Richard Neville was no longer alive.

Me? I am no better than any of the others. I have no knowledge of him personally, and whereas I found large chunks of *Oz* unreadable, I was impressed by his book *Playpower* and in the passages about him in Tony Palmer's book he struck an undeniably heroic figure against the same sort of establishment malice which had (as alluded to above) turned me against my parents twenty years back.

His book *Hippy Hippy Shake* was entertaining, even though its hedonism left a slightly bitter taste in one's mouth, but I remember being told that the movie that was made from it was so bad that several of the major figures portrayed refused to let it come out. In July 2007, in a piece for *The Guardian*, feminist author Germaine Greer vehemently expressed her displeasure at being depicted, writing, "You used to have to die before assorted hacks started munching your remains and modelling a new version of you out of their own excreta." Greer refused to be involved with the film, just as she declined to read Neville's memoir before it was published (he had offered to change anything she found offensive). She did not want to meet with Emma Booth, who portrays her in the film, and concluded her article with her only advice for the actress: "Get an honest job."

So where is this taking me? I truly don't know, but if there had not been a Richard Neville, there might well not have been a *Gonzo Weekly* magazine. I first read *The Trials of Oz* whilst on holiday with my patients back when I was a Registered Nurse for the Mentally Subnormal [RNMS] nearly thirty years ago, and it was one of the sacred texts, together with *A Series of Shock Slogans and Mindless Token Tantrums* by Penny Rimbaud et al, that set me on the path that I am on now. But when I finally read the *Schoolkid's Oz*, I thought it was puerile bollocks, and was massively underwhelmed.

And I too find it hard to adjust to the fact that I have woken up this morning to a planet on which Richard Neville was no longer alive.

So, if I may:

"He was loved he was hated he was cherished despised
There were rivers of tears when the Oz editor died
But love him or hate him I cannot decide
What to make of old Nev this man of our times."

Hare Bol Mr Neville

GOD SAVE US
ELASTIC OZ BAND

OUTCRY AS OZ EDITORS ARE JAILED
Labour MPs attack 'act of revenge'
Daily Telegraph

FURY OVER OZ JAILINGS

Angry MPs join the wave of protest
The Sun

OZ: OBSCENE! BUT WHY THE FEROCIOUS SENTENCES?

Fury as three editors are jailed
Daily Mirror

Oz sentences — Labour MPs sign protest
Daily Express

COMMENT

MPs condemn OZ gaolings as 'Establishment revenge' *The Guardian*

Demonstrations and protests against 'Oz' jail sentences

'Shocked MPs protest: It looks like revenge'

STORM OVER OZ SENTENCES
Daily Mail

Apple are donating royalties on this record to the Oz Obscenity Fund

In Mitigation

So what was *Oz?* And why was it so important?

OZ was an underground alternative magazine. First published in Sydney, Australia, in 1963, a second version appeared in London, England from 1967 and is better known.

The original Australian *OZ* took the form of a satirical magazine published between 1963 and 1969, while the British incarnation was a "psychedelic hippy" magazine which appeared from 1967 to 1973. Strongly identified as part of the underground press, it was the subject of two celebrated obscenity trials, one in Australia in 1964 and the other in the United Kingdom in 1971. On both occasions the magazine's editors were acquitted on appeal after initially being found guilty and sentenced to harsh jail terms. An earlier, 1963 obscenity charge was dealt with expeditiously when, upon the advice of a solicitor, the three editors pleaded guilty.

The central editor throughout the magazine's life in both Australia and Britain was Richard Neville. Co-editors of the Sydney version were Richard Walsh and Martin Sharp. Co-editors of the London version were Jim Anderson and, later, Felix Dennis.

In early 1966 Neville and Sharp travelled to the UK and in early 1967, with fellow Australian Jim Anderson, they founded the London *OZ*. Contributors included Germaine Greer, artist and filmmaker Philippe Mora, illustrator Stewart Mackinnon, photographer Robert Whitaker, journalist Lillian Roxon, cartoonist Michael Leunig, Angelo Quattrocchi, Barney Bubbles and David Widgery.

With access to new print stocks, including metallic foils, new fluorescent inks and the freedom of layout offered by the offset printing system, Sharp's artistic skills came to the fore and *OZ* quickly won renown as one of the most visually exciting publications of its day. Several editions of *Oz* included dazzling psychedelic wrap-around or pull-out posters by Sharp, London design duo Hapshash and the Coloured Coat and others; these instantly became sought-after collectors' items and now command high prices. Another innovation was the cover of *Oz* No.11, which included a collection of detachable adhesive labels, printed in either red, yellow or green. The all-graphic "Magic Theatre" edition (*OZ* No.16, November 1968), overseen by Sharp and Mora, has been described by British author Jonathon Green as "arguably the greatest achievement of the entire British underground press". During this period Sharp also created the two famous psychedelic album covers for the group Cream, Disraeli Gears and Wheels Of Fire.

Sharp's involvement gradually decreased during 1968-69 and the "Magic Theatre" edition was one of his last major contributions to the magazine. In his place, young Londoner Felix Dennis, who had been selling issues on the street, was eventually brought in as Neville and Anderson's new partner. The magazine regularly enraged the British Establishment with a range of left-field stories including heavy critical coverage of the Vietnam War and the anti-war movement, discussions of drugs, sex and alternative lifestyles, and contentious political stories, such as the magazine's revelations about the torture of citizens under the rule of the military junta in Greece.

In 1970, reacting to criticism that *OZ* had lost touch with youth, the editors put a notice in the magazine inviting "school kids" to edit an issue. The opportunity was taken up by around 20 secondary school students (including Charles Shaar Murray and Deyan Sudjic), who were responsible for *OZ* No.28 (May 1970), generally known as "Schoolkids OZ". This term was widely misunderstood to mean that it was intended for schoolchildren, whereas it was an issue that had been created by them. As Richard Neville said in his opening statement, other issues had been assembled by gay people and members of the Female Liberation Movement. One of the resulting articles was a highly sexualised Rupert Bear parody. It was created by 15-year-old schoolboy Vivian Berger by pasting the head of Rupert onto the lead character of an X-rated satirical cartoon by Robert Crumb.

OZ was one of several 'underground' publications targeted by the Obscene Publications Squad, and their offices had already been raided on several occasions, but the conjunction of schoolchildren, and what some viewed as obscene material, set the scene for the *Oz* obscenity trial of 1971.

The trial was, at the time, the longest obscenity trial in British legal history, and it was the first time that an obscenity charge was combined with the charge of conspiring to corrupt public morals. Defence witnesses included artist Feliks Topolski, comedian Marty Feldman, artist and drugs activist Caroline Coon, DJ John Peel, musician and writer George Melly, legal philosopher Ronald Dworkin and academic Edward de Bono.

At the conclusion of the trial the "OZ Three" were found not guilty on the conspiracy charge, but they were convicted of two lesser offences and sentenced to imprisonment; although Dennis was given a lesser sentence because the judge, Justice Michael Argyle, considered that Dennis was "very much less intelligent" than the others. Shortly after the verdicts were handed down, they were taken to prison and their long hair forcibly cut, an act which caused an even greater stir on top of the already considerable outcry surrounding the trial and verdict.

The best known images of the trial come from the committal hearing, at which Neville, Dennis and Anderson all appeared, wearing rented schoolgirl costumes.

At the appeal trial (where the defendants appeared wearing long wigs) it was found that Justice Argyle had grossly misdirected the jury on numerous occasions and the defence also alleged that Berger, who was called as a prosecution witness, had been harassed and assaulted by police. The convictions were overturned. Years later, Felix Dennis told author Jonathon Green that on the night before the appeal was heard, the *OZ* editors were taken to a secret meeting with the Chief Justice, Lord Widgery, who reportedly said that Argyle had made a "fat mess" of the trial, and informed them that they would be acquitted, but insisted that they had to agree to give up work on *OZ*. Dennis also stated that, in his opinion, MPs Tony Benn and Michael Foot had interceded with Widgery on their behalf.

Despite their supposed undertaking to Lord Widgery, *OZ* continued after the trial, and thanks to the intense public interest the trial generated, its circulation briefly rose to 80,000. However its popularity faded over the next two years and by the time the last issue (*OZ* No.48) was published in November 1973 Oz Publications was £20,000 in debt and the magazine had "no readership worth the name".

We are publishing these magazines in these collected editions, partly as a tribute to the late Richard Neville (1943-2016) and partly because we believe that they constitute a valuable socio-political document reflecting the counterculture of 1967-74. This collection has been made available due to its historical and research importance. It contains explicit language and images that reflect attitudes of the era in which the material was originally published, and that some viewers may find confronting. However, we have taken the decision to blank out a very few images which would be seen as unacceptable in today's society.

Times have changed a lot in the past half century. The magazine's obsession with pornography, for example, has not stood the test of time very well, and some of the typography is so muddy as to be unreadable. Every effort has been made by the present publishers to clean up the typography, but in most cases it proved to be impossible, so we have left it as it was. The *Oz* readers of the late 1960s were unable to read it. Why should the present generation be any different?

Some of the pictures in the original magazine, especially artwork by Martin Sharp, was printed so it could fold out into a poster. We have therefore included these twice - as per the original pages so they can be read easily, and as extrapolations of the original artwork. Richard Neville stipulated in the extract from the notorious *Schoolkid's Oz* reproduced below that the material in these magazines could be used for any purpose, and we are taking him at his word.

Peace and Love

Ronnie Rooster
September 2016

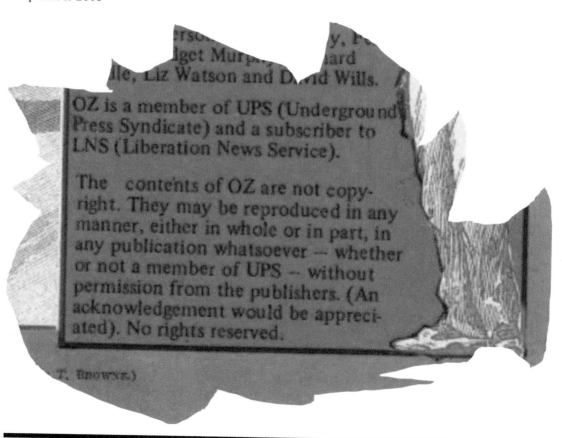

...rso... ...y, ...
...iget Murp... ...ard
...le, Liz Watson and D...id Wills. ...

OZ is a member of UPS (Underground Press Syndicate) and a subscriber to LNS (Liberation News Service).

The contents of OZ are not copyright. They may be reproduced in any manner, either in whole or in part, in any publication whatsoever — whether or not a member of UPS — without permission from the publishers. (An acknowledgement would be appreciated). No rights reserved.

T. Brown...)

man aged 45 picks you up on the road in his sports car, seems
asonably intelligent and personable and offers you £100 to
end the night with him. Would you accept?

at depends on how broke and randy you are at the time, of
urse, but for small town sociologist, Professor Jessie Pitts, it
uld tell a lot about his son.

ofessor Jessie Pitts is surveying hippies, and is currently comb-
g Formanterra, London and Paris with a fourteen page question-
ire. He is able to detect his subjects by "gut feeling" - a
flex response to the presence of hippies.

the top of the questionnaire is the warning, "This question-
ire is nosy but anonymous.....it is part of a research project
the radical wing of the youth movement. Much is written
out it but the true facts are very scarce indeed. Hence this
estionnaire, which cannot claim to ask all the right questions
...You may add whatever comments you think might in-
ease communication."

ommunication between whom? Pitts' questionnaire is chaotic,
nfused, incoherent. He asks whether 'hippies' (as identified
"gut feeling") believe in God, Psychiatry, Numerology,
eories of violent revolution etc. He asks questions about
enstruation, orgasm, whether drugs make sex better, the diff-
ence in technique between squares and hippies and he asks
hat many questionnaires seem to be heading towards but
ever quite ask: "When did you last have intercourse?"

is a plaintive, if useless, scholarly project, for Jessie Pitts.
e is a middle-aged, American college professor who has a
ersonal problem. His eldest son dropped out of Harvard and
ecame a hippie.

Once upon a time Jessie was a Trotskyite and later he served
time in the American Air Force. He admits, quite openly,
that life is a drag and that this is "right and proper". He sees
the American educational system as, very rightly, a process
where people can learn to tolerate being bored 75% of the time.
If you cannot learn to be bored then you become crazy and he
has designed a little table in his questionnaire to prove this.

It asks the subject to record any feelings of being outside his
body, living a scene he has lived before, feeling somebody is
watching him although nobody seems to be around, feeling
somebody is in his mind or to record any odd sensations of
lights and sounds.

Professor Pitts' reasons for doing the survey are to prove what he
already thinks. He will prove this quite easily because he has
designed his questionnaire with that state of mind, he will
analyse with that state of mind and he will interpret with that
state of mind. So if a balding sociologist aged 45 picks you
up on the road in his sports car, seems reasonably intelligent
and personable and offers you a 14 page questionnaire, ask him
for £100.

3

OZMOSIS

AND I'M SURE IT WOULDN'T INTEREST ANYBODY OUTSIDE OUR SMALL CIRCLE OF FRIENDS

Jim Haynes - seneschal of the Arts Laboratory, the hippies Burlington House, is having second thoughts about the all night marathon movies he runs Saturdays. Quite a few afficionados have found the 5/- admission makes it a cheap way to spend the night together.

The other Sunday, Digger Jim appeared at the head of the stairs, surveyed the ranks of somnolent cineastes, shouting, 'This place is not a fucking doss house', and threw everyone out.

Baroness Wootton of Abinger is studying the pharmacological, social and legal aspects of LSD and Cannabis, along with other members of the sub-committee of the Standing Advisory Committee on Drug Dependence, established by the Home Secretary and Health Ministers.

POISON

Maybe a change in the law is on the way. A BBC 2 team researching a programme on the cigarette giants have seen a test market pack of hash.

In Boston, terminal cancer patients are being administered LSD. "We found that to a certain extent we could relieve the fear of death,' says one of the researchers.

Mussolini's widow, Rachel, is claiming a war widow's pension. She stands to collect some $300,000 in back payments under an Italian law which awards pensions to winners and losers alike.
If the government fail to recognize her husband's self styled title of Marshal of the Empire, she will sue for a pension as the widow of a WW1 corporal.

Here, where we can have any radio we like like, as long as it's crack, the NDO may be wearing McLuhan T shirts beneath their Burton suits, but Radio One sure isn't wonderful. Meanwhile on the West Coast, in the sunshine, Los Angeles's 55th radio station, Radio Boss Angeles, call sign KHIP is tuned in and seems to turn on.

Imagination dead, imagine. Imagine Jimmy Young competing with this sort of sound:

'Turned on, Kay-HIP-ied Boss Angeles is tuned in to fifty thousand clear channelled watts of flower powered KHIP Brother Humble Mind here with sounds from deep beneath the KayHIP revolving antik atop the KayHIP studios in downtown Boss Angeles PLASTIC MAN LOVES YOU BABY KayHIP time 8:21 psychedelic seconds past the hour and 98.6 KayHIP mushrooming degrees on the outside. Hey Boss KayHIPped Flower Children! Get your Humble Mind Astrological LP and Hopi Life Map for just 25 Boss cents and a self addressed stamped envelope sent to: Ankh Trip Kit, KHIP, Boss Angeles, California, attn:Department Head. Do it now! Pssssychadellllliiick!!!!! A country gets the radio it deserves.

London's looned, Formantara's folded and S.E. Asia seems too far away- next place may be Prague.

Capital city of a communist countri that's never had a revolution, Prag on the verge of its first at the hand local and imported provos.

Everything illegal is available - ba a flourishing black exchange for do

Hard currency brings three times th official rate. Grass and dex are pus on the streets by characters straight of B movies. Trams run for a penny meals are 2/- and accommodation

Most money changes are also exper trading drugs for Czech crowns or and dealers stand nonchalantly on street corner looking exactly what Drug Squad man thinks a dealer sh look like.
Local films are out of sight, all sta owned, ten cents reserved seats. U fortunately there is a compulsory n

Stretch the legs and bend your right foot and keep it over the right thigh. Now extend the left leg and grasp the left foot with the right hand. When the left foot is firmly grasped, pull the right foot with the left-hand until you touch the left ear with it. Repeat this three times, alternately and then get out of Vietnam.

For those beyond the generation gap, posters outside Rank cinemas confirm the compensations of age.
ENJOY YOUR RETIREMENT AT THIS CINEMA IN THE AFTERNOON ALL STALLS SEATS 9d.
It is believed, Bertrand Russell, 94, has not so far taken advantage of Rank's offer to Look at Life.

Radio may be audio tactile in the Land of the Free but abortion law is still back in the days of the bike spoke. The Society for Humane Abortions, one of a number of groups which disseminate information about illegal abortions counsels its members to eat stewed prunes before and after the operation - in large quantities. In California on Monday an inventor died when his prune de-wrinkler blew up.

reel - they lock the doors. And C the accommodation agency do a r line; in castles to get stoned in.

own' down, 'Zeta' next to be z Despite genteel regrets expressed 'The Times' Ton's demise may ha

4

...VENTOR DIES AS PRUNE DE-WRINKLER BLOWS UP

...t to do with the fact that those alleged
...ife swappers in the sensational October
...ssue were in fact professional models...
...ho have had some difficulty since the
...ppearance of the issue explaining
...ey were not really wife swappers at
...II. Though it is believed their solic-
...ors pointed out to Town that a suitably
...arge sum might help them explain all
...hat much easier.

T T T

...eta have their problems too........

...lotho sensed danger. The tattooed eye
...elow her left breast glowed faintly.

...ow! Kerplunk! "Jeeps, it's my oldies, "
...he cried.

...lommy and Daddy are exceedingly wroth
...at Clotho unclothed. As she is not yet
...l and thus still their baby daughter,
...eta are in trouble. The next five issues
...lready printed which all contain un-
...lothed Clotho, may have to be junked.

...ead next week's 'Private Eye' for a
...low by blow of the demise of OZ.

INVENTOR

Reuben Tice
decided to give the
world the gadget it
had been waiting
for . . .

A machine for taking
the wrinkles out of
prunes.

But he died before per-
fecting his new scientific
contribution to society.

Cylinder

His prune de-wrinkling
machine exploded and
killed him yesterday.

Police found him dead in
his workshop in Monterey,
California. Around him
were the remains of his
shattered machine — and
half a pound of wrinkled
prunes in a cylinder under
high pressure.

Part of the machine —
the long valves — had
...year-old...

From JOHN SMITH
New York, Sunday

head-k... b... ...ly
Tice, a skilled engineer,
who ran an electrical business
in Monterey, was a well-
known ... as a creative
inventor.

He developed a method
of electrical heating which
is used in systems... ...
ing under-floor wiring.

He also perfected a store
to chill ...

It is... ...al that he may
have got his latest idea
from w... ...n... ...com-
mercial which discusses
the possibility of removing
wrinkles from prunes.

"It was an inquisitive
sort of guy," said Mr. Hill-
hun.

"It's the sort of thing
that would appeal to him.
Sadly, his latest final
experiments ended in
failure.

The police found on the
workshop floor against the
... prunes as still as wrinkled
as ever.

ANN BENSON

People keep disappearing. All those odd
characters the assassination brought to light so
pointedly—where are they now?

The lucky ones left Dallas, New Orleans,
country long ago and, we hope, have found rest in
pier climes, presumably terrestrial. Others, not so
lucky, dragged their heels or didn't leave their tracks
and thus had to stay in home territory, so to speak.

Well, coincidences—like accidents—will happen.
It's true that a fusty old London insurance firm did an
actuarial study and pronounced a thirty billion to one
chance that 20 people associated with the assassination could expire within three years, but you know the
British. Always depressing.

We won't for a moment dismayed by their lugu-
brious calculators' logarithms and the scratchings
and checkings of that poor old country fellow—what
was his name?—Penn Jones.

Because, no matter how much you know it's easy
to stay out of trouble if you just look sharp and learn
by the experience of others. The simple rule is: Don't
do the things they did.

Don't eat or drink anything that might contain ar-
senic. (R.I.P. Robert Perrin.)

Don't walk along highways traveled by speeding
cars. (R.I.P. Rose Cheramie.)

Don't pilot planes. (R.I.P. Hugh Ward.)

Don't look like your brother. (R.I.P. Eddie Bena-
vides.)

Don't fall into plate glass windows and cut your
throat. (R.I.P. Hank Killam.)

Don't let people inject you with things. (R.I.P. Jack

Don't help people (like Ferrie) learn how to inject
mice with cancer cells. (R.I.P. Dr. Mary Sherman.)

Don't let people like Ferrie do anything, in fact.
(R.I.P. David Ferrie del Valle.)

Don't get bombed, especially if people know you
take sleeping pills. (R.I.P. Dorothy Kilgallen.)

Don't aim a pistol behind your left ear with your
right hand. (R.I.P. J. Garrett Underhill.)

Don't get arrested by the Dallas police. (R.I.P. Lee
Oswald, Jack Ruby.)

Don't ask for a private cell if arrested. (R.I.P.
Nancy Jane Mooney.)

Don't sit around in police stations waiting for
news. (R.I.P. Bill Hunter.)

Don't stand around outside automobile showrooms
waiting for customers. (R.I.P. Albert Guy Bogard.)

Don't step out of the shower with your knife in
someone's chest. (R.I.P. Jim Koethe.)

Don't drive a car in Dallas. (R.I.P. William
Whaley.)

Don't drive a car outside Dallas. (R.I.P. Lee
Bowers.)

In fact, don't drive a car at all without checking
the wheel lugs first. Mort Sahl always remembers to
do this now, and he's still with us as this goes to press.

Oh, yes—and don't get between anyone and Jim
Garrison.

Postscript: We know it's a little hard to remember all these former people formerly connected with
the case. Their former identities are detailed in Garrison's Playboy interview (October '67) and Penn
Jones's Ramparts article (November '66).

Paul Lawson

Dear Sir,

I have just today obtained a copy of your filthy magazine and I have sent it straight to the Chief Inspector of Police in Glasgow to request that action be taken to ban the sale of this piece of stinking filth which you call a magazine. May God help you to see how you are helping to corrupt the youth of this nation. I would remind you that one day you will stand before Almighty God to give an account of your life.

Yours,
Rev. Gordon Kerr,
Clarkhill,
75 Clifford St.,
Glasgow S.W.1.

Dear Sir,

Your readers might be interested to know of a vicious smear campaign against several British subjects held in Geneva on charges of smuggling hashish. So few of our cargo amongst British holidaymakers stayed, and most while they are held in prison with little chance of communicating to the outside world about the charges, as all letters are heavily censored. During the five days they were kept without foods and were allowed very little sleep. One of these was whipped with a leather thong on the soles of his feet to try to extract information on his alleged international crime syndicate connections, and one of the girls was threatened with having her face screwed into the night bells. The Greek lawyers demand £750 for the defence of three of the prisoners, and so far £600 has been raised by friends. The Foreign Office have agreed to transmit this money, although they have been generally unhelpful throughout, and most of what has been done for these people has been done with difficulty by friends in this country.

A defence fund has been started, and any contributions would be gratefully received at Westminster Bank St. Ives, Huntingdon, cheques etc. being crossed GREEK FUND A/C.

Yours faithfully,
Elaine King,
Fenstanton
Huntingdon

Dear Sir,

We thank you for your order placed for typesetting items for your publication. We return herewith two letters sent for setting as we feel that we cannot ask our girls to undertake typing of this nature. We trust that you will find someone of a more broadminded nature.

Yours faithfully,
J.R. Chadsworth (Mrs.)
for and on behalf of
R. CHARLESWORTH & CO. LTD.
Fitzwilliam Street,
Huddersfield

Dear Sir,

Yours is a truly incredible publication and certainly destined to rank equally with any other avant-garde magazine of any other time! What makes me so sure as this judgement is the amazing difference in standards between the various articles.

Take your last issue for example. The Dylan analysis, The "Malik" interviews and the "Cock-up Spaniels" were all stimulating and profound. Yet what can be said for "Other Scenes" or "Blueprint for a beautiful conclusion"? The latter article was at its best vaguely amusing and hopeful but at its worst the most hopeless, muddled and slapdash piece of writing I have ever encountered. Please let quality take precedence over quantity and don't subject your faithful readers to any more of this.

Yours hopefully,
R.J. Hall,
St. Johns College
Oxford

Dear OZ,

With reference to Whitman and Cowley.

A manifesto as such is not required as this would be no more than the statement of a personal dogma on the part of a minority.

Some sort of gathering together of ideas would be useful to all as an aid to clarifying their own ideas. This need not be book of rules, nor even a highway code.

"Now, tell me young hippy. What really are your beliefs?"
"Well, um, err..."
"Love"
"Love?".
"Love."

I would suggest that the 'Love Generation' would find themselves somewhere among the manifestos of Marxists, Anarchists, Humanists and hinterhors. The order in which these are placed being varied to suit the individual.

Yours in the above order,

Michael Kenward,
30, Ferndale Road
Oxford.

Dear Sir,

Previous issues of OZ have generously offered advice on how to take trips and where to find travel agents. There's also the question of setting out on the longest trip of all.

The renewed euthanasia controversy centres on whether doctors ought to be allowed to despatch their more unfortunate old patients: a rather passive, bureaucratic approach.

Suicide might seem as easy as falling off a log, provided it's a high enough log. But human nature being

---

what it is, there are big snags. True, OZ readers are unlikely to be paralysed by traditional and conformist condemnations of suicide, whether deriving from Christianity (which sees despair as dishonest and blasphemy), or from a vague contempt for the weak, or from totalitarianism (which denies the individual any sovereignty over himself) or from the mechanical and empty promises of dogmatic optimism. And though suicide recently ceased to be a crime, your friendly neighbourhood bobby won't exactly lend you a helping hand.

Still, the bogey of suicide is fear. As Jean Gabin ponders in French Can Can: "Shall I jump from the window? I'm scared of heights. Shall I shoot myself? I can't stand noise. Shall I gas myself? It's been cut off". So he goes on living. Worse, the apathy, clumsiness and fear which make life unbearable also block off suicides requiring anger, skill and courage. By definition, those who most need to commit suicide, can't.

Or both it.

There's probably some truth in the generalisation that those suicide attempts which failed were secretly meant to. But the generalisation is too consoling to be convincing. Many suicide attempts fail, through clumsiness, or fear, or bad luck leaving the suicidist worse off than ever. To take two cases from among my acquaintances: A very quiet girl, too well-behaved for her own good, was strolling in the park one Sunday morning when, on an impulse, she climbed into the locked ladies' lavatory and drank half a bottle of Harpic. While delirious, she slashed at her face and throat with broken glass to try and cut away the pain, but survived this too. Her vocal chords were so badly burned that she'll never speak above a whisper. And she's still too well-behaved for her own good. Another girl, after an unhappy love-affair, took so many sleeping pills that she vomited them up and survived with a permanently damaged brain. Such failures often breed despair or acquiescence presenting a repetition of the attempt.

It's sometimes assumed that while suicide was alright for the Ancient Romans any such need has been abolished by modern medicine, the Welfare State and psychotherapy. But, despite the medical profession's phoney reassurances, the body rapidly acquires resistance to painkilling drugs, especially when, as is the rule, they are inexpertly or inadequately applied. You don't have to look far in the N.H.S. for cancer patients in constant agony from

---

JUST LIKE BEIN' BORN STONED

innumerable side-effects, all the way down to the fact that, bedsored as large as saucers make people scream with pain whenever they're moved (as they have to be, to stop them spreading). For all those proud old ladies and gentlemen, being stopped, pushed and humiliated in old folks' homes up and down the country, wouldn't suicide be a nobly Roman way out, and a revenge.

with deterrent possibilities? (Otherwise one can foresee the headline: "Home Secretary Closes Old People's Home After Anonymous Letter Alleges Executive Use Of The Cane"). Again, if Russian or Chinese bombs landed to windward of love in one fine evening, you'd need your ultimate fix to hand, no On The Beach nonsense about awaiting a Government Prescription. Or a sudden road accident might well deliver you, for years, or life, into the hands of doctors and nurses who stop you reading because books make a clutter, and they'd rather make you a docile vegetable for life than have any untidiness in the ward.

Spiritual reasons for suicide may be perfectly valid. What are you to do when year after year you come to love-ins, wearing your Perfumed Garden badge, and still nobody talks to you, because you really do have spiritual bad breath? and you deserve to be lonely? or if your mind is a losing battle against something that it can't help being disgusted by? "Shot? so quick, so clean an ending! Oh that was right led that was brave" said Housman, But isn't it still right if you're a coward and need, like Keats, to "cease upon the midnight with no pain"?

It's chemically feasible. Allied secret agents had cyanide in a false tooth if torture proved too much, and passed over in a few seconds.

The obvious snag is, of course, that an easy-suicide prescription is also an easy-murder prescription. Maybe the final solution is establishing Auto-Euthanasia Agencies. Here you file your application, wait a few weeks, are offered various alternatives (pot, a priest, "hospitality

---

No. 8   Jan 68

London OZ is published weekly monthly by OZ Publications Ink Ltd., 38A Palace Gate, Terrace, London W8. Phone 603 4205. FAR 1969

Editor: Richard Neville

Deputy Editor: Paul Lawson

Design: Jon Goodchild assisted by Virginia Clive-Smith

Company Accountant: Andrew Fisher

Advertising: Penny Service FLA 3785

Subscription etc: Louise Ferrier

Pusher: Felix Dennis

Photography: Keith Morris

Contributions: Martin Sharp, David Widgery, David Reynolds, Jim Anderson.

Distribution: Moore-Harness, 11 Lower St. London EC3. CLE 4882

Printing:

Printed Web Offset by Shell Dale (Carlisle) Ltd. Tel Carlisle 25/63/4

BANG! YOU'RE DEAD...

OTHER SCENES

Lively underground Newsletter published from wherever the Editor, John Wilcock, happens to be. Distribution 20 times a year in Europe & USA. Contributions to PO Box 8, Village Station, New York 10014, USA; 3grs or $10 for November 1967 to February 1969

WHAT IS THIS SKULL-SHAPE MACHINE? SOME WEIRD ILLUSION? BUT NOW ITS LIMBS ARE DISSOLVING! AND WHO IS THE ROBOT WHO APPROACHES? ARE YOU FRIEND OR FOE?

'prostitution" by dedicated dreamgirls); but where, if you insist, you are at last provided with a sweet, a small room, a single bed and a "Do Not Disturb" notice to hang, briefly, outside.

The pressure of over-population, and the increasing loneliness of everybody, especially the aged, make some such step just as inevitable as World War III.

Pending enlightened government action, it wouldn't be at all surprising if private enterprise decided to do what they can. Is there a potential black market in death pills? Can cyanide, or some equivalent, be prepared in the home, from, say, weedkiller? Facilities for instant self-disposal may be everywhere at hand, given a little medical or specialist knowledge, available on the grapevine. Could one hire a companion-executioner to despatch one in one's favourite circumstances, without loneliness?

If some of the energy devoted to extracting LSD from bananas, old socks or peals of thunder were devoted to pushing the idea of do-it-yourself euthanasia, it is quite probable that death, and life, would lose many terrors, and acquire new dignity.

RAYMOND DURGNAT
London, N.W.1.

Dear Sir
You recently published an article on McLuhan which I feel failed to cover his more interesting discoveries. When McLuhan says the medium is the message he is really saying that the medium is as important as the message in that it is the media, or the extensions of man which cause change irrespective of content or message.

He considers how the invention of electricity and then television has turned night into day and the world into a village.

Now when McLuhan talks about messages or content he often uses the word programme. He says that the media are being programmed with 19th century information. If on the other hand we are to use all the information discovered by 20th century philosophy and science in the various media we now possess he considers that much of our way of life would alter. He claims that the war in Vietnam would not be being fought for a start and that classrooms would be obsolete. Presumably the war in Vietnam might have been avoided by greater understanding of Marx (long suppressed by all media) and the classroom might become obsolete through the use of television at home and making the world into a playground rather than simply a medium for the motor car only.

I think a line from Peter, Paul and Mary's recent record sums up our present use of media.

'But if I really say it' the radio won't play it.'

McLuhan, like Vance Packard, is concerned with the way society is conned into unawareness. All that those ads want us to do is buy crap, and all TV wants us to do is believe LBJ is right.

McLuhan loves the consensus rather than the point of view. That is, he prefers collective involvement and understanding using information obtained from all sources and approached with rationality. That presumably includes government.

It is so wonder that McLuhan is hailed as a prophet of the new society because he has done a lot to smash the fucked up concepts of the old Victorian bourgeoisie.

With love and many thanks for all the information your medium contains.

Andrew Benway.
Brighton.

Dear Sir
I was recently given a copy of your issue No.6 by an ageing, hippy-manque friend of mine, who led me to believe that it was far superior to the well-known grub-sheet "Private Eye", I am deeply grateful to him, for he has saved me wasting 2/6 on the biggest load of boring old scrofulous crap to come my way in many a long day.

Comparison with the "Eye" is ludicrous, the layout and artwork present as much challenge to P.E. as a 1924 Bovril advert. Nasty microscopic type in a whiter shade of puce, with Art-Nouveau-cast-off artwork that was fashionable for decorating boutiques with about six months ago. And the content is laughable - compared with the "Eye's" wit and attack your contributors whine petulantly like a crowd of fifth-formers whose Headmaster has told them to stop wanking. LBJ, H.Wilson, etc., etc., etc., are unlikely to lose much sleep after reading "Oz". And while P.E. can take the piss out of the Beatles in their latter stages of flower-senility and out of venal con-men like the idiot-grinning Maharishi Whatsisname, you can only publish articles about being cool on acid under the guidance of "gurus". Gurus-schmurus!

As to be expected, you make O.K. noises about Vietnam, and I'm sure it's a great comfort to the Vietnamese peasants in their troubles to know that the Beautiful People smoking pot 3000 miles away in Katmandu are right behind them. However, I doubt whether the exploited classes of the world (such as the poor sods gathering the marijuana harvest for Haight-Ashbury under a 120-degree broiling sun at ½ an anna per hour) will go overboard for the far-reaching social reforms proposed by your anonymous bearded phony - keeping the Tube open after 11.30 p.m., abolishing TV licences and the £50 travel allowance, etc.

I doubt whether you will publish this - the double-breasted, cowbell-less businessmen who no doubt own or back Oz Publications Ink (Ltd., I notice, which can hardly be called "Beautiful" will hardly want the boat rocked while there is still a little juice to be squeezed out of the Hippy Cult and the secondary-modern dropouts who find it such a compensation for their mediocrity and personality-defects.

In conclusion, I enclose the Linsey Prize for Wet Loony of the Month (a Spontex "Moppit" sponge) and request that it should be shared equally by Chester Anderson and Daniel Sporri (the retread Dada-ist).

Yours faithfully,
A W Munsey
Barnes Common
SW 13

cc sent to the Eye, Greek St.

Dear Sir
You may have received the original of the enclosed copy letter.
It is a joke.
It was sent by a Mr. T. Nunn, of 2 Cavendish Mansions, N.W.10, and represents his views not mine.
Good luck with OZ.
Yours sincerely
Arthur Munsey
11 The Elms
Barnes Common S.W.13.
P.S. I am writing to Private Eye to the same effect.

Pot

A Message for Ingrid Superstar, age 17, 5'10", slender build, Caucasian. Distinguishing features: "blonde wavy shoulder-length hair" front tooth chipped.

Your father CANNOT forcibly put you into military school. He CANNOT take you away to Sonora, Oregon and put you into a foster home. Please come back. You do not have to see your father again. Everything's cool now. We all miss you. Your Staudel Imperial XV is here. Come back so we can play Monday Dew without feeling sad. Come back! Call your mother at home or at 8SL.

Anyone knowing the whereabouts of my daughter please call her mother, Mrs. Constance Von Schaeffer at (213) SL 5-9441 after 5 p.m.

SWEATERS
ONLY £2 POST FREE!

GREAT BRITAIN DRINKING TEAM

'MAY PEACE BE THROUGHOUT ISRAEL' MOSHE DAYAN

SEND NOW for warm, long sleeved, fleecy-lined sweaters with crew neck. Design can be worn on chest or back.
Sizes OS and M. Sent within five days, satisfaction guaranteed. Send £2 postal order, money order or cheque to R. R. Box ?? OZ Magazine 38A Palace Gdns Terrace London W8.

7

Fig. 5.—Assaying upon Charcoal.

NEW:FROM PENTHOUSE

A REVOLUTIONARY PROJECT IN MAGAZINE PUBLISHING

The PENTHOUSE FORUM provokes more interest, more correspondence and more stimulating discussion than any other feature in British publishing. It reflects this nation's sexual habits and interests, its fears and its fantasies, with an authentic cross-section of the individual men and women whose personalities and experiences form the basis of our social attitudes. It is human, intimate and, above all, candid! No other publication, conceived in our time, could have created a public platform of such liberal *and liberating* proportions.

Unfortunately, editorial and space limitations make it impossible to present the full panorama of enlightened argument and discussion that this section deserves. To overcome these restraints and to satisfy the mounting demand created by the innumerable letters that may never see print in these pages, the editors of Penthouse have prepared a totally different publication, a magazine devoted exclusively to readers' correspondence and the personalized discussions, comments, questions and answers arising therefrom. Published monthly, **Forum** Supplement will dramatically extend and develop the areas already covered in Penthouse while introducing many more not yet touched on. **Forum** Supplement will continue to promote that vital lifeline of communication between individuals and the society in which they live. It will act as a contemporary encyclopaedia of human conduct and experience, covering every aspect of our socio-sexual development as a nation, and providing—through the informed comment of social, theological, legal and medical authorities—THE FIRST PERSONAL ADVISORY SYSTEM EVER PUBLISHED ON THIS SCALE IN BRITAIN!

forum:

AVAILABLE ON SUBSCRIPTION **ONLY**

Initially, **Forum** Supplement will not be available to the public at large, but *only* on subscription and in strictly limited editions. The cost is £3 a year. To ensure that you do not miss a single valuable issue (each one of which will become an immediate collector's item) reserve your subscription NOW by filling in the coupon provided below:

SUBSCRIPTION COUPON : Please enter me as a subscriber to Forum Supplement for one year and send me 12 issues. I enclose cheque/cash/postal order for £3 (U.K. rate, postage included).

Send coupon with remittance to Subscription Department, Penthouse Magazine, 170 Ifield Road, London, S.W.10

PLEASE PRINT NAME & ADDRESS

NAME

ADDRESS

DESTINED TO BECOME THE MOST POWERFUL AND CONTROVERSIAL SOCIO-SEXUAL ARBITER OF OUR TIME . . . .

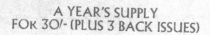

A YEAR'S SUPPLY
FOR 30/- (PLUS 3 BACK ISSUES)

People get annoyed because OZ isn't laid-out like the 'New Statesman'.

'You publish some extraordinary articles,' they say, 'but no one can take them seriously when they're printed upside down in circles in purple ink.'

Yes, they can. That's why OZ is banned at Parkhurst Prison. The library committee take OZ very seriously. The police in Picadilly take OZ seriously too. That's why they cautioned the newsvendor for selling OZ. (He doesn't sell it anymore.) And the man who sent the editor 24 cakes of Coal Tar soap takes OZ seriously. (We wish more people would send us soap – you can't have a bath with abusive letters.) Best thing to send us is 30/-.

Rubbish from past issues:

Michael X and the Flower Children . . . The Poetry of Bob Dylan . . . Letter from a Greek Gaol . . . The Coca Cola King of Kathmandu . . . Mark Lane's famous exposé of the BBC . . . Peter Porter's 'Metamorphoses' . . . Toad of Whitehall . . . The Great Alf Conspiracy . . . Mind Benders of Mayfair . . . How to take acid. . . .

Plus **Angelo Quattrochi** on De Gaulle, Italy and Russia . . . **David Widgery** on Guevara, the quality Sunday's, hippies . . . **Anthony Haden-Guest** on Girodias . . . **Ray Durgnat** on Marshall McLuhan, suicide and sex . . . **Jonathan Aitken** on himself . . . **Elizabeth Smart** on picking her nose.

OZ SUBSCRIPTION OFFER

12

'Russia, you have bread,

The Russian revolution began well. Killing the czar (God on earth), giving the land to the people who worked it (justice), and using man's resources for the common good, not for the benefit of the few (socialism).

The Russian revolution meant well. Confiscating churches and building schools. Asking that each man worked for the common good, each according to his capacities. Promulgating freedom of the mind and the freedom of love, the two freedoms which make man beautiful.

At first, the Russian revolution gave bread and shelter, as much as it could, but soon took away freedom of mind and freedom to love.

In the beginning it was a revolution by the people (peasants and workers) for the people. It developed into a revolution for the Russian people, made by the party.

He who thinks that the Russian revolution was made so that half a century later baggy trousered and neck tied Russians could live in pigeon holes called apartments and read Pravda, and that Russian housewives could raise well behaved and reasonably fed brats who will land on the moon; deserves to be shot by a firing squad of underfed, barefoot South Americans, using American rifles and Russian bullets. Save the Chinese ammunition.

Marx's analysis was correct; only, history side-stepped it by making the first revolution in a predominantly agricultural country. Instead of the workers taking power and developing socialism from the correct beginning: the appropriation of the means of production by the workers and

but no ★ Roses'

Angelo Quattrocchi.

their representatives, the Russian revolution had to rely on party cadres. Trotsky's forced exile was the beginning of the end. The party elite soon became the party apparatus and the substitute for democracy by the people.

Stalin decided that the Soviet Union could be built; but it had to be the Soviet Union first, and socialism second.

Sad, that the first socialist revolution had to begin in such a country. Bad, that Lenin died so soon.

Because the revolution is made by those who need it, as the Russians did fifty years ago. They saved their revolution from the enemies surrounding them, well and good. Then they were supposed to start building a socialist state. Millions of Stakhanovs (Stakhanov is the mythical worker who worked harder than anybody else — a hero of production) slaved in good faith, convinced that one ounce of Russian steel was good for the people. But he was cheated and discovered it in the early thirties. He discovered that one ounce of steel was good for Russia, yes, but not necessarily for the people. In the effort to make Russia impregnable socialism was thrown overboard. It was either grim work or Siberia — or both.

WAS IT NECESSARY?
WAS IT INEVITABLE?

The production of red flags has risen with every quinquennial plan, comrades, over the last fifty years; they could almost clothe the naked of the world.

Maybe Marx was wrong, and the true proletariat is not the working class which has accepted the crumbs of industrialized systems, east and west alike, but the peasants. The peasants who made the Chinese revolution, in spite of Stalin, against Stalin. The peasants who fight in Vietnam, the peasants who die of starvation in our name.

"Let us produce more" sing the songs of the new era, bastard socialism, so there will be plenty for us, and surplus for India. That Russian comrades, is not socialism.

Yes, there are historical necessities. Like the destruction of the anarchists in the Spanish Civil War. Like displaying Stalin's photograph and silencing Eisenstein. Like supporting Chang Kai Shek instead of Mao, like handing out rhetoric with the one hand and purges with the other.

And yet your people, who couldn't be trusted to talk, who couldn't be trusted to read, who couldn't be trusted to think, fought Nazism with the desperation of the just; with the determination of the simple.

And then a new Machiavellian god made its appearance at Hiroshima, a god of death and vengeance, an all embracing god spelling total annihilation, justifying all quiesence.
BUT DOES IT?
When the state which called itself socialist was strong enough not to be afraid of its life (it took forty years), when Stalin receded rapidly into the shadows of the dark past, then you discovered the perfect justification of your betrayal. The internal sins were no more, you proclaimed, they belonged to Stalin and to Stalin only. But atomic disaster called for prudence, injustice couldn't be eliminated, only outwitted.

Therefore, "let us produce more," you said, under the umbrella of the bomb, which we have as well as you, we will bury you in tons of butter, which we now produce for the benefit of our children who are Russian and therefore socialist. Elegant silver silhouettes guarantee our might, let's even try to get to the moon; who gets there first will be the winner, we'll celebrate the day by distributing rice and rifles at reduced prices, a token of our associated concern for the state of the rest of the world.

But in the rice fields of China, other peasants have rediscovered simple words, words carefully buried within the Soviet encyclopedia, murdered in camps in Siberia, the grave of Russian socialism.

Old and simple words like: redistribution of land, socialism for the oppressed, all over the world. "Too late," said the Russians, "we will help you, but be reasonable, the Godbomb makes it all impossible. You have made it by yourself, when no-one was watching, but the others have to wait, we cannot take the risk, frankly, it's become too dangerous."

"And what about Algeria? what about Cuba?" asked the Chinese, asked the poor.

"But" says the voice of Russian reason, "look what has happened to the Congo, to Indonesia — you must all wait until we are good and ready."

And the Vietnamese are waiting, and the Indians are waiting, and the South Americans are waiting, and Che Guevara is dead. And Russia, the socialist Mother Russia, bleeding for her children discovers a new way, a pacific way.

The peasants say, "Every time we rise the bombs fall — either we don't have enough rice or we have the bombs falling on our heads, what sort of umbrella is that?" and they say, "The godbomb was supposed to be impartial but we can't afford to be impartial, we can't afford to wait".

Every time a peasant dies of an American bullet, Mother Russia's heart bleeds, but indeed she knows that there is only one way now, to produce more. More butter to bury her enemies, and more cannons so the enemies will respect her. Then she can afford to send some to her poor relations in distress, Vietnam — yes, Guatemala, Bolivia, Colombia, Venezuela — no.

This is what is necessary if you want to build socialism in one country — this is how it started:
Take over the economy so it doesn't run for profit, and choose the priorities, hospitals before cars, schools before tanks, (war is profitable, that is why a capitalist country is, so they say, 'war mongering', and a socialist country, even Russia, is not). Who chooses the priorities? It should have been the people, but, in Russia, it was the party. The party which represented the people in the beginning, but fatally lost them. Stalinism was an aberration, a direct consequence of the lack of democratic decision.

Everybody knew that socialist Russia had to be defended. They defended splendidly at first, the peasants and workers who became the people's army over night and defeated the professionals, the White Army and the mercenaries from every Western country.

Socialism calls for public ownership of land and industry as the one basic measure to implement social justice. It is not an end but the beginning. If they believe in what they are doing, and participate in the decisions, the Stakhanovs are countless. One way pointed to the continuation of the revolution, the other to the strengthening, at all costs, in the name of socialism, of the Russian state. When people didn't count the hours they worked (the Stakhanovs — and now the Chinese workers and peasants) they were already in a state of socialism.

As soon as enough food is produced, make it free, enough houses, make them free. When basic needs are satisfied people give their best, the meaning of property (its mine, its yours) shrinks and eventually has no meaning at all. Luxury is a driving force only where there is poverty, or fear of poverty.

Russia has enough to make food and shelter and public transport free, so that everybody could participate with joy, (yes, they would, work is only what you are compelled to do). But they have not done it. They do nothing. On the contrary. They have reintroduced substantial differences of distribution and have made money artificially important. Grim, grey idiots perpetuating a party machine bent on its survival, paying lip-tribute to the struggles going on in the world, measuring the stock market of fear, sparing bullets for the Vietnamese. Proclaiming that production is the means, and consumption its end.

If only they had made bread and shelter and travel free, and love with no strings. . . . . .

Fifty years, fifty years, and countless defeats, and humiliations, and deaths, and miseries, and fears, to defend the socialist state which hasn't even begun, to become good consumers and silent workers. To become the sort of people who want cars and a good career for their children. In the name of socialism. Where are the soviet writers? where the soviet poets? Where the new arts which should have come from the new man? Where is the new man?
The revolution was made for joy and beauty, for bread and roses, so that a man could go hunting in the morning, fishing in the afternoon and recite poetry at night (Marx, only slightly re-edited). Fifty years later it is a mean, miserable society,

pompous and worried, selfish and unimaginative, capable, even, of the last sparks of the western world, unashamed of imitating its values.

The richest capitalist countries, with their absurd over production and their supreme unconcern for the oppressed, already contain the seeds of their own destruction. The supreme irony, there where capital is god and profit his prophet, of the young — who refuse the unnecessary, pointing to the qualities of poverty and survival. Ask the philosopher what you need to take with you, a cup, for water? Not necessary, your two hands will suffice. Through meanders of error and ideological capitulation the revolution that-should-have-been has bred a country of the most pallid, anaemic and sad bourgeois. Russia has accomplished, fifty years after, what no other country will ever reach — a perfect bourgeois state.

Where has all the hate gone? The hate of injustice, the hate of poverty, the hate of oppression, the hate of money. They parade it on the first of May in the missiles and guns which rid them of guilt and fill us with fear.

Where has all the love gone? The love of humanity, the love of roses, the love of life, to each according to his needs? Gone into the classrooms where knowledge is a means of achieving status, yes, status — in a socialist country.

What happened to the dreams of free love, of sexual liberation and the obliteration of the family? And why, fifty years later, do they still need religion, the opium of the masses?

Oh yes, it will take a long time, such a long time that we will all be dead before we will have a chance to judge.

Meanwhile, look at that portrait of the young Russian mother, baby in one arm shovel in the other, proudly leading you to the future — and if you study and work and behave you'll have a better apartment than your neighbour, in secula seculorum.

MAN WANTS TO BE KIND, ONLY, HE CAN NOT

Because I have to rise in life, because my superiors are difficult, because one has to eat, because I have a mother, a sister, an aunt, a child, a car, a mortgage, a party card, a position, a dacha.

Because I haven't a house, I haven't enough to eat, most of my children die, there isn't enough water for the village, the crop this year was bad, the taxes are too high, the moneylender has taken away my cow, because we don't know what will happen to us.

Russia, you have bread, but no roses. Russia, man isn't kinder to man, and fifty years have passed. Will the Chinese do better? Will they do it quicker? Their kind of hate seems right — their time for love hasn't come yet. Or should we wait for new signs among the rabble of the overfed, because there where the world is craziest, the new buds will appear.

Russia, the sleeping beauty who slept too long, woke up dead. As dead as all the revolutions-which-should-have-been and were not, dead as all the loves which should have blossomed and did not, dead as the hopes of people who still have to fill their bellies, dead as the hopes of people who still must fill their hearts.

And look at you. When evening falls in Moscow, they dream of coloured telly, an American sized screen, where Ivan could perform once more, his Chekov, and feel gratified.

And at Zima, the remotest village, the mujik now working in the state co-operative, tells himself that he is happier than his father, which he is, but wonders, when the vodka has been good, why his eternal wife nags, why life is so drab in his socialist head, in his socialist family, in his socialist country.

WHAT RUSSIA COULD DO TODAY

1) free food, free houses, free transport.
2) abolish marriage, abolish the party card.
3) complete freedom of speech and publication.
4) the highest paid shouldn't get more than double of the lowest paid. Money mustn't be an incentive.
5) no compulsory political training in schools, it's mummyfied, waste.
6) free cinemas, theatres, books and newspapers.
7) referendums on major issues (Vietnam war) with alternative solutions stated.

THE ONLY THING WHICH NEED BE COMPULSORY, AS FROM NOW, IN RUSSIA, IS WORK

8) in order to avoid excessive specialization and formation of elites and castes everybody should work at a factory or field, for a small part of the year, say two months.

THAT IS BECAUSE SOVIET MAN DOES NOT PARTICIPATE IN STATE DECISIONS AND IN THE BUILDING OF SOCIALISM AND THEREFORE IS STILL SELFISH AND CONSIDERS WORK A CURSE, NOT A PRIVILEGE.

THE ULTIMATE AIM OF SOCIALISM IS TO ELIMINATE MONEY

(everybody will take what they need, no less no more, and they will restrain themselves for the sake of the community, if necessary) AND STATE (the goals will be the same for all man, socialist man will do no harm to his fellow man, he will not have any interest in doing so, self-discipline will be more than enough, no need for the state and its apparatus then).

If you can have what you need and want (food, shelter and love) you will not need to possess (possess what? a better car, a better baby?). Start from there, we will very quickly need to own, it will start from commodities (sleeping bags I can't think what.)

Do you have to own the woman (man) you love? It will be also free love, love without ownership. What chains it down now? the limitations imposed by the family, and the selfishness (ownership) necessary to survival. Jealousy is selfishness applied to man's sentiments.

That is why communities which do not respect money-ownership, see the hippies, are said to be 'promiscuous'. That is also why they are unconsciously revolutionary. Take the basic needs only, refuse the rest, and you'll discover freedom of the sentiments. But it's upside down, you'll have to have a society which frees from hunger and injustice first.

17

Poems — Stories — Photos — Posters

LONDON MAGAZINE - 5s. Monthly

is blowing in the mind

Fly high and follow

the poets who matter

the critics that count

Pop — Books — Painting — Plays

Buildings — Sculpture — Poetry — Films

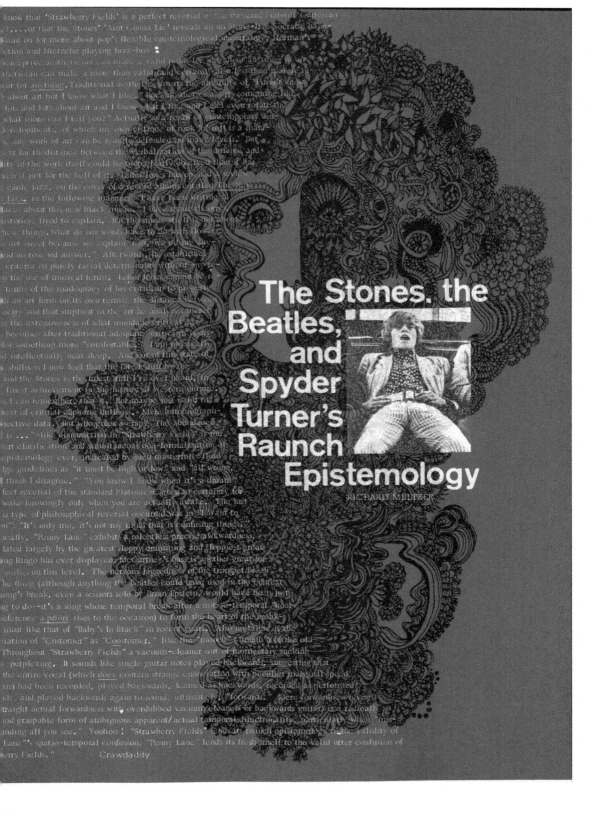

The Stones, the Beatles, and Spyder Turner's Raunch Epistemology

RICHARD MELTZER

know that 'Strawberry Fields' is a perfect reversal of the standard Platonic-Cartesian of . . . or that the Stones' 'Aint Gonna Lie' reveals an un-Stone-like Socratic hang. Read on for more about pop's flexible epistemological uncertainty, Herman's ction and Nietzche playing fuzz-box ≩

ceptive aesthetician can make a valid point for practically anything, this stician can make a more than valid and extremely less than invalid nt for anything. Traditional aesthetics asserts the diversity of "I don't know about art but I know what I like." Rock aesthetics asserts something like lots and lots about art and I know what I like, and I can even relate the what more can I tell you?" Actually, as a result of contemporary aes-developments, of which my own critique of rock itself is a manif n, any work of art can be readily defended on many levels. But ext for the distance between the verbalization of the aesthetic and ity of the work itself could be more easily observed than it has ven if just for the hell of it. LeRoi Jones has operated in avwr garde jazz, on the cover of a record album entitled The New Jazz, in the following manner: "I have been writing eas about this new black music. I have made theori istories, tried to explain. But the music itself is not about fe's things. What do our words have to do with flowers? s not sweet because we explain it so. We'd as soon nd no rose wd answer." Afterward, he establishes criteria on purely racial determinants without any ref o the use of musical terms. LeRoi Jones cannot be re terms of the inadequacy of his criticism to present h an art form on its own terms; the distance betwee oetry and that implicit in the art he analyzes is t s the extensiveness of what mundane critical des becomes after-traditional-adequate criticism is dis for something more "comfortable." I am physically d intellectually near sleep. And out of this state of s dullness I now feel that the latest stuff by the and the Stones is the finest stuff I've ever heard, th finest achievement in the history of W. tern culture s I can remember, that is. But maybe not valid in t text of critical euphoric dullness. Mere autobiograph-jective data, but who gives a crap. The abundance is . . ."-like construction in "Strawberry Fields" is the ert clarification and simultaneous non-formalization of epistemology ever, indicated by such masterfull fluid lge guidelines as "it must be high or low" and "all wrong, think I disagree." "You know I know when it's a dream fect reversal of the standard Platonic-Cartesian certainty for wake knowingly only when you are actually awake. The last is type of philosophical reversal occurred was in "I want to u"; "It's only me, it's not my mind that is confusing things. ically, "Penny Lane" exhibits a relentless precise awkwardness, lated largely by the greatest sloppy drumming and sloppiest great ng Ringo has ever displayed, McCartney's bass is another great tor nuffier on this level. The nervous jaggedness of the trumpet break he thing (although anything the Beatles could have used in this context ong's break, even a scissors solo by Brian Epstein, would have been just g to do--it's a song whose temporal break after a not-so-temporal "hour ference a priori rises to the occasion) to form the heart of the break-most like that of "Baby's In Black" in recent years. Also nostalgic is the ation of "Customer" as "Coostomer," like the "moooo" (literally) of the old Throughout "Strawberry Fields" a vacuum-cleaner sort of momentary sucking s perplexing. It sounds like single guitar notes played backwards, suggesting that the entire vocal (which does contain strange enunciation with peculiar marginal speed ons) had been recorded, played backwards, learned as backwards, recorded as performed rds, and played backwards again to sound, ultimately, "forwards." Mere forwardness (even traight actual forwardness with overdubbed vacuum cleaners or backwards guitar) is a radically nd graspable form of ambiguous apparent/actual temporal directionality, particularly when "mis-nding all you see." Yoohoo! "Strawberry Fields" lends its raunch epistemology to the validity of Lane"'s spatio-temporal confusion: "Penny Lane" lends its fresh smell to the valid utter confusion of erry Fields."   Crawdaddy

Silver Rings

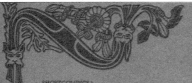

COME UNDERWATER

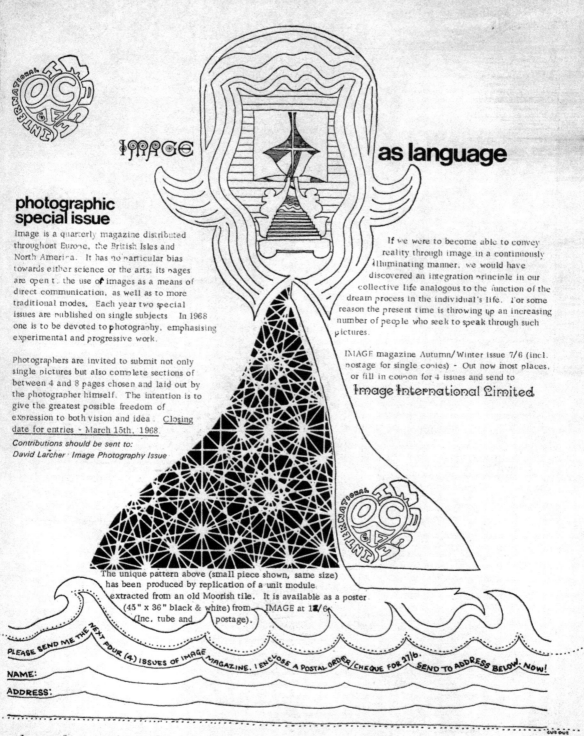

IMAGE as language

photographic special issue

Image is a quarterly magazine distributed throughout Europe, the British Isles and North America. It has no particular bias towards either science or the arts; its pages are open t. the use of images as a means of direct communication, as well as to more traditional modes. Each year two special issues are published on single subjects In 1968 one is to be devoted to photography, emphasising experimental and progressive work.

Photographers are invited to submit not only single pictures but also complete sections of between 4 and 8 pages chosen and laid out by the photographer himself. The intention is to give the greatest possible freedom of expression to both vision and idea. Closing date for entries - March 15th, 1968.

Contributions should be sent to:
David Larcher : Image Photography Issue

If we were to become able to convey reality through image in a continuously illuminating manner, we would have discovered an integration principle in our collective life analogous to the function of the dream process in the individual's life. For some reason the present time is throwing up an increasing number of people who seek to speak through such pictures.

IMAGE magazine Autumn/Winter issue 7/6 (incl. postage for single copies) - Out now most places, or fill in coupon for 4 issues and send to

Image International Limited

The unique pattern above (small piece shown, same size) has been produced by replication of a unit module extracted from an old Moorish tile. It is available as a poster (45" x 36" black & white) from IMAGE at 12/6 (Inc. tube and postage).

PLEASE SEND ME THE NEXT FOUR (4) ISSUES OF IMAGE MAGAZINE. I ENCLOSE A POSTAL ORDER/CHEQUE FOR 27/6. SEND TO ADDRESS BELOW. NOW!

NAME:

ADDRESS:

Image International Limited, 20 Gerrard Street, London W.1. Telephone GErrard 0281

Other Scenes

lican, Americans for Democratic WHAT?)

It is obvious to most of the world by now, if not in America itself, that the United States stands behind most fascist dictatorships, most countries where a strong minority (particularly the military) is in power. It is obvious, therefore not only that these dictatorships be defeated — almost certainly by armed force — but that THIS American government is the evil octopus that must be wiped out, or at the very least totally removed from office. There is still too much of a tendency for American "liberals" (also known as judas goats) to feel that something can be done through polite representation requests. Bullshit. Johnson and his shithead aides are murderous bullies who, like all bullies, respect only toughness.

"Power is seized and held in the capital", writes Debray, "but the road that leads the exploited to it must pass through the countryside." And he goes on to point out that if you want success and not just dialectics you must remember the historical priorities. "The people's army will be the nucleus of the party and not vice versa. The guerilla force is the political vanguard and from its development a real party can arise.

"That is why the guerilla force must be developed if the political vanguard is to be developed."

YOU CANNOT BUILD ENOUGH PRISONS... OR DIG ENOUGH GRAVES... TO STOP THE GUERRILLA'S VIOLENCIA! VIVA LA REVOLUTION!

Revolution in the Revolution

Regis Debray's

book will remain as a blueprint for revolution for at least a decade to come. Historically it occupies much the same position as Mein Kampf once did: a plan of action—a prediction and projection of just what is going to happen in the world for the next ten years or so. And, like Mein Kampf, it will probably be largely ignored because of the context in which it is presented.

This is the age of the revolutionary, as even the dimwitted fatcats who rarely leave their airconditioned homes are aware. But revolution, suggests Debray, must be total not just a coming to terms—a compromise— with the enemy. Who is the enemy? Obviously the people who own most of the world's material possessions and intend to keep them with the help of cops, armies, politicians and fascist-type publishers—all the repressive structure that will try to kill and at least jail anybody who tries to take it away from them.

In Latin America, whereof Debray writes, country after country is in the hands of a greedy few while hundreds of thousands work and starve to allow these inequities to continue. Debray's thesis, "Revolution In the Revolution" (Monthy Review Press, $4), says in effect that resistance movements too often take the form of self-defense. A group of exploited tin-miners sick of being hounded and badgered in their remote company town decide to fight back to earn the right to be left in peace, for example. They earn this right—for a time—but at the cost of being marked down for future extermination or repression. They have acted to secure their perimeter, only to make it clear to the bosses that they are contained within that perimeter and can be polished off at any convenient time.

The answer? Total guerilla warfare—to break out and destroy the enemy, in this case the military government. It is useless to get hung up on a political structure and try to negotiate, as all anti-Vietnam war protestors should have realised by now. (The recent American for Democratic Action congress decided that although they were opposed to the war they were even more opposed to LBJughead losing to a Repub-

"That is why at the present juncture the principal stress must be laid on the development of guerilla warfare and not on the strengthening of existing parties or of the creation of new parties.

"That is why insurrectional activity is today the number one political activity."

And that is why, incidentally, Debray is posing such a threat to military and police-state governments. He says that each country must find its own type of revolution but these are the general theoretical principles. And his knowledge comes from the experience of Castro and Guevara who inevitably will see in a score of Latin American countries the revolution that they earlier brought to Cuba.

it or because they're happy to keep their names in print for any reason at all.

A typical Warhol column item:

43-23-37 XXXX, was cornered by three vicious lesbians in the women's washroom of XXX's the other night. We got the story from one of the lesbians. It went like this: 'You dropped XXXXXXXX because you don't like men, honey?' Then they advanced on her until she was backed into a stall with the door locked. XXXX, in case you didn't know it, is not a real big girl even though she looks statuesque, and was scared for

The NY Times quoting a recent sociological survey on hippies home life came to the conclusion that hippies' kids tend to ignore their parents rather than fight with them. 'How can you rebel sexually against a mother who will be happy to fit you for a diaphragm at the age of fourteen?' one asked.

under- ground confiden- tial: world wide exclusive

by Andy Warhol

Andy Warhol is experimenting with a new medium - the run of the mill scandal column. But like all things Warhol does there is a difference. By taking an established form and converting it, he is proving once again the essential interchangeability of forms in the present social culture.

His avenue of expression is via a new New York tabloid, Downtown, whose major content is gossip columns about the Manhattan art and social set. Andy's column at first appears to be merely a replica of the type of thing that the sex and scandal tabloids have been running for years. The kind of crap that everybody knows is made up in the office, libelling movie stars and other ego-happy figures who never bother to sue either because it isn't worth

her life. She really got the chills when one of the lesbians started climbing over the top of the stall. Just then another woman who is really a female impersonator came into the washroom and XXXX was able to leave with her virtue intact. . . .

In the Warhol version the XXXX XXXX's are filled in with the name of Andy's current super star, Viva, but apart from that every single word of the item appeared in another tabloid with some other name appearing where the X's are. Naturally enough, Downtown's readers don't know the background so they come to either of two conclusions: 1 That Warhol writes as lousy a scandal column as everybody else, or 2 That the items are true!

≈ Aquarius

Every New Yorker inhales toxic materials to the equivalent equivalent of smoking 38 cigarettes a day according to Moment in the Sun, a newly published book which is significantly subtitled A Dial Report on the Deteriorating Quality of the American Environment.'

More and more American heads who want to avoid the draft have been joining the Neo American Church which wants to legalize acid as a sacrament. Once a member you can apply for ordination as a minister and theoretically be exempt.

Win...
£100!

Edward
de Bono

I am offering a prize of £ 100 for the best example of the use of lateral thinking sent to the publisher of the book by January 1st. Any number of examples may be submitted. They may take the form of a story, an anecdote or any other capsule form. The examples may be from personal experience, from literature or specially designed. Should the examples be good enough the best ones will be published as an anthology so the source of borrowed examples must be fully stated.

Many years ago when a person who owed money could be thrown into jail, a merchant in London had the misfortune to owe a huge sum to a money-lender. The money-lender, who was old and ugly, fancied the merchant's beautiful teenage daughter. He proposed a bargain. He said he would cancel the merchant's debt if he could have the girl instead.

Both the merchant and his daughter were horrified at the proposal. So the cunning money-lender proposed that they let Providence decide the matter. He told them that he would put a black pebble and a white pebble into an empty money-bag and then the girl would have to pick out one of the pebbles. If she chose the black pebble she would become his wife and her father's debt would be cancelled. If she chose the white pebble she would stay with her father and the debt would still be cancelled. But if she refused to pick out a pebble her father would be thrown into jail and she would starve.

Reluctantly the merchant agreed. They were standing on a pebble-strewn path in the merchant's garden as they talked and the money-lender stooped down to pick up the two pebbles. As he picked up the pebbles the girl, sharp-eyed with fright, noticed that he picked up two black pebbles and put them into the money-bag. He then asked the girl to pick out the pebble that was to decide her fate and that of her father.

Imagine that you are standing on that path in the merchant's garden. What would you have done if you had been the unfortunate girl? If you had had to advise her what would you have advised her to do?

What type of thinking would you use to solve the problem? You may believe that careful logical analysis must solve the problem if there is a solution. This type of thinking is straightforward vertical thinking. The other type of thinking is lateral thinking.

Vertical thinkers are not usually of much help to a girl in this situation. The way they analyse it, there are three possibilities:

1. The girl should refuse to take a pebble.
2. The girl should show that there are two black pebbles in the bag and expose the money-lender as a cheat.
3. The girl should take a black pebble and sacrifice herself in order to save her father from prison.

None of these suggestions is very helpful, for if the girl does not take a pebble her father goes to prison, and if she does take a pebble, then she has to marry the money-lender.

The story shows the difference between vertical thinking and lateral thinking. Vertical thinkers are concerned with the fact that the girl has to take a pebble. Lateral thinkers become concerned with the pebble that is left behind. Vertical thinkers take the most reasonable view of a situation and then proceed logically and carefully to work it out. Lateral thinkers tend to explore all the different ways of looking at something, rather than accepting the most promising and proceeding from that.

The girl in the pebble story put her hand into the money-bag and drew out a pebble. Without looking at it she fumbled and let it fall to the path where it was immediately lost among all the others.
'Oh, how clumsy of me,' she said, 'but never mind—if you look into the bag you will be able to tell which pebble I took by the colour of the one that is left.'

The above story is a good example of the use of lateral thinking. Many people on hearing the expression have an instinctive understanding of the nature of lateral thinking. Few use it consciously and deliberately but many recognise occasions when it has proved effective.

Vertical thinking has always been put forward as the only effective form of thinking — at least for scientific and practical affairs. Vertical thinking is the traditional logical, sequential, mathematical, Aristotelian type of thinking. But you cannot dig a hole in a different place by digging the same hole deeper. Effective as vertical thinking is for developmental purposes it is quite inadequate for generating new ideas and new ways of looking at things.

Lateral thinking is 'the other sort of thinking' but it is no less effective than vertical thinking even in practical matters. The difference between vertical and lateral thinking is a fundamental one and it is based on considerations of the system organisation in the brain.

The immense effectiveness of the human brain depends on its being organised as an iterative self-maximising two stage memory system. This is the type of system that creates order out of disorder but imposes an old order rather than recognise a new one. This is the type of system that makes everyday life possible but adventure difficult. Life would be awkward indeed if one had to analyse all the possible interpretations of the sound before jumping out of the way of a motor car horn. Instead the most probable interpretation totally dominates all others. In a system with a normal distribution of probabilities (figure 1) the most probable would be slightly ahead of something less probable. A self-maximising system on the other hand is a dynamic system and the most probable is always far ahead of any other (figure 2).

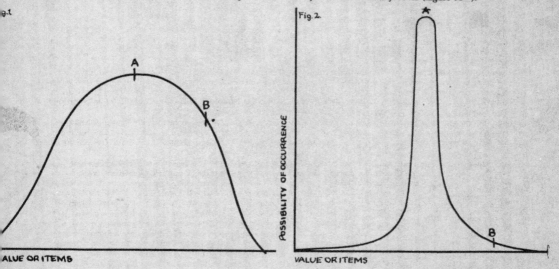

The simplest example of a self-maximising system is an empty glass. Push it slightly and negative feedback brings it back to its original position. Push it very slightly more and it takes off on its own positive feedback and reaches the limit position. Combine these self-maximising properties of the brain with a memory system (and this has to be a two stage memory system in view of the limited attention span of a self-maximising system) and one ends up with a very rigid — but immensely practical — form of information storage.

No matter how far back one takes the ordinary logical process there must be an initial stage of perceptual choice. No matter how excellent the logic may be it is the perceptual choice that will decide how easily the problem can be solved. In vertical thinking one accepts the most obvious choice and then works from it with great application in the hope that by sheer effort one may earn a solution. In lateral thinking one continually shifts the initial perceptual choice and quite often very little logic is required when one makes the right choice.

In some circles it is fashionable to regard the brain as a statistical computer. This can be a misleading idea for while statistics are based on probability the brain is based on preferability. Scatter water randomly on a preferability surface and you will end up with a few deep holes.

The effect of the rigidity and inevitability of perceptual choice is shown in the following visual problem. The problem is to draw the outline of a shape which can be divided into four identical pieces (size, shape and area) by a straight line. The outlined shape should be capable of being cut out of a postcard and the four piece separated by one straight stroke of the scissors. The solution is shown on page 29.

The disadvantages of high-probability vertical thinking are inseparable from the advantages since they are but another way of looking at the advantages. Lateral thinking is an attempt to escape the self-maximising properties of the brain system in order to generate new ideas. It is interesting that in the higher reaches of computer programming the importance of random inputs (one aspect of lateral thinking) is being recognised. This is interesting because for many people computers are the epitome of sterile logical sequential thinking.

With logical thinking the context develops first and then a point develops from this; with lateral thinking the point arises first and then the context develops to support it (it is in the nature of the brain to develop a context for whatever is held in consciousness). The experts who relied on the Clerk Maxwell laws of electro-magnetic radiation were correct when they told Marconi that the wireless waves would not follow the curvature of the earth but would stream off into space. Foolishly, Marconi believed that since the Atlantic ocean was only a longer distance than his previous successful attempts at wireless transmission, he would merely require a more powerful transmitter, a more sensitive receiver. Marconi succeeded. He made his point and eventually the context, taking the form of the re-discovery of the Heaviside layer – arose to support that point.

Traditional methods of thought like traditional mathematics are arbitrary and for the most part unrelated to the system structure of the brain. People were content with Euclidean geometry until Riemann and Lobachevsky came along and showed that other geometries were possible. Our mathematics are still based on mechanical principles such as $2 + 3 = 5$ (or some modular variant). It is perfectly feasible to base a mathematics on the notion that $2 + 3 = 3$. Such a mathematics would be biological rather than mechanical.

Some of the fundamental differences in attitude between vertical and lateral thinking are indicated in the following points:

Vertical thinking is sequential and proceeds step by step along a path. Lateral thinking may make jumps and then fill in the gaps or it may saturate the field and allow a pattern to develop on its own.

With vertical thinking each step must be justified and rest firmly on the preceding step (this is so fundamental a basis of logic that if one were to try and explain logic to a dog who had suddenly become capable of it one might well start with this notion). In lateral thinking the steps do not have to be justified until the end just as bridge spans may not be self-supporting until they meet in the middle.

With vertical thinking one chooses the most probable approach and then proceeds from this. With lateral thinking one moves sideways generating as many approaches as possible and then scanning across them all.

With vertical thinking one blocks off certain pathways with negatives. With lateral thinking all pathways and avenues are used.

The categories and definitions in vertical thinking are rigid spatial separations. With lateral thinking the separations are in time not in space.

In vertical thinking one concentrates and excludes interference. In lateral thinking one not only welcomes but makes use of random influences.

These are but some of the differences between vertical and lateral thinking. They are detailed here precisely because they are rather obvious to anyone who has been involved in the so called creative process. But they are derived not from a description of the creative process but from a consideration of the functional behaviour of the brain as a biological system.

Lateral thinking is used consciously or otherwise a good deal by creative people and a consideration of the basis of lateral thinking can extend this use and allow it to be more deliberate. Unfortunately lateral thinking is very little used in the scientific or practical field. Scientists become unhappy that the process is not more predictable and more firmly under control. They do not seem to realise that a method which is not completely under control can nevertheless be effective. If a girl plays roulette with her boyfriends money but keeps her winnings she is not likely to refuse to play on the grounds that she cannot tell on precisely which play she is going to win. Vertical thinking promises a minimum solution and often breaks the promise, lateral thinking increases the chances of a maximum solution but makes no promises.

Once one gets away from the semantic antics of descriptive word play then it becomes possible to start making predictions. One such prediction which arises from the very nature of lateral thinking is that there is an optimum amount of emotionality for creativity. Less than this optimum (peak) or more than it would inhibit creativity.

Even those people who habitually use the general concept of lateral thinking tend to use it in a vertical way. Lateral thinking is not a substitute for vertical thinking but a complement. It is a disruption of the probability patterns of the brain in order to allow a temporary re-forming. It is a vertical characteristic of the mind to form rigid dichotomies and then choose one or the other: certainty/possibility; definiteness/fluidity; stability/change; saneness/excitement; security/adventure; square/pop. The mind finds great difficulty in usefully oscillating from one to the other as polarisation is so fundamental a characteristic. The brain is capable of lateral thinking for the same reason that it is capable of humour. Both define the system. It would be very sinister if a computer could be constructed that could laugh.

In both this article and in the book, 'The Use of Lateral Thinking' the description of lateral thinking has been very general. The intention is to provide a focus. Lateral thinking is a definite type of thinking, not a set of rules, or techniques or theories and there is a danger in detailing such peripheral matters.

 The Use of Lateral Thinking by Edward de Bono. Published by Jonathan Cape 18/-

When a group of 100 people were given this problem the reactions were as shown in the figures:

35% could not produce a figure, I.

50% produced one or other of the variations shown under II. These are obviously wrong since if they were to be cut out of a postcard a stroke of the scissors would only divide them into two halves.

produced either one or the other of the variations shown under III. Both these are correct.

Only 3% produced what seems to be by far the most elegant solution. The difficulty here is that the pieces are not treated symmetrically but one serves as a base for the other three, V

The apparent difficulty with this simple task is that immediately the problem is stated there arises a 'perceptual choice' of a square divided into four quarters as shown in the figure. The two erroneous versions proceed from this image as shown, V. ④ ②

If, however, the problem is stated as being one of assembling four identical pieces around a straight line then there is no difficulty and the thing proceeds as shown in the last figures, VI.

i

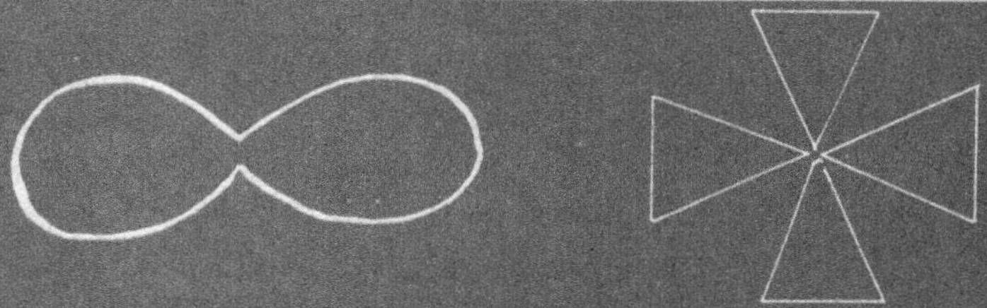

ii

iii

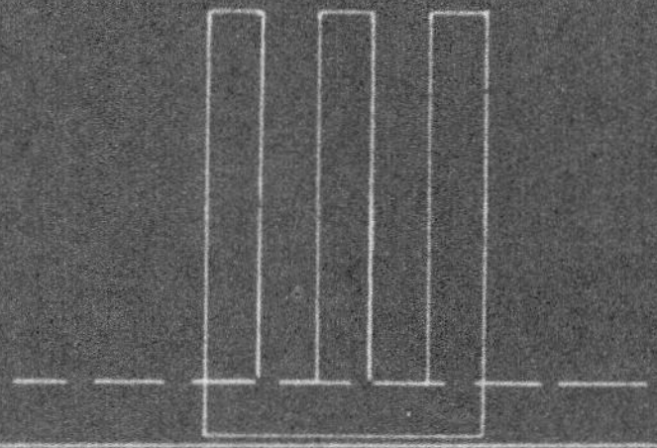

iv

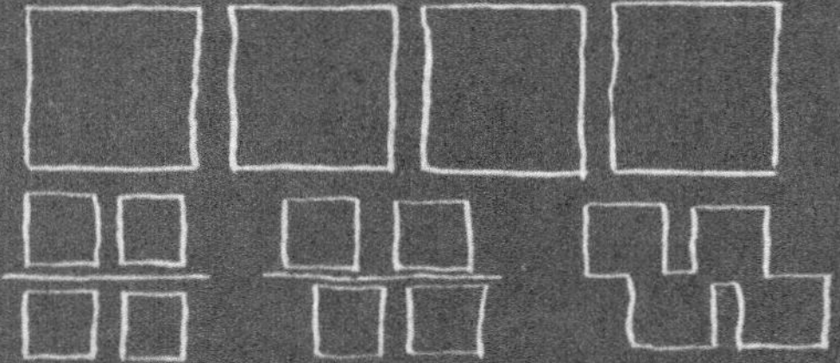

vi

EPILOGUE

Rhubarb, rhubarb, rhubarb. Clink and shuffle. Cough.

Shut up, people. Quiet, now.

ha ha ha ha ha ha ha ha ha ha

One minute studio. Ta.

Start the clock.
Start the clock.

　　　　　Cough.
　ha ha ha ha ha ha

Clink, scrape and ha ha ha ha ha.

Very nervous....

Don't worry. Just the same as when we rehearsed, you know.

Thirty seconds.
Cue VTR.
Thirty seconds.

Cue announcer ident.
Right. Christian Affairs number seventy two, 365. Take one.

　　　　　Good luck, children.

Fifteen seconds.

....Ten, nine, eight, seven, six, five, four, three, two, one - cue grams and up caption.

Cue announcer.

In tonight's Christian Affairs, the Reverend David Summers, Vicar of All Saints' Chelsea, and director of Christian Bodies, talks to Derek Iverson of the Sunday Times	Symphony No.5 in C. B/hoven. First move. Columbis 33c 1051 On the first chinagraph mark.

Change caption.

Change caption.

Luverly.

Coming to you, two. Ready. Kill grams. On you, two. And .... -er cue Derek.

Good evening. Today is the first anniversary of the Christian Bodies Movement, and tonight we have **(stand by, three; soon on you - tighter on him than that, luv.)** the director of the organisation with us in the studio. He is **(on you, three)** the Reverend David Summers.

Hello.

(**back to you, two**) First of all, sir, there is one question that I feel we must put to you straight away. (**on you, three**) And that is about the new branch of Christian Bodies, the Do-ers. We've heard a lot about them lately - in the Press and so on -**(tighten in, three. Slowly, slowly. Swinging. Don't knock him off his bloody chair)** tell us something about it.

(**I'll buy that. Hold it just there, Fred, three**)

Well, it's hard to say what we do, really. I mean, (**tighter, three; nice grotty close-up**) the whole object of Christian Bodies(**Stand by with caption, one**) is to help, you know. Our new headquarters (**one**) in Chelsea in the - er - picture there, is open day and night to help the really needy. We look after the body as well as the soul there.

Two-shot, three. Bit tighter, can see that hole in the cyc....he's a natterer. We'll be here all blinding night

　　　three,

Yes, but what we want to know is something of what you are doing there.

Well, first of all, we deal with the - er - poor, the homeless, and the - um - outcasts of society.

Like the Salvation Army in a way?

Not unlike it, no. We have eighty two beds and a

kitchen which are in use twenty four hours a day ...

(**I want a mid-shot, two. Keep his collar in for the image if anyone switches on at eleven forty six at night. Bit too close. More collar, doll.**)

And our main purpose is to extend the warm hand of Christian fellowship to those who really need it. It is not enough just to get up in a pulpit and preach at people. The Do-ers feel that is it truly practising Christianity as it was intended in the - er - first place.

(**two**)

(**Stand by, telecine**)

Sounds most rewarding.

It is rewarding work. I have thirteen volunteers at the moment, but I do need more.

What about money? I mean, the headquarters alone must cost a small fortune to run?

Ah-ha, we are fortunate in having, if you like, a
sponsor. A wealthy and well-known business friend
pays rent and overheads. Er - this is Independent
Television, isn't it, so I'd better not mention his
name, eh?

Ha ha ha ha ha ha

(Gawd. Telecine, that's it. Right film, one hopes?
Stand by, announcer, for voice over film)

We have some film of your hostel home. Let's look
at it together and give the viewers some idea of what
you are doing there.

and rhubarb and rustle.

(When we get to the film, kids, I want one to cover all
the captions as planned. Three, nice tight shot of the rev.
I vant his reaction to the film. Which is a load of
excrement, anyway. Damm, missed the cue. Cue announcer)...

The Borough of Chelsea is usually
associated with the wealthy, the
affluent, and the slightly odd.

Property there is now worth a fortune
and it would hardly seem the place
for
a voluntary charity organisation.

(he missed that on run-through, too)
But in this vast Georgian house
just off the King's Road **It's about
half a poxing mile from the King's
Road - we had to walk there with the
Arriflex, mate)** there is a group of
people whose constant task it is
to help and succour **(what?)** the
needy and the distressed.

Lofty and well-aired dormitories for
the bedless....

(hold it, announcer, until they
clear this shot. The bod on the right bends
down)

(who's been using my po?)

(in you go)

a modern kitchen.....
and a small chapel. Plain and simple,
but a home for as long as it is
needed.

Here we see our guest for the evening,
David Summers, the Director of
Christian Bodies, at his desk.
Each day, he says, about thirty
people come to him in distress.

Lame dogs, ex-gaolbirds, alcoholics,
television directors) homosexuals,

(roll telecine. In after five, announcer)

**(like the berk wo writes these
scripts)** fellows - all sorts of hapless
human beings. **(thirty sex to
end of film. Ta)** Here we see
some of the satisfied customers of
David Summers. This man was
going to commit suicide.... This
woman took to drink and
prostitution when she lost her
only.... **(I wish we had admags
back)** and this boy was well on the
way to becoming a sexual pervert....
(talking about Sydney again)

This is the Christian Bodies, the
bo-ers, in action. Doing a daily
job, working all hours for little
return, save the knowledge that
they are helping their fellows.

(five sex to end of film)

From this work in Chelsea, and
the inspired efforts of this
group, must surely come further
understanding of the needs of
others.

(on you, three)

I didn't know I looked like that.

Well, on that bit of film we saw the sort of place you
work in and a little of the work you do. Of course, it
would take a much longer programme than this
epilogue to fully explain what you do there, but can
you give us, briefly, what your aims and objects are?

**(he's taken a deep breath. He'll waffle on now, the old
soandso)**

Er, well, to start with, may I quote from my own script?
The script that I learn my own daily part from?

Of course.

16 mm mute

(I think he's going for the bible on the table. Watch it, one.
If he does, I want a nice tight shot of the movement, you know)

Thank you.

(there he goes. Grab it. Nice....and....tight....and....
pan....with the....book. I'll come back to you, three,
straight away. Got to get some bloody movement into
this thing. How are we for time, Myra? One. Pan up....
slow, darling. Slowly. On you, three)

I take my cue

("I'll have unnatural sexual relations with my
discarded heavy duty footwear) from Romans, chapter nine.
And if there be any other commandment, it is briefly
comp - comprehended - in this saying, namely, that thou
shalt love thy neighbour as thyself. As far as we are
concerned, the Do-ers of C.B., there is no better way of
showing our love for our neighbour than by going out and
doing something about it. Something tangible. The body needs
aid as much as the soul. I mean, how can a soul think
clearly in a careworn body, or a starved one, or an unloved
one? This love thy neighbour thing is the whole fulcrum
of the Christian letter. And love should not be
something you put on the bottom of a letter - it is
something you do. Hence the name, Do-ers. It all
started when I was a young curate in Wigan....

(they'll have closed when you've finished, you old clown)

Er, I was sick to death of hearing people talk, talk, talk
(you're jesting, for a certainty) about helping others,
but not doing a single thing about it. I was determined
that when I had a church of my own and a little - er -
ecclesiastical authority I would start a practical unit of
help and aid. Only when I came to All Saints' was I able
to do this.

So this is a dream come true, so to speak?

Yes, a dream come true. I know there are lots of other
similar groups doing the same work, and that our modest
effort is not unique, but this is all to the good. The
more the merrier, I say.

(wind Derek up and give the old boy a poke up the
roodscreen too. We've got the closing prayer yet)

(tighten in, three. Stick your four inch in his mush and
put the fear of Murphy into him)

Well, I see our time is nearly up. Can you (stand by,
Harry, with the prayer caption for one. The one with
the open book thing. Tighter and kill that chalk mark)
- er - as we ask all our guests on these programmes, can
we ask you to leave us with a prayer for the end of the
day?

I have one here.

Cough. ruffle, riffle, scraps. Ahem. rasp. Cough.

(on you, two. Just look at the pigging caption, will you?
Graphics? I've shot 'em)

O, Lord God, maker of mankind and ordainer of our
destinies, grant that we grow more to know our fellows
and that we serve thee through kindness and ministration
to others. Help us to help. Give us strength where there
is weakness   And give us faith where there is
ignorance and fear. And embrace us in thy care that
we may pursue these charities with all the might of thy
hand and with all the courage of thy blessed crucifixion.

(sounds like the end. Amen. Come on - amen)

And bless us, Lord, in all the works we do in thy name.
Amen.

(right. Stand by, announcer, for closing chat. Wide
shot, one: on you, one. Pull out slowly - slowly, for
crying out loud)
          (cue announcer and stand by grams)

In Christian Affairs tonight (cue   Symphony No.5
grams) the Reverend David Summers, in C.
vicar of All
                                                     Symphony No.5

In Christian Affairs   (cue
the Reverend David Summers   grams)
vicar of All Saints' Chelsea, and   Symphony No.5
director of Christian Bodies,   in C.
talked to Derek Iverson of the   B'hoven.
Sunday Times.   First move.
                                                     Columbia 33c 10?
                                                     Second chinagram
(fade grams....and cue announcer)   mark

Next week at the same time, Christian Affairs goes to
Leeds to see what the young people are doing for the old
age pensioners of the city. (up grams)

(....six, five, four, three, two, one - out. Fade sound
and vish. And another converted savage bits the dust)

All over?

Rasp.

Hold it. Let's see if we are clear with VTR.

All clear. Ta muchly, people.

Well, David, if that was your first time, you
certainly did a fine job. Very professional. We'll
have you in Coronation Street yet.....

                              Ha ha ha ha ha ha   Cough

Thank you, Derek. I think it's a wonderful way of
talking to people, this TV.
                         Are you joining us upstairs for a c
                    Oh, yes, please.
Right. This way, then.
    It's quite chilly when they turn out all the lights.

Yes. We'll go to the visitors' room. I think that we
have got to

                              FADE

Some readers complained about the space OZ 7 gave to Michael Malik. A particularly vocal critic was a beautiful Jamaican girl, Melinda, who is questioned below.

What do you think of Michael Malik's twelve months' gaol sentence?

I think, frankly, it should have been longer. He should have been deported, except that Trinidad won't have him back. The newspapers must stop publicising Michael X in the same way they stopped publicising the mods and rocker Brighton riots. The Press should ignore him and when he realises that he will get no more publicity, he will either shut up or he will start doing something constructive for negroes in Britain who have a genuine problem.

Don't you think he is?

No, he's doing a lot of harm; he's creating a situation which doesn't really exist. He's trying to force the issue, he wants to be a hero, as Stokely Carmichael is, just for his own personal gratification, to the detriment of the negroes in Britain. I think Malik's putting voice to a lot of submerged hatreds ...if you present any group of people with an unpleasant person they will automatically hate him and what he stands for and Michael X is trying to identify himself with all the negroes in Britain, which is wrong. The day his compatriots appeared on television a lot of harm was done. I think a lot of white people went round thinking: "You bloody nigger, I know what you're really thinking behind that calm facade - go back to your own country."

Do you think that black people are discriminated against in this country?

I don't know because I don't live in the predominantly coloured areas of Manchester and Birmingham. I think in London there is very little discrimination. If one wants to find discrimination, one will. There are cases obviously of discrimination in housing, the same way as there are cases of discrimination in anything - but there is also discrimination against Greeks, Jews, the Irish and everyone.

Are you an Auntie Tom?

Yes, by Malik's terms, I am an Auntie Tom, which means that I choose to first find out the sort of life the English live, find out how they want me to live and abide by their wishes - this is their country, not mine.

But if you're going to settle here and have children, as many coloured people are, isn't it in their interests for you to try and eradicate inequality?

Yes, but inequality has been and is being eradicated by legislation (which I don't terribly agree with). Inequality stems from ones basic inferiority or inadequacy to cope with a situation - I think a lot of the immigrants who are here now are inadequate or considered inferior because they have not had the opportunities of the people living right next door to them - when their children are educated and go and look for jobs, if they are qualified, I would think that they would have exactly the same opportunities as anyone else. If we find

in ten years' time that there is a large number of unemployed West Indian youths who grew up and were educated in Britain, then is the time to say whether there could be a colour problem and what do we do with it. I don't think the situation exists now that Malik says exists - that is discrimination, negroes being killed, negroes being spat upon constantly - he says constantly - .... I think there are isolated cases and if he wishes to have on his platform the negroes who have been discriminated against and spat upon and are bitter, then he will have a very loud voice to proclaim his cause.

There is much evidence of blatant discrimination. There is a recent, much publicised, example of whites banding together to prevent a West Indian from buying a house.

There was a letter to The Times subsequently, in reply to this very subject, saying that if a man wants to sell a house and there are three people who want to buy it and the man who wants to sell the house has a particularly nice garden which he wants to keep up - yet his first and highest offer is from someone who doesn't particularly care for gardening and he says 'no thank you' - this can be construed as discrimination. I think in the case you mention there was discrimination, but on the other hand, other tenants in the street were interviewed and asked if they would mind having a coloured neighbour, and I think sixty percent of them said 'No, not at all, it wouldn't matter to me' - this depends - I'm sure a lot of people if asked would they like a Jewish neighbour or an unmarried mother with six children living in the room above would say no - everyone has their prejudice and they're quite entitled to it.

Have you ever suffered severe cases of discrimination?

Yes, looking for flats. Ninty percent of the people I rang said no - they did not want West Indians - they were extremely polite - and I finally found a flat in a very respectable area and the landlord said 'Certainly you can move in'. I asked whether the other tenants or the neighbours would mind, and he said if anyone in the house objected, he'd move them all out and fill the house with negroes.

You're not very bitter about the fact 90% didn't want West Indians?

No - but how can I explain it? - it was like trying to get the sort of job I wanted for a year and a half. Nobody felt that I was as qualified as I said I was. Eventually one person did say: 'O.K. we'll give you a try'. Ninety percent of the people I asked refused me - this could have been on the basis of colour, but I don't think it was. I think it was simply their own apprehensions about whether or not I was qualified to do the job. Why be bitter?

What is your reaction to teenage racial segregation?

Well, I encountered exactly the same sort of situation in Jamaica ...the Chinese only marry the Chinese, and if a Chinese girl marries a non-Chinese boy she is considered an outcast, usually by both societies - hers and her husbands - the same with the Indians in Jjamaica, the same with the darker skinned Jamaicans and the lighter skinned Jamaicans - if you're a white Jamaican, you do not marry a coloured Jamaican, or you try your best not to, because you are looked down upon. Why should this not be so in Britain, particularly when these children's parents have got prejudices, and do not feel that their son or daughter would be doing well to marry or go out with a coloured boy or girl - I don't see how the negro in Britain can say "Why the hell won't you let your daughter go out with me" when in fact he would not be able to go out with a white girl in his own country.

Do you want to marry a black or a white person?

I just want to get married to someone who loves me very dearly . . . .

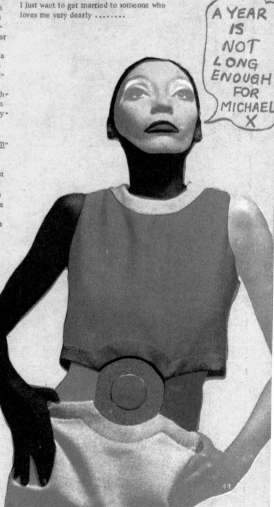

A YEAR IS NOT LONG ENOUGH FOR MICHAEL X

49

SPECIAL EDITION

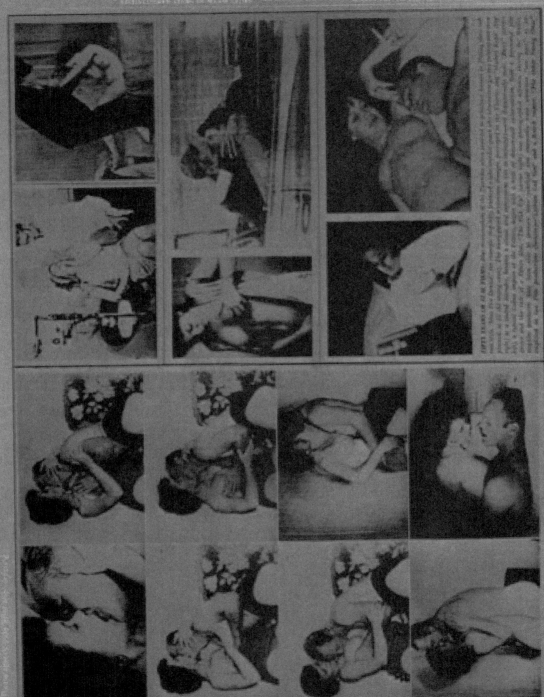

BULLETIN NO 12

It was five years ago that I attached myself to the Cambridge group that started the psychedelic movement. In those days we didn't use the word "psychedelic" much – the accepted phrase was "consciousness-expanding drugs", or more briefly, "mushroom", since the Harvard group worked mainly with psilocybin. There was a whole new world in the mushroom, so we said – the key to a stronger, richer human life soon to be made available to every man. We were messianically dedicated, full of the happy excitement of sharing a soon-to-be-public secret that was going to save the world.

Were we like today's novice acidheads? It is hard for me to tell, because my perspective has changed so much. To my younger, naiver eyes, the mushroom people were idealistic as children, brave as Christian martyrs, and full of wisdom. They were an indissoluble family, destined to go forward, hand in hand, to win souls and bring in the Kingdom.

I have no idea what has become of most of them. They are not in the movement any more. Some of the conservative fringe members are still conservative fringe members. Some went "straight". A few flipped out of psychedelics into Meher Baba or some other form of occultism. The original, most enthusiastic members just disappeared, sometimes turning up briefly in this city or that, but no longer activists. The leaders, Leary, Alpert and Metzner, apparently unmoved by the fact that their own group had fallen apart, went out to preach LSD as the key to love and consciousness-expansion, to new starry-eyed kids, forming new groups that fell apart in turn.

For two years I have been publishing a bimonthly Bulletin which concentrated on facts: names, dates, addresses, the correction of rumors, etc., and in which editorializing was kept minimal. I am changing that policy, because I have slowly come to realise that I do readers a disservice to report on things like the Neo-American Church, the League for Spiritual Discovery, the psychedelic shops and so on, as if I took them seriously. Most of the psychedelic projects I have reported in past Bulletins have flopped, even though the more obvious losers were screened out before printing. Those that remain are a caricature of the psychedelic vision, a mockery of the idealism of youth. If the utopian vision of 1962 was too good to be true, it does not follow that what came out of that had to be this bad.

The word "psychedelic" is ruined; it might as well be scrapped by those who still wish to speak earnestly about their experience. Psychedelic now means gaudy illegible posters, gaudy unreadable tabloids, loud parties, anything paisley, crowded noisy discotheques, trinket 54 shops and the slum districts that patronize them. There

was something I used to mean by psychedelic, but if those posters are psychedelic, that other thing isn't. Put "psychedelic" down along with "community," "love," "religion" and other good words the hippies, with the help of Leary & Co., have corrupted.

Whatever happened to the Neo-American Church Boo Hoos whose names I used to publish (and what will happen to the new ones)? Art Kleps, "your Chief Boo Hoo," went to Florida where he knew there was a warrant for his arrest, got raging drunk, picked a fight with his ex-wife and passed out in a railroad station where he was picked up by police and, when his identity was learned, held on the old charge. (This is what he means when he writes in his recent bulletin, "This is not a good test case too messy.") I made the mistake of feeling sorry for him and raised $1000 for his bail, only to have him retreat into Millbrook and refuse to appear for trial, thus causing me to lose most or possibly all of the bail money. He is able to get away with this because psychedelic people have such short memories, and because they apparently do not expect their leaders to be trustworthy.

Not the least consequence of all this is the loss of the possibility of trust. A sensitive person can no longer distribute LSD after seeing how it is used. One can no longer buy LSD – the dealers cannot be trusted. It is unlikely I will ever go anybody's bail again. No old head expects much of any newly announced psychedelic project (unless it goes commercial, and then it may become big and rich, but irrelevant).

Vacant-faced kids drop by the Psychedelic Information Centre and ask, "what's happening?" Pressed for what they mean, they usually turn out to be looking for a rock band or maybe a shop selling buttons, or news of the latest busts. I have nothing for them that they want, and they go away puzzled – they thought I had a Thing here, but it turns out to be just a few publications, no flashing lights, so it isn't hip.

There's still the same thing happening, of course, that's been happening since psychedelics became available: the possibility of having an experience that will reawaken a person to the basic truths he understood as a child, and point the way to becoming a better man or woman. (But even this possibility is cut off for many of the kids – they have had 100 trips and are jaded. Thus we have pathetic rumors about drugs "stronger than acid.")

That would be the only psychedelic happening that I'd be interested in – if a few people could be helped to lead better lives with the aid of psychedelics. If the Indians can do it with peyote, it should be possible for us – if we could just get clear of the cultish, flashy, idiotic pseudo-underground.

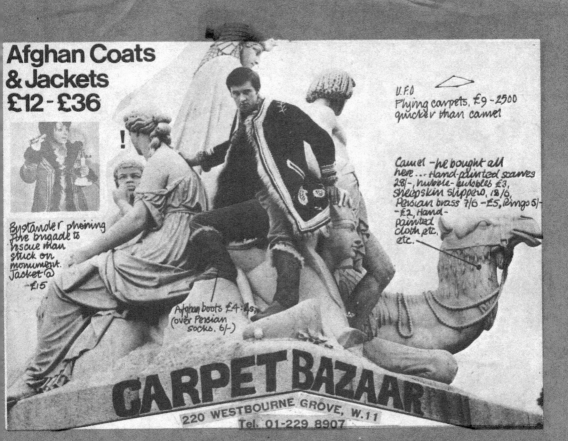

Afghan Coats & Jackets £12 - £36

!

Bystander phoning the brigade to rescue man stuck on monument. Jacket @ -£15

Afghan boots £4·45, (over Persian socks. 6/-)

U.F.O ⟶
Flying carpets, £9 - 2500 quicker than camel

Camel - he bought all here... Hand-painted scarves 28/-, nubile-autobles £3, Sheepskin slippers, 18/6, Persian brass 7/6 -£5, Rings 5/- -£2, Hand-painted cloth etc, etc.

CARPET BAZAAR
220 WESTBOURNE GROVE, W.11
Tel. 01-229 8907

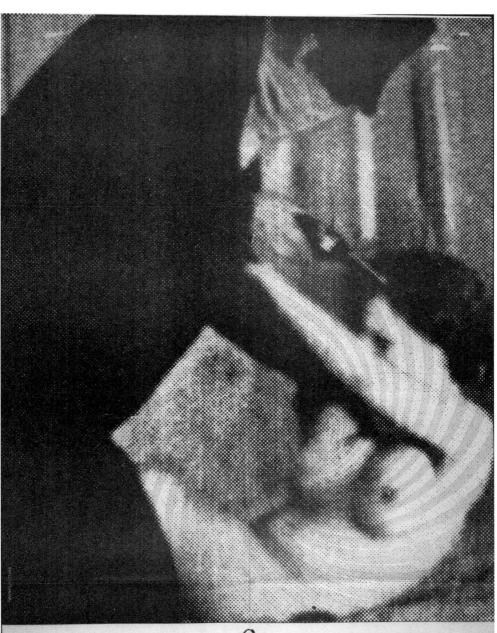

'WHILE DAD'S AWAY, MUM WILL PLAY'

GEUVARA IS DEAD... LONG LIVE GEUVARA!

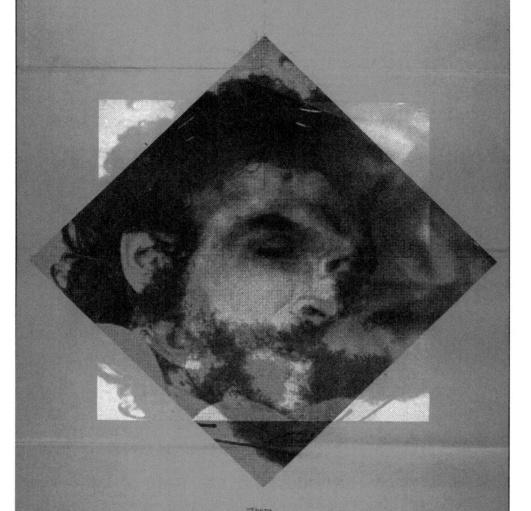

"There
is no defin-
ition of socialism
which makes sense for us",
said Che Geuvara, "but the
abolition of exploitation of one
man by another". Or of one country by
another. The West is Billy Bunter in a world
of Oliver Twists and Geuvara saw no boundaries;
for exploiters are running free in Athens and Djakarta,
Saigon and the Congo. So he taught tin miners to throw
dynamite, mountain Indians to use their traps for war. The Doctor
took up a carbine (yet lagged behind the geurilla bands of the Cuban revolution to care for the wounded on both sides). Men like Geuvara are too big
and angry for our world of typewriters and soft hands; too big for the courtroom of
Camiri, too honest for those fat men in the Kremlin who ordered their parties to betray the
geurillas and whose revolution goes on in drapes and velours, and too serious to live into middle age

2/6

DYLAN

SONG POEMS   NEW STUFF

"FREEZE-OUT"

THE MILLION DOLLAR BASH

Well the big dumb blonde with her wheel gorged
turned to the friend of hers
with his cheques all forged
and his cheeks in a chunk
with his cheese in the cash,
theyre all gonna be there at
that million dollar bash
Ooh baby , ooh ee,e . . . its that
million dollar bash

Everybodys ridin out to over there
and back
the louder they come
the bigger they crack
come now, sweep clean
dont forget to flash
we're all gonna meet at
that million dollar bash
Ooh baby, ooh eee . . . its that
million dollar bash

Well i took my counsellor out to the barn
silly nellie was there
she told him a yarn
then along came jones,
emptied the trash
everybody went down to that
million dollar bash
Ooh baby, ooh eee . . . its that
million dollar bash

Well ive hit her too hard
my stones wont take
i get up in the morning
but its too early to wake
first its hello
goodbye
then pushing
then crash!
but we're all gonna make it at that
million dollar bash
Ooh baby, ooh eee . . . its that
million dollar bash

Well i looked at my watch i looked at my wrist
i punched myself
in the face
with my fist
i took my potatoes
down to be mashed
then i made it on over
to that million dollar bash
Oohooh baby, ooeee, oohoo baby ooheee
its that million dollar bash   ©

TINY MONTGOMERY SAYS HELLO!

Well you can tell everybody down in ole Frisco
Tell em Tiny Montgomery says hello.
Now every boy an girl gonna get their thing
Cause Tiny Montgomery's gonna shake that thing!
Tell em everybody down in ole Frisco that Tiny Montgomery's comin
                    down to say hello

Skinny-Moo and T-Bone Frank
They're all gonna take on down by the Bounty Bank
One bird book, and a buzzard and a crawl
Tell em all Tiny Montgomery's gonna say hello!

Scratch your dad and do that bird
Suck that pig and bring it on home.
Paint that dream and nose that dough
Tell em all that Tiny says hello!

Now he's the King of Drunk and he squeezes too . . .
Watch out, Lester . . . take it Lou
Join the Monk, the CIO
Tell em all that Tiny says hello!

Now bitch that gig
And play it blank
Tell em to go on out and gas that dog.
Track on in
Flower that snow
Take it on down
Begin to grow
Now play that load
An pick it up
Take it on in
In a bottle truck
Three legged man in a hotlip hold
Tell em all that Montgomery says hello!

Well you can tell everybody down in ole Frisco
Tell em all that Montgomery says hello!   ⑤

I SEE MY LIFE COME SHINING

They say everything can be replaced
yet every distance is not near
so i remember every face
of every man who put me here

I see my life come shining
from the west unto the east
any day now
any day now
I shall be released

They say every man needs protection
They say every man must fall
yet i swear i see my reflection
some place so high above this wall

I see my life come shining
from the west unto the east
any day now
any day now
I shall be released

Now you all see standing
in this lonely crowd
a man who swears he's not to blame
all day long
i hear his voice shouting so loud
crying out that he was framed

I see my life come shining
from the west unto the east
any day now
any day now
I shall be released   ©

CRASH ON THE LEVEE

Crash on the levee mama
waters gonna overflow
swamps gonna rise
slow boats gonna roll
Now you can train on down
     to Williamspoint
you can bust your feet
you can rock this joint
Aah mama
aint you gonna miss
     your best friend now
You gonna have to find you
another best friend somehow

Now dont you try to move
you're just gonna lose
there's a crash on the levee
and mama you been refused
Well its sugar for sugar
and salt for salt
if you go down in the flood
its gonna be your fault
Aah mama aint you gonna miss
     your best friend now
Yes you gonna have to find yourse
another best friend somehow

Well the high tides risin
mama dont you let me down
pack up your suitcase
mama dont you make a sound
Now its king for king
queen for queen
theres gonna be the meanest flood
that anybody seen
Oh mama aint you gonna miss
     your best friend now
yes you're gonna have to find your
another best friend somehow

OZMOSIS

USO *A Home Away from Home*
— 2 —

just managed to get the flames out before it blew up. I heard later one of them was on acid at the time. what a trip!

Two of my buddies, Rick & Steve got busted last week for grass. They're really watching us now man, but there's piles of stuff around as well as lots of hash. There've been days when the whole base smelled like Tompkins Sq. Park. The grass comes from Cambodia, I've heard, but anybody who's been in Saigon says it's as easy to score as to get laid and often both at once. Out in the field we get mostly hash because R+R in Saigon has been restricted lately, and hash is so much easier to stash in a spot check. There are opium dens in S. incidentally, a couple right across from the Caravelle and supposedly operated by the Cong. But I don't dig that shit. Pot's fine for me and most of the other guys around, who can at least thank the Army for one thing — turning teen into heads. Some days everybody for miles around seems stoned. They've all got those sunny grins on their faces, you know, and we salute each other — "Peace!" It really breaks us up.

RVNAF (the S. Vietnam gov. radio station) now has some teenybopper disc jockey chick called Mai-Lan, which means M

Paul Lawson

John Steinbeck II, just back from Bien Hoa, embarrassed the Pentagon and his super hawk dad when he revealed that 75% of American troops stayed stoned throughout their Vietnam year. It only costs fifteen dollars. Unreported so far in England, the fact that troops going on R & R, rest and recreation leave, in nearby Asian capitals, are marketing Viethash to pay for the holiday. Even Sydney's lackadaisical drug squad have been embarrassed into arresting an Ally a day.

If your eyes were up to reading, Lisa Bieberman's Psychedelic News Sheet No. 12, last issue, you might still be relishing her axe-job on Arthur Kleps. Kleps is the Chief Boo Hoo of the Neo American Church, the post-Leary religious organisation whose sacrament is peyote and whose ministers or Boo Hoos, seminary a five dollar note, are required by their faith to turn people on—sure grounds for a draft deferment. Kleps hits back hard at Bieberman in the latest issue of Divine Toad Sweat, the 'Dilated House Organ of the Church.'

Lisa Bieberman: You may have seen Lisa's muckraking bulletin or her article in the New Republic. I agree with much of what she has to say about the movement, and would only add, "so what?" Most people in the movement are fools for the same reason that most people in the telephone book are fools—statistical probability. Lisa has always tested the behaviour of others against some imaginary standard of correct behaviour appropriate to her own fears and limitations, rather than trying to asses the alternative and do what is possible with what is at hand. I am no more a standard Hippie than she is, but I enthusiastically advocate this life style for the majority of young people today. Conversely, although I am about as Red as you can get without being a tomato, I am quite happy to number among my closest friends some millionaires whom I consider to be blood-sucking parasitical imperialist conspirators. Lisa, and too many of the Hippies she finds so repugnant, share a common infantile conceit, they consider their tastes more important than their policy, and even, in extremis, wholly define their policy as the extension of their tastes. As for her personal attack on me, all I can say is (1) the bail money she solicited has not been forfeited or used to pay a fine as of the present date (2) almost all of it was raised from friends of mine who know that I know that they know that I know, etc. etc.—It would be an insult to ask, "May I borrow the $100 you put up for a few months to pay the fine, or would you rather see me in prison?" (3) If I am forced by necessity to pay the fine out of the bail money, it will only amount to $500 or so and the people who need cash in hand at once will get their contribution back at once (4) Lisa seems to think the circumstance of my being picked up passed out drunk in the Sarasota Railroad Station is evidence of moral iniquity and mental dengeneracy so desperate as to make public disclosure obligatory. I should be, I suppose, "disgraced" in the eyes of all those Sunday School superintendent acid heads out there to whom Lisa so coquettishly addresses herself ("Look Ma, I take drugs!". Yes, folks, I had, indeed, on that occasion, more-or-less voluntarily, rendered myself unconscious in a public place (no private place was available). How about that? Some people, of course, lead affectional lives so rigorously ordered and curcumscribed that they never experience losses, anguish which may verge on the unbearable. I have noticed that these people very frequently end up rendering themselves dead in private places. To each his own.

Mixed media. Secker & Warburg, Studio Vista and almost every book publishing house have begun publishing film scripts. While moviemakers like Peter Whitehead, and Ian Cameron have begun publishing books. On films. Our McLuhen award goes to Whitehead and Andrew Sinclair's, Lorimer Publishing, who have corned the market in Godard and the more memorable classics and will be bringing out a title a month for the next three years.

Not all the good movies in town are at the New Cinema Club, which is getting round the censorship hangup, though their Chelsea Girls is a very bland strip of celluloid. The uncut version is expected to be presented by the BFI in conjunction with the Arts Lab soon. Meantime try and take in Alain Jessua's 'Comic Strip Hero' at the Cinephone.

3

BLOW UP!

The photograph is the one taken by Mary Moorman with her Polaroid camera as President Kennedy was being assassinated.

David Litton, a graduate student at UCLA, made an examination of the Moorman photo in 1965 and discovered the man shown in the series of blow-ups. He is holding a straight object in his hands and possibly may have actually fired a frontal shot at the President's car as it came up the street. This can not be determined from this photo but it is important to note that the existence of this man at that time and place contradicts the Warren Commission report on the assassination, which denies that anyone stood behind this wall or the picket fence.

This photograph proves the presence of at least one man, No. 5, half hidden behind the wall on the knoll, at the time of the shooting. The published Warren Commission documents do not reveal the presence of any individual behind the wall or fence at that time, either in an official capacity or otherwise; and Joseph Ball, senior commission counsel (who identifies himself as being in charge of this area of the investigation), explicitly denies that anyone was there.

Since the subject area of the knoll is generally consistent with that designated by most witnesses as the source of at least one shot, No. 5 man must logically be considered an important suspect. This would be true even if it were not a fact that he appears to be holding a straight object.

The photograph and surrounding circumstances demonstrate graphically and powerfully the urgent need for a complete reinvestigation of the assassination of President Kennedy.

Reprinted from the Los Angeles Free Press, No. 176, Dec. 1, 1967.

(Re: OZ No 3, Mark Lane.)

Is this one of the Kennedy Assassins?

Why doesn't the 'Moorman Photo' appear as a Warren Commission Exhibit?

Who is this man?

What is the straight object he appears to be holding in his hands?

Why is he on the grassy knoll, half hidden behind the wall at the time Kennedy was shot?

Why does Counsel Joseph Ball insist that there was no one either behind the wall or the picket fence?

7.

DRAWING BY RICHARD HEFFEREN
M.I.T. GRAPHIC ARTS SERVICE

2. **3.** **4.** 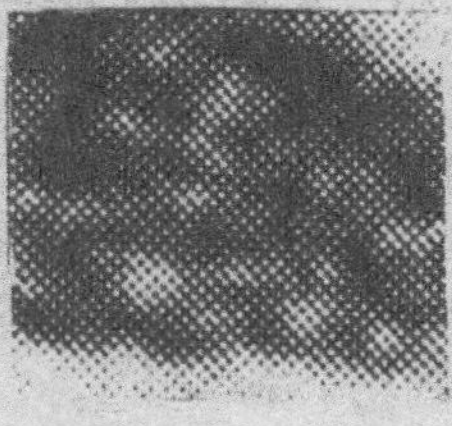 **5.**

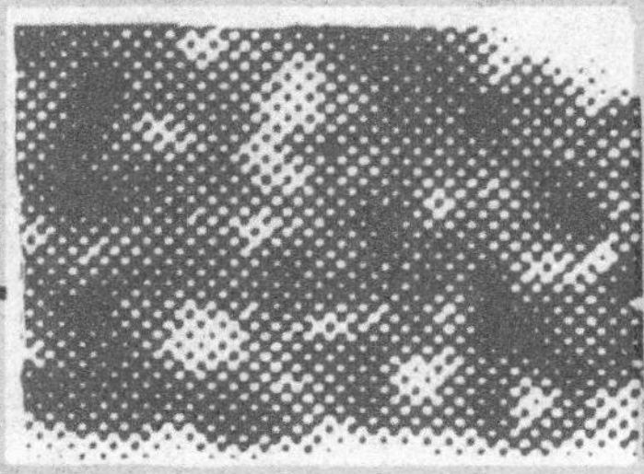

6. Stand back a few paces to view.

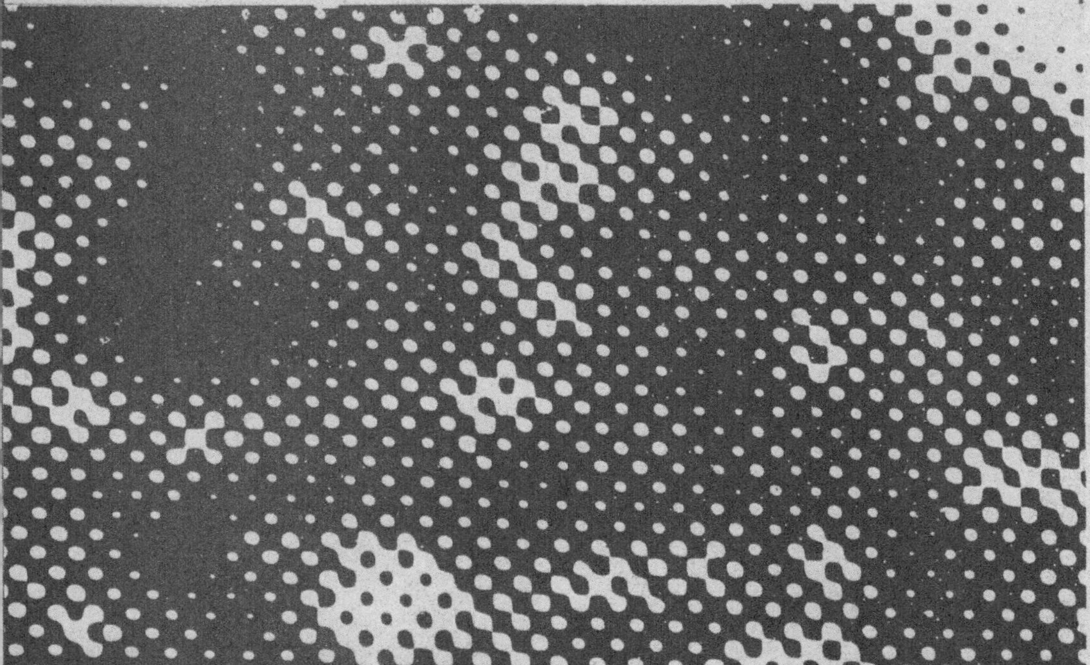

The DIGGER THING is your thing ....IF YOU ARE REALLY.....

Unless we can wipe out the menacing mountain of evil karma accumulated by the human race, it will soon crush out love, freedom, enlightenment and all that is beautiful in the world. To avert this catastrophe we must act quickly, for time is not on our side. It cannot be overemphasised that delay will surely spell doom of the love revolution.

TURNED ON!

Alex Lowsiewkee

The modern diggers are the dharma descendants of the Diggers who tilled common land and practised sharing in the England of 1649 and whose declared aims were to 'lay the Foundation of making the Earth a Common Treasury for All' and to create a new society in which all would 'as one man, working together, and feeding together . . . not Lording over another, but all looking upon each other, as equals'. But without reference to any historical affiliation, the term 'digger' may simply be defined in the present day revolutionary context as 'a person who digs love, freedom and sharing and acts on his understanding'.

The first of the modern diggers emerged from the hippie community in the autumn of 1966 in the Haight-Ashbury district of San Francisco. They made history there by dishing out free food to all comers, running a free store called 'The Free Frame of Reference' where goods were given away free, providing crash pads in their communes for dropouts and distributing a free newsheet (Communication Company, San Francisco).

This pattern of action has been taken up in one way or another by diggers in other cities and towns on the North American continent. The digger movement is spreading fast over...

CONTINUED

there and diggers are now developing land-based love communes where they grow their own food, and even building their own 'drop cities'.

Over here in England we are lagging behind - but we'll soon catch up. However when moving into the third phase of the love revolution, we must appreciate that the circumstances existing here are somewhat different from those in America. So, although we can learn a lot from the experiences of our American dharma brothers and sisters, it may be necessary for us to evolve a somewhat different course of action.

As I see it, the most essential and urgent thing is the creation of love communes, each with its own land, houses and means of production for primary as well as secondary goods.

At present most of the land, houses and means of production are in the hands of the state and private capitalists, so we have to play their money-game and score bread to buy these things (or rather *retrieve* these things, for they belong to everyone by right of birth and our share has been filched from us).

When we've got the communes on the groove, we'll support and expand the whole of Hipville by giving away some of our surplus produce free to hippies and diggers in need of them, and by selling the rest in hippie shops, preferably at prices which will appreciably undercut those of the profiteering hucksters of Squareville. The bread obtained from the sale will go partly to support those hippie shops and hippie enterprises which have to survive in the grab-world of straight society, and partly to reinvestment in land, etc. for the communes.

We'll automate our means of production and do our own scientific and technological research as soon as possible. And when we've done that, we could easily flood the market with cut-price and free goods because we would be unaffected by the hassles of big-profit margins and engineered scarcity which string out the squares.

The potential of the love economy is limitless, and we'll realise more and more of it as we devop our love communes. Meanwhile let's

wise up on what a love commune really is.

What Is A Love Commune?

A love commune is a group of diggers practising together the digger dharma of love, freedom and sharing. It is a nucleus of the love society and has a love economy. It is interlinked with other love communes all over the world in a love network.

For the digger dharma to be a concrete reality within the love commune, all diggers must be hip to certain fundamental points of the dharma and practise these within their love communes. The following are some of these points whose reification characterises the fully-developed love commune.

Point On Love In The Love Commune In Full Flower.

(1) There is love in everyone for all sentient beings.

(2) In everyone there is the openness and nakedness of love and complete freedom from all square hangups.

(3) Everyone has arrived at that enlightened state of expanded awareness known as yung-huo (in chinese). This is a state best described as freedom from possessive or clinging attachment to things.

(4) In everyone there is sympathetic and compassionate understanding for the failings and deficiencies of others.

When these points are realised, there will be true communion between the diggers of the commune. Love communes are powered by love and it's love that makes what's human divine.

Points On Freedom And Sharing In The Love Commune In Full Flower.

(1) The love commune is an anarchistic organisation without any authoritarian hangups. This means it has no place for such megalomanic frauds and con-men as leaders and bosses and quack gurus.

(2) All work as far as possible is shared by all. There is no swindle like a permanent 'division of labour' which inevitably leads to division of people into different classes.

(3) All knowledge and enlightenment are shared and made available and free to all. This means that there is no monopolistic professionalism. This means diggers can and will evolve into versatile or even universal cats and chicks with their beautiful potentialities maximally realised, and thus become the forerunners of the fully aware and enlightened beings of the coming Aquarian Age. And each digger contributes to the love commune according to his or her ability.

(4) All material goods of the commune are shared out to each digger according to his or her need or, when the goods are abundant, simply made available and free to all.

(5) All drudgery, toiling and moiling are automated out of productions so that everyone can have as much leisure as possible to do his or her own thing.

(6) Everyone is free to do his or her own thing on the understanding that he or she does not shit on the freedom of others.

(7) To ensure true personal freedom, no one is treated or regarded as the property of another - this applies to children as well as adults. No one has

any 'rights' over another and parents have no 'rights' over their children.

(8) The freedom, well-being, education and enlightenment of children are the responsibility of the whole commune.

(9) To ensure true sexual freedom, the sexual relationship between a couple is treated as a mutual arrangement which is freely entered into and which may be of as long or short a duration as is convenient to both parties. It may be freely broken at any time by either party and both may then make new arrangements with new parties - a current arrangement automatically cancelling out a previous one. The sexual arrangement is regarded as entirely the concern of the couple involved and is not subjected to the unsolicited interference of a third party. All sexual matters are freely discussed and openly illustrated and demonstrated as desired.

(10) There are neither putdowns like laws, rules and regulations nor putons like pharisaic respectability and morality and 'holier-than-thou' attitudes. The lifeways of the diggers are always entirely a matter of love and understanding.

The foregoing points, if fully realised, will raise the practice of freedom and sharing to a new high in human society.

Practical Side-Issues And The Revolutionary Praxis.

The diggers of each love commune will work out for themselves the practical details not only of the diggers' dharma but also of certain side-issues which may arise from their particular environment.

For example, in the early days of love commune development it may be of value or even indispensable for some communes to have weekend or part-time diggers. Again it may be useful or necessary for some diggers to learn kung-fu and/or judo and/or karate for self-defence against the brutal violence of thugs, bullies and other crooks and evil elements, including sadistic fuzz.

If our revolutionary praxis is a living and tuned-in one, it can easily cope with such side-issues. To keep the praxis evergreen and always in tune and in touch, it is essential to have a revolutionary critique and a revolutionary dialogue among the diggers to ensure that each and every practical detail pertaining to the praxis will be both meaningful and effective.

The London Diggers' Love Commune.

With this point in view, my dharma comrades associated with *OZ* magazine, *The International Times* newspaper, Family Dog Productions, The Arts Laboratory, The Tribe of The Sacred Mushroom, The Hyde Park Digger Movement (The Flower Children), The 192A People and The Exploding Galaxy, and myself invite all love revolutionaries to join us at the first open forum of The London Diggers' Love Commune, which will be convened to discuss the launching of the commune. We also invite everybody to the commune's first 'Breaking Ground' ceremony to be held on a subsequent occasion. If you are interested and would like to participate in the forum and/or the ceremony, please write to:
Diggers,
c/o OZ Publications Ink Ltd.,
38A Palace Gardens Terrace,
London W8.

OZ NO 9 February 1968

London OZ is published approximately monthly by OZ Publications Ink Ltd, 38a Palace Gardens Terrace, London W8. Phone: Bay 4623 . . . 727 1042.

Editor: Richard Neville

Deputy Editor: Paul Lawson

Design: Jon Goodchild assisted by Virginia Clive-Smith

Creative Consultant Andrew Fisher

Advertising: Penny Service at FLA 5785

Subscriptions: Louise Ferrier

Pusher: Felix Dennis

Photography: Keith Morris

Contributors : Martin Sharp David Widgery, David Reynolds, Julian Manyon Lynn Richards

Distribution: Moore-Harness Ltd, 11 Lever Street, London EC1 Phone: CLE 4882.

Printing: Steel Bros (Carlisle) Ltd. Phone: Carlisle 25181/4. Printed Web Offset.

Typesetting: Big O Press Ltd, 49 Kensington High Street, London W8. Phone: 937 2613/4

WE'RE BACKING THE WORLD

Dear Sir,

Although suicide is no longer a crime, it remains an offense to aid , abet or counsel suicide in specific cases. Raymond Durgnat's letter in the last issues of your journal almost arouses the wish that the encouragement of suicide in general should be subject to the same penalties. He will no doubt attempt to shelter behind the distinguished poets from whom he quotes. But this would be to take these verses outside the context of their authors' obvious concern with the betterment of human life. Great art is on the side of Life, never of Death.

Yours sincerely,
David Holbrook

Dear Sir,

I am not in the least surprised that your correspondent Raymond Durgnat has failed to find a suitable suicide prescription.

His article is garlanded with quotations from various kinematograph entertainments and from such such minor literary figures as Messrs Housman and Keats. If he had turned aside from these pootling foothills, and directed his attention towards my towering plays, he would immediately have found the recipe he requires.

In 'The Millionairess', which I presented to the world almost one-third of a century ago, Epifania Fitzfassenden, nee Ognisanti di Parerga, approaches her solicitor, Julius Sagamore, with a similar request, and is immediately gratified with the following instructions:

'You will have to sign the chemist's book for the cyanide. Say it is for a wasp's nest. The tartaric acid is harmless; the chemist will think you want it to make lemonade. Put the two separately in just enough water to dissolve them. When you mix the two solutions the tartaric and potash will combine and make tartrate of potash. This, being insoluble, will precipitate to the bottom of the glass; and the supernatant fluid will be pure hydrocyanic acid, one sip of which will kill you like a thunderbolt.'
Time spent on the enjoyment of the loftier peaks of English literature is never wasted.
Yours,
G.B.S.

Raymond Durgnat replies:
So stalwart an exponent of the life-force as Mr Shaw cannot but command one's respect. He has, perhaps, had a little difficulty in understanding the problems of the weaker candidates for suicide,

with whose plight I probably find it easier to identify: with those who could hardly face the complex task of conning a chemist of asking for cyanide in a nonchalant voice, of looking as if they have access to a garden with wasps' nests.

Dear Sir,

After reading John Wilcox' 'blue print for a beautiful community (OZ No 7) - almost arose from apathy to comment - J.W.'s enthusiasm for freebie dogma overpowered his capacity for reason (assuming he has one) and faith in politics and willingness for compromise with the Establishment, in the last paragraph was excrutiatingly nauseous. Despite these emotional reactions I was silent, not wishing to shatter the tranquil intellectual progress of your readers and amigos.

Come OZ No 8, and remarkable Angelo Quattrochi's sermon upon the freakdom of Russia (which has rushed nowhere slow) stating criticisms and targets supernaturally parallel to my own. Russia is now fast retracting within its own A.M.M. shell. The Gremlin has decided that it is now prepared to undergo a nuclear attack (vis civil exercises resumed) and has redetermined to undermine PEACEFUL co-existence.

With more unstable regimes, an expanding wipeout gang, population explosion, germ warfare, famine, race war, Chinese missiles etc. ad infinitum, posing a mushroom threat to the very continuance of man; the time has come for a radical ideological change . . . NOW! It should be intolerable to us to contemplate the total eradication of life on earth. (see 'Words' by J-P Sartre)

Leo Tolstoy, a religious anarchist, had a solution which Ghandi

proved practical in India in the forties: He advocated rule by Love, i.e. abolition of organized authority. This would mean the free association of individuals, no armed forces, courts, prisons or written law. Hippies believe in a peaceful transition to anarchy Regis Debray & Che Guevara demand revolution,as do 'Tomorrow' on their last record. It is not these aims which require debate only the methods advocated for achieving them. Peaceful anarchists like Tolstoy proposed refusal by the people to
1) render military service
2) to pay taxes
3) to recognise the courts and the police;
while Guevarian radicals proposed armed insurrection and revolution by the people at the 1877 & 1907 International Anarchist Congresses. Their common purpose . . . the collapse of the established order!
Assuming that the world 'civilisation' is truly doomed these are the alternatives facing us: extinction, revolution, or transition peacefully. This first is ludicrous and the other two are dependent upon how much time we feel we can spare. Hippies are a long term solution whereas the Revolutionaries believe the problem to be more urgent, thereby requiring more radical action. It remains to be seen which method humanity will choose, provided it has time to do so!

Yours sincerely,
N.A. Megson (optimist)
Solihull,
Warwickshire.

Dear Sir,

I would have thought that such a lavish presentation as your Che Guevara fold-in merited a bit more attention than it obviously received.

I can visualize your design and layout people congratulating each other over their latest neopsychedelic, total man, super-hero creation.

'Are you sure it's Gee- Eee- Ewe? who cares, man they'll know who he is. We'll explain all that at the bottom, and we'll throw in g - e - urillas just to really upset everyone.'

'Men like Guevara are too big and angry for our world of typewriters and soft hands.'

You said it and I bet He'd puke if he could see the hollow tribute you've paid him.

Yours,

J. Russell Wimbush
13 Ladbroke Cresc.,
London W.11.

All advertising enquiries to Penny Service at FLA 5785.

SUBSCRIBE NOW!

In No. 24 . .
Berlin Commune/ Sedition Goes On
Belgium Experimental Film Festival.
The Nature of Vision by Jeff Nuttall
Roy Lichtenstein interview
ALL THE NEWS THAT FITS WE
PRINT.

To: INTERNATIONAL TIMES 22 Betterton St., WC1

I want to be an iT distributer ....

I want to be an IT girl ....

I want to sell advertising space for IT ....,

I WANT TO SUBSCRIBE TO IT AND ENCLOSE AT
LEAST £2 ....

(or equivalent amount) for One year ....

NAME ....

ADDRESS ....

....

MEN IT CAN BE DONE

Now available --- MAGNAPHALL ---
a sound and successful method
of improving virility and increasing
the size of the male organ. A method
which is absolutely SAFE , involves no
drugs or apparatus and is GUARANTEED
MAGNAPHALL has helped thousands of
men, all over the world. There is no
longer a need for any man to envy the
sexual vigour or proportions of others.
You don't have to believe us --
we can send you such PROOF as will
convince even the most skeptical.
For full details of how MAGNAPHALL
works and positive proof of it's
success, in strict confidence and with
no obligation, write to:-

RAVENSDALE PRODUCTS LTD.
SECTION T
SPRINGFIELD ROAD,
LONDON. N.15.

DO YOU WANT MORE OUT OF YOUR SEX LIFE?

We have an extensive range of items
designed to increase the intensity of
sexual pleasure. Many of these have
never before been available in this
country. If there is something that
you may have heard of, but can't
get - try us . . .

ROOM 3

Pellen Personal Products LTD.
47 Muswell Hill Broadway, London N.10

From Michael X, Swansea

The last time I sat down to write I had no idea where the writing would lead: a book, however, came out of it. In that document I find that I was consistently accusing myself. Well to that I say 'beautiful' for the more I accuse myself the more I have the right to judge you. Better yet I make you judge yourself, which makes it that much less necessary for me to do it.

Don't matter where I start from. It can be called a bad start, but still let us compare feelings. I would like to say let us compare facts. But then I may take offence as what you present to me as fact, and here lies one of the strange dichotomies that arises whenever we speak to each other. So, like I said to the judge, (in Reading) I have no doubt that some of the things I say may sound offensive to your ears, but please bear in mind that your words may unknowingly have been an assault on my ears all my life. Nonetheless, these words must be spoken for with meaningful dialogues we may yet be able to contain the conflagration.

At this precise moment I visualise myself talking to people: black people, white people; and, this is important, the others, for so many people to-day are in the strange state of limbo. I would like to describe what I mean when I say white people. They include some folk with black skins with thoughts as grey as the majority of anglo-saxons and of course the majority of anglo-saxons, they are white people.

It seems strange to me that I use two words like 'White Monkeys' and white people get very offended, when in point of fact that is being quite kind, for I could have said 'white man' and that is probably the nastiest thing that a black man could call another human being, and daily, they, the grey ones, hear it and never even get slightly upset.

To-day I look back at that trial in Reading and I see what was really needed were interpretors, for during this monumental farce the judge invited me to come and stand two or three feet away from him. Me, who has always said that there is more of us than them. Yes, me, who sincerely believes that there is only one way to go when you are sure you are going, and that's taking one of them with you. That judge could not have understood a word I was saying for all that he had between him and his maker was those two or three feet of empty space. Judges, I believe, are the main bastions of grey thought. The greys are few but they are powerful. They have succeeded in

splitting us in so many bits that it isn't funny. They create mythical alliances and we see them as real. For example when the word 'White' is used in relation to racial issues all the pink people, all the pale faces together with the greys see themselves as a monolithic group and act accordingly. This unique power of persuasion, through which the greys have ruled for centuries I call the grey super power super structure. It claims almost every media of mass communication. It is almost unbeatable, for people are naturally attracted to that which is strong. And all the pink idiots identify there.

How many pink or pale faced readers will actually renounce this alliance and come and fight the good fight with us, for man, for free man? No. I have heard them: 'you are right, but . . .'. Please, please, ask yourselves this for anyway you care to look at it there is more us than you.

And still they pretend not to understand for they see finally that truth is facing them, so they ask 'What is really wanted is apartheid in reverse, isn't it?' How can I answer after trying so hard to show the many shades of man.

So I evade the question, for I know they will be no better off if I say 'No' in reply. Instead we talk a bit about South Africa and they say that apartheid is abhorrent. I make my final plea - can't you see now why our struggle must be international? What are we going to do when black people begin to storm Johannesburg, Durban, Capetown? What role are you going to take then? For it is obvious that this country will go the way of protecting its financial interests in South Africa, which in effect means protecting the grey thinking South Africans. We cannot wait until D-Day to organise ourselves. It is crystal clear that it is the duty of all clean thinkers to be ready to oppose or at least to neutralise the greys.

There you see one example of why we must move now. Letters or even a big advertisement in The Times condemning the action of the British government will not be enough. At this point I will have to fight you too, for then the end will be near and in that sea of faces one cannot identify individuals. When that happens all is lost. Your cause and mine. Just think this is only one example of many such situations around the world. Now I see the problem, they say, but you put it badly, if you will change the language . . . . Allah be merciful. Give me patience.

Give me guidance. Just like the prayer was unheard. Out goes my cool. Instead a torrent of words 'What else must I change?' Why don't you do some changing too? Why is it always me who must change? No. I will not change. This is how I have twisted and turned to please you. I have done your building for centuries. Now I put my foot down. You will have to look at me in the eyes with truth this time or all that you have worked for will go. I can give no more. Naught have I and since that is the legacy for my children like it was for my father and his father before him, so it will be for you and yours. In this world there are two kinds of people - the takers and the took. We have been took. You have always told me what I wanted, now let me tell you what I want . . . .

MICHAEL

Justice Partial, Your Lies Are Showing

The week before Christmas, Michael Abdul Malik was taken from Swansea goal to make his fourth court appearance, this time before Lord Chief Justice Parker at the High Court of Appeal. Mr. Pain Q.C. Counsel for the Defence, did all the talking, finding four grounds for appeal.

For a start, in the light of 'The Sunday Times' article which described Malik as taking to politics after an unedifying career as brothel-keeper, procurer and property racketeer 'the trial should not have proceeded. Mindful of his career Mr. Pain neglected to press the obvious: that Justice Parker had in this same court a fortnight earlier fined the owners of 'The Sunday Times' £5,000 for contempt of court and was now backpedalling. Though the article was likely to have caused an unfair trial', declared Milord Parker, 'in the opinion of this court it did not have that effect'.

Secondly Mr. Pain cited the Reading prosecution's choice of evidence as showing the jury that Malik had been in prison before. Thirdly he showed how the Recorder had failed to put the case fairly to the jury. On the question of Michael's intent the Recorder had presented the jury with a bogus simplification: 'did Malik understand what he was saying or didn't he? Michael's defence in fact rested on his being of a different background and so using the words in a different sense to that understood by the white majority. For a full hour Michael had explained at his Reading trial why the oppressed cannot and must not

accept the culture of their oppressor, how the white man had subverted the black. The Recorder left all that out in his summing up to the jury. The accused was getting personal; the court had listened in absolute silence.

Q.C. Pain made an awkward point for a liberal advocate: that Michael's complaints and abuse related to the system, not to individuals or as the law has it, a section of the public distinguished by colour'. Parker, whey-faced and tight-smiling, didn't need to be told this. He dug what was in question, his own top job in that system, and what he had to do with this political criminal, shut him up.

Lastly Defence suggested to Parker it would be a help if he could lay down some precedent for this type of case. Wasn't Michael's sentence of one year excessive for a first offence under the Race Relations Act; hadn't the four coloured speakers tried on the same charge at the Old Bailey been fined £30 with one 2 year, binding over? Parker would not be drawn. Defence had failed to pose an intriguing problem for his learned mind to work upon. Each case must be dealt with individually. Parker replied and dismissed all four grounds for appeal.

Rather patronisingly Pain suggested that the coloured people had very little political experience and so lacked the background to English public life of an Englishman's sense of what is reasonable and what is not. Had Michael's original speech actually endangered the public peace, did we read that Reading rioted? Or had some chunks of misreported speech disturbed the media-believers' peace of mind? Either way the Race Relations Act was a good stick to beat down a man not deceived by it.

Question for the Establishment: Is Michael Abdul Malik backed by an organisation ready to execute the speaker's calls for action?

Question for the public: If Michael Abdul Malik is fishing in troubled waters (see Political and Economic Planning Report now before Parliament) will the spread of legal oil do more than calm the surface? Discrimination in public places has roots in the private prejudice of individuals. How do you legislate a change of heart?

Guy Gladstone
721 Fulham Road,
London S.W.6.

Open letter t o Castro by Angelo Quattrocchi

Compagnero Fidel,

Back in the Sierra you promised to transform all Cuba's prisons into schools, the army barracks into hospitals.

The Batista tyranny over your country made you first a political opponent, then a guerrilla, and finally a victorious leader - and a Marxist statesman.

Some come to Cuba to see if you have built, if you can build, the schools and the hospitals which you promised. Others come to see how Cuba bears the blockade; what the Cubans eat, what they wear, how they cope. Those who come with small minds - and small questions - leave with their small answers, for the overfed philistines of the world: the Cubans cope well.

Many come claiming that Cuban socialism is subsidized by Russia (and China?) and therefore its achievements and significance are very limited.

You do not need to answer them; they are often the ones who deal in South African gold, they choose their friends.

But I came with different questions, and other hopes.

The hopes of European Marxists; hopes destroyed by Stalin, killed in Hungary, mocked by revisionism.

Seemingly impossible hopes that a change in society means a change in man. The other world, China, has offered us negative hopes: it can only teach us humility, no more.

Cuba, the hostage of the future, suggested more than a geographical diversion. From the start, it promised more than a revised edition of the socialism of the means and the capitalism of the heart. In words made pathetic by our long wait and our historical impotence, we hoped, not only for social justice, but for socialist happiness.

Our questions were simple, and therefore very difficult to formulate. 'When exploitation of one man by another ends,' said Che, 'socialism begins.'

But that is only the beginning; the Russians decided that it was all, and when man's heart didn't change, affirmed that nothing else could be done - and late - pretended that all had been. A socialist dropout of historical proportions.

The Chinese have had to wait for us all, while we ride the ferocious paper tiger, judiciously imparting phosphorous death to the struggling. But Cuba, privileged by its own smallness, its unique position, can go further. The two old hopes of Marxism, elimination of money

and the obliteration of the family, are in sight.

Money means a reward for egoism. It is an unnecessary incentive for a free, happy and responsible man.

Family means egoism applied to emotions. A free and happy man does not need to own other people he enjoys them.

Now in the West, young people freed, by chance, from the fear of necessity, are tentatively striving to get rid of these bonds. They are achieving little but offering an image of what our future could be.

Cuba could make reality of their dreams. I am not mistaken: the young work-brigades on the Isla de Pinos are already that future.

But the morality of production must not be allowed to over-ride the ultimate morality of the revolution: human happiness.

Let us speak simply and sincerely. Life is not easy in Cuba - hard work is necessary. Young Cubans are enthusiastic and give their energies to the work in hand. Their society must not only be just, it must also become beautiful. They must invent it, and for that they don't need money, only total freedom of choice and decision, whenever and wherever possible.

A few brigades of ideological dissenters from Europe, the young who have discovered the way of the future through moral dissent, could help.

You, Fidel, could invite them to come. Some will, I know, go next summer to work, they could form the first international brigade of the new revolution. Ask them.

They would not come for love of money, only for love of the revolution - which means love.

Dear Sir,

As a free-lance writer and, at the moment, also an instructor in Magazine Journalism (at Univ. of Iowa), may I say that rarely have I seen a more confused, confusing, botched-looking, noxious, sloppy, tasteless or incoherent magazine than yours. Keep up the good work!

Yours admiringly,

Bob Perlongo
School of Journalism,
University of Iowa,
Iowa 52240, USA.

Dear Sir,

Many congratulations on the success of your magazine 'OZ', biggest confidence trick of the modern age. You are very fortunate in having discovered such a large section of the public who are so naive as to be seduced into buying your superficial magazine.

As a new reader I expected to discover something which, if not revolutionary, may at least be termed original. Regrettably I failed to find this. Certainly, your ideas about sex are completely opposed to the norms of society, similarly your attitude to drug-taking. However, all this proves is that you are able to look at the values of society and decide that yours will be exactly the opposite, hardly a very mature attitude. Constructive thinking is evidently beyond your ability and you are merely able to find fault with the ideas of others, something which is not beyond the most simple-minded

I therefore sympathise with those who think they are discovering some new philosophy in your magazine for they are sadly mistaken.
Yours etc.,

Sheila Ladd
University College,
Glamorgan.

You are making money out of Flirt with your magazine, the So called OZ and I am glad to see the "people" Newspaper is about to do something about this and about time too, there are others of this work's about to become, Anyway at this SLUSH!

In the beginning God created the heaven and earth. And the earth was without form, and void; and darkness was upon the face of the deep, and the Spirit of God moved upon the face of the waters. And God said: Let there be light; and there was light. And God saw the light that it was good.

Genesis 1.1-4

I believe that there have been civilisations in the past that were familiar with atomic energy, and by misusing it they were totally destroyed.

Frederick Soddy

Observing that the human young needs a long period of care and protection, Anaximander concludes that had man always been as he is now, he could not have survived. Therefore he must have been different, that is, he must have evolved from an animal which can fend for itself more quickly. Later, Darwin explained the theory of evolution in terms of natural selection from a universal ancestral organism.

Bertrand Russell, 1959

It may be that other forms of humanity, or rather other thinking beings, made their appearance and disappeared. They may not have left visible traces, but their memory is preserved in legends . . .

Ten thousand years ago an enlightened civilisation controlled the world. It set up in the Frozen North zones of deportation. Now what do we find in Eskimo folklore? References to tribes being transported to the Frozen North at the beginning of time by giant metallic birds. Nineteenth century archaeologists always scoffed at these 'metallic birds'. And what do you think?

Louis Pauwels/Jack Bergier, 1960

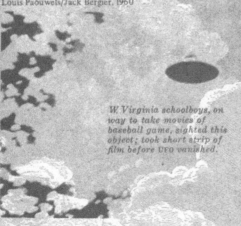

W. Virginia schoolboys, on way to take movies of baseball game, sighted this object; took short strip of film before UFO vanished.

No matter how cheerful and unsuspicious my disposition may be, when I go to the American Museum of Natural History dark cynicisms arise the moment I come to the fossils or old bones that have been found - gigantic things, reconstructed into terrifying but 'proper' Dinosaurs. On one of the floors below they have reconstructed the DODO. It's frankly a fiction . . . but it's been reconstructed so cleverly and so convincingly . . .

I think we are property. I should say we belong to something that once upon a time this earth was no man's land, that other worlds explored and colonised here and fought among themselves for possession, but that now its' owned by something . . .

I suspect that, after all, we are useful - that among contesting claimants adjustment has occured, or that something now has a legal right to us, by force, or by having paid out analogues of beads for us to former owners of us - and that all this has been known, perhaps for ages, to certain ones upon this Earth, a cult, or Order, members of which function like bell-wethers to the rest of us, or as superior slaves or overseers, directing in accordance with instructions received from Somewhere else - in our mysterious usefulness.

In the past, before proprietorship was established, inhabitants of a host of other worlds have dropped here, hopped here, wafted sailed, flown, motored - walked here, for all I know - been pulled here, been pushed; have come singly, have come in enormous numbers; have visited occasionally, have periodically, for hunting, trading, mining, replenishing harems; have established colonies here; far-advanced peoples, or things, and primitive peoples or whatever they were; white ones, black ones, yellow ones . . . We are not alone; the Earth is not alone.

Charles Fort

The recognition of our eternal ignorance does not lead back to religion. In fact the acceptance of our incorrigible ignorance puts us far above the religions. The latter know the ultimate answer to everything. The explanation of everything is embodied for them in a three letter word beginning with G and ending in D, with an O in the middle.

Hans Elias, 1966

It seems certain that the world stands at the threshold of a new Age and that life on our planet in all its forms is enduring the birth pangs that precede a new dispensation . . . In the villages of West Somerset there still exists a tradition which says that: The Day will come when Jesus the Christ will come striding up the lanes from Cornwall on His way to Avelon.

Wellesley Tudor Pole, 1951

How can men be prevailed upon and empowered to make the radical changes in thinking and living which are indispensable for man's survival and for his evolution into a higher state of being?

Talk would be incomplete without mention of telepathic messages purporting to be coming from the inhabitants of other planets, many of them beyond our solar system, which reflect an apprehension that we may, by some foolhardy act set fire to the earths outer atmosphere, which consists largely of helium. These messages are being received in different parts of the world and are generally accompanied by invitations to the effect that our activities have long been observed by these friendly and highly evolved visitors from outerspace, who are ready to welcome us into their interplanetry brotherhood the moment we show signs of becoming a little more civilised. In fact, their purpose in coming is to help their brother man on planet earth as the new age dawns. The principal governments of the world know about these things, but are at present somewhat confused. Clearly nothing is more likely to result in a dramatic transformation almost overnight of the worldwide ordering of affairs on earth than the enforced admission by governments, that government as we know it, including the whole gamut of our national self-defence system, is outdated. Many things are being kept from the peoples of the world which they need to know at this time, but all doubts will soon be replaced as our visitors from outer space begin to show themselves in greater numbers all over the world. Anthony Brooke, 1965

Secrecy results from the nature of the thing kept secret, and is not necessarily imposed by those who know.

Louis Pauwels/Jack Bergier, 1960

It would clearly be vain to study approaches to human unity and the creation of a planetary society in a narrow perspective divorced from the total stream of our evolutionary development and from significant universal cosmic facts which are widely impinging themselves upon our consciousness at this time. Although there may be need to give careful consideration to whatever institutions, frameworks and laws we may envisage for our world society, it is equally indispensible and even more important to direct our concern to the spirit of our world community in its individual and collective expression and in particular to the ways and means of effecting the release of those infinite divine resources which, like the power locked up in the atom, lie virtually asleep at the core of our individual being. It is an awakening of these latent powers which alone can give glory and meaning to life on earth. Without such an awakening any 'peace' and 'unity' brought about by external arrangements of a formal character will be without substance and will certainly not meet the deepest aspirations of the heart and soul of man.

Anthony Brooke, 1967

He who seeks to aquire knowledge must first know how to doubt, for intellectual doubt helps to establish the truth.

Aristotle, 360 BC

...was a small creature, with a normal human ...e, from 1 meter to 1.20 meters tall; he was ...aring a transparent suit that covered him ...npletely: he reminded me of a child ...apped in a cellophane bag.

One of the things, it seems to me, that most of us most eagerly accept and take for granted is the question of beliefs. I am not attacking beliefs. What we are trying to do is to find out why we accept beliefs; and if we can understand the motives, the causation of acceptance, then perhaps we may be able not only to understand why we do it, but also be free of it. One can see how political and religious beliefs, national and various other types of beliefs, do separate people, do create conflict, confusion, and antagonism - which is an obvious fact; and yet we are unwilling to give them up. There is the Hindu belief, the Christian belief, the Buddhist - innumerable sectarian and national beliefs, various political ideologies, all contending with each other, trying to convert each other. One can see, obviously, that belief is separating people, creating intolerance; is it possible to live without belief? One can find that out only if one can study oneself in relationship to a belief. Is it possible to live in this world without a belief - not change beliefs, not substitute one belief for another, but be entirely free from all beliefs, so that one meets life anew each minute? This, after all, is the truth; to have the capacity of meeting everything anew, from moment to moment, without the conditioning reaction of the past, so that there is not the cumulative effect which acts as a barrier between oneself and that which is.

J Krishnamurti, 1954

Sun turning round - graceful motion
We're setting off with soft explosion
Bound for a star fiery ocean
It's so very lonely
You're a 100 light years from home
Freezing red desert turned to dark
Energy here in every part . . .

Mick Jagger, 1967

The question . . . is not whether there is intelligent life in space but: is there intelligent life down here on earth?

Max Lerner, 1967

I saw a great star most splendid and beautiful, and with it an exceeding multitude of falling sparks which with the star followed southward. And they examined Him upon His throne almost as something hostile, and turning from Him they sought rather the north. And suddenly they were all annihilated, being turned into black coals . . . and cast into the abyss that I could see them no more.

Hildegard of Bingen, 1195

It seems amazing that man was so philosophically advanced in such ancient times. The mere fact that any culture in those days could deduce the correct explanation for the whiteness of the Milky Way is astonishing! There seems to be more mystery about early man than any anthropologist has guessed.

Joseph F Goodavage, 1967

The *Daily Express* published an interesting account from their representative in Moscow, Mr. Roy Blackman, who wrote to say that Russia is to open the world's first UFO detection agency. He went on to tell how it was revealed over the weekend that a Soviet scientific commission will in future investigate all corroborated sightings of UFOs over the Soviet Union. The commission, he said, is headed by Air Force General Anatoli Stolyerov. The establishment of the agency, added Mr. Blackman, represents a rethinking by Soviet scientists on flying saucers, which have always previously been ridiculed, and he concluded his piece with a reference to the Zigel article, and the new appraisal revealed therein.

One of our friends, recently in Moscow, had given us prior notice, in a letter dated October 25, that a permanent commission had been established on October 18. We also understand, from other sources, that General Stolyerov's No. 2 is the distinguished Dr. Zigel, and that among others the committee includes an unnamed Russian cosmonaut and 18 scientists and astronomers. There will also be 200 qualified observers throughout the country, and the Commission will be particularly interested in persistent reports from the Caucasus, the Urals and Central Asia.

On November 9, 1965, 80,000 square miles of America was plunged into darkness by the failure of the Northeast Power Grid. The magnitude of such a failure; its consequences and its forbidding potential demanded and received instant investigation and general world-wide puzzlement and requests for explanation.

Quick answers were given and hastily retracted.

One early explanation was that a line break near Niagara Falls was the cause. This proved not to be the case. The blame switched to power lines near Clay, NY. They were not at fault. Investigators turned their attention to trouble in the Montezuma Marshes near Syracuse. Everything ship-shape. Ultimately the cause was said to have been a malfunctioning tripper at the Sir Adam Beck No 2 plant, in Canada. But authorities admit today that the real cause of the disastrous blackout remains a mystery.

The utility companies, the Air Force and the press made little mention of the reported UFO sighting that afternoon of November 9. Two commercial airline pilots spotted two disc shaped objects flying over Pennsylvania. In pursuit were two jets. At 4.30 p.m. a tremendous burst of speed carried the UFOs out of sight. At 5.30 p.m. a brilliantly glowing light was seen coming down over Syracuse, NY. At that same time 36,000,000 people were plunged into the Great North Eastern Blackout. Two huge fireballs were reported by two sets of reliable witnesses at this same time; one over the airport at Syracuse; the other above the power lines leading to the generating plant at Niagara Falls.

"Lamentation," by the Belgian artist A. M. Rener. Professor C. J. Jung observed that the shape of the "flying saucer" was commonly depicted by artists, generally associated with fantastic themes.

Joseph F Goodavage, 1967

"BUT EVEN MORE UNTHINKABLE, TO EARTHLINGS, IS THE WORLD OF CYBORGIA, IN MACABRE LABORATORIES OF ITS LIVING MACHINE INHABITANTS..."

THE MAN-THING IS NOT PLEASED BY ITS NEWLY-GAINED IMMORTALITY!

VERY, VERY STRANGE!

NO, NO, NO! I WOULD RATHER BE DEAD THAN EXIST AS 'HALF-MAN AND HALF-MACHINE' IN AN ALIEN LABORATORY!

On November 4 Jose Alves of Pontal was fishing in the Pardo River near Pontal. The area was deserted, the night quiet with only a slight breeze blowing from the east. Suddenly Alves spotted a strange craft in the sky, apparently heading towards him. He watched, transfixed, as it closed in with a wobbling motion and landed. It was so near he could have touched it, he said. The object appeared as two wash-bowls placed together, looked to be about ten to fifteen feet in diameter. He was too frightened to run. Three little men, clad in white clothing with close-fitting skullcaps, emerged from a window-like opening in the side of the small craft. Their skin appeared to be quite dark. Alves stood terror-striken, watching the small creatures collect samples of grass, herbs and leaves of trees; one of them filled a shiny metal tube with river water. Then, as suddenly as they had come, they jumped back into their machine, which took off vertically as swiftly and silently as it had come. Residents of Pontal, who heard Alves story when he came back to town, told the press he was a quiet man who lived only for his work and his family. He had never heard of flying saucers, and he was sure the little men were some kind of devils.

Coral E Lorenzen, 1967

We are no longer living in an age where progress is assessed exclusively in terms of technical and scientific advances. Another factor has to be considered, the same that was envisaged by the Unknown Elite in olden days who showed that Liber Mundi was concerned with 'Something else'.

Louis Paouwels/Jack Bergier, 1960

A man travelling across a field encountered a tiger. He fled, the tiger after him.

Coming to a precipice, he swung himself down over the edge. The tiger sniffed at him from above. Trembling, the man looked down to where, far below, another tiger was waiting to eat him. Only the vine sustained him.

Two mice, one white and one black, little by little started to gnaw away the vine. The man saw a luscious strawberry near him. Grasping the vine with one hand, he plucked the strawberry with the other.

How sweet it tasted!.

A Zen story

No man can reveal to you aught but that which already lies half asleep in the dawning of your knowledge.

The teacher who walks in the shadow of the temple, among his followers, gives not of his wisdom but rather of his faith and his lovingness.

If he is indeed wise he does not bid you enter the house of his wisdom, but rather leads you to the threshold of your own mind.

The astronomer may speak to you of his understanding of space, but he cannot give you his understanding.

The musician may sing to you of the rhythm which is in all space, but he cannot give you the ear which arrests the rhythm, nor the voice that echoes it.

And he who is versed in the science of numbers can tell of the regions of weight and measure, but he cannot conduct you thither.

Kahil Gibran, 1926

More ancient writings have been lost than have been preserved, and perhaps our new discoveries are of less value than those that we have lost.

Atterbury

On September 14, 1957, Ibrahim Sued, a well-known Rio de Janeiro society columnist, reported a strange story which startled the readers of his column in the newspaper 'O Globo'. Under the heading, 'A fragment From a Flying Disc,' he wrote:

We received the letter : 'Dear Mr. Ibrahim Sued. As a faithful reader of your column and your admirer, I wish to give you something of the highest interest to a newspaperman, about the flying discs. If you believe anything said or published about them. But just a few days ago I was forced to change my mind. I was fishing together with some friends, at a place close to the town of Obatuba, Sao Paulo, when I sighted a flying disc. It approached the beach at unbelievable speed and an accident, i.e. a crash into the sea seemed imminent. At the last moment, however, when it was almost striking the waters, it made a sharp turn upward and climbed rapidly on a fantastic impulse. We followed the spectacle with our eyes, startled, when we saw the disc explode in flames. It disintegrated into thousands of fiery fragments, which fell sparkling with magnificent brightness. They looked like fire-works, despite the time of the accident, at noon, i.e. at midday. Most of these fragments, almost all, fell into the sea. But a number of small pieces fell close to the beach and we picked up a large amount of this material - which was as light as paper. I am enclosing a small sample of it. I don't know anyone that could be trusted to whom I might send it for analysis. I never read about a flying disc being found, or about fragments or parts of a saucer that had been picked up. Unless the finding was made by military authorities and the whole thing kept as a top-secret subject. I am certain the matter will be of great interest to the brilliant columnist and I am sending two copies of this letter to the newspaper and to your home address.'

From the admirer (the signature was not legible), together with the above letter, I received fragments of a strange metal . . .

The magnesium in the samples analyzed, which was absolutely pure in the spectrographic sense, represents something outside the range of present-day technological development in earth science. In fact, the metal was of such fantastic purity that even to see it symbolized on paper is unbelievable. Even the infinitesimal quantities of 'trace elements' usually detected by spectrographic analysis - traces so small they could not possibly be detected by any other analytical method - were not found. Thus, the magnesium in the samples was absolutely pure in the spectrographic sense - with a percentage of 100. X-ray spectrometry and X-ray diffractometry by the powder method confirmed the results of the spectrographic analyses - the metal was pure magnesium. Again, no impurity was detected to introduce irregularities in the crystal lattice. The presence of any impurity of any interstitial atoms would change the regularity of the crystal lattice, thus causing crystal imperfections that would be revealed by the X-ray method. Therefore, on the basis of the chemical analyses the conclusion was that the magnesium in the samples was of absolute purity, in the sense that any other possible constituents which could be present would be present in such an infinitesimal amount as to be beyond the reach of any known method of chemical analysis.

We know very little about metals completely free of impurities and imperfections, simply because they are never found in nature and, in most cases cannot be prepared in the laboratory. It is not too difficult to refine a metal to 99.99% purity (which means there is something else besides the metal to the extent of 1 part in 10,000), but once beyond this point the going gets rough. For every 9 we tack on after the decimal point following the first two 9s, the cost increases tenfold, sometimes a hundredfold. This is so because involved, delicate and time-consuming crystallization operations are required so that the final product becomes more precious than gold.

On the basis of this evidence, it is highly probable the metallic chunks picked up on the beach near Ubatuba, in Sao Paulo, Brazil, are extraterrestrial in origin. This is indeed an extremely important and almost incredible conclusion. But on the basis of the findings of these chemical analyses there is no other alternative. As staggering as the implications may be, this appears to be the only acceptable explanation. Therefore, the magnesium samples analyzed must represent 'physical evidence' of the reality and extraterrestrial origin of a UFO destroyed in an explosion over the Ubatuba region. They are, in fact, 'fragments' of an extraterrestrial vehicle which met with disaster in the earth's atmosphere, as reported by human beings who witnessed the catastrophe. The gratifying aspect of this case, however, in that we do not have to depend on the testimony of witnesses to establish the reality of the incident, for the most advanced laboratory tests indicate the fragments recovered could not have been produced through the application of any known terrestrial techniques.

Coral E. Lorenzen, 1962. Olavo T. Fontes, M.D.

The Solar system is not a structure that has remained unchanged for billions of years; displacement of members of the system occurred in historical times. Nor is there any justification for the excuse that man cannot know or find out how this system came into being because he was not there when it was arranged in its present order.

Actual phenomenon observed in Basel on August 7, 1566. The dark, round objects seen to be fighting each other. (Collection Wickiana, Zurich Central Library)

All human conceptions are on the scale of our planet. They are based on the pretension that the technical potential, although it will develop, will never exceed the terrestrial limit. If we succeed in establishing inter-planetary communications, all our philosophical, moral and social views will have to be revised. In this case the technical potential, become limitless, would impose the end of the rule of violence as a means and method of progress.

Lenin to H G Wells, 1920

'I saw a big disk, some eight to twelve meters in diameter, pass over my property at Jouy-sur-Morin, spinning as it flew and giving off a reddish-violet light together with a whistling sound somewhat reminiscent of the approach of a jet aircraft. The machine was at an altitude of about four hundred meters and hovered above me for more than twenty minutes; thus I had plenty of time to study it well. It then departed in the direction of Coulommiers.

As a former manager of the Aero-Club of France and having served in the airforce, I have not been the victim of a hallucination, and this machine was not a balloon, but a thick circular wing that hovered over one spot, then moved off at very great speed, climbing steadily as it did so.'

G Farnier, FSCE, 1954

FLYING SAUCER REVIEW

Vol. 13. No. 6 November/December, 1967 13th Year of Publication

BRITAIN'S BUSIEST UFO DAYS

The Moth Man

Perhaps the weirdest creature of them all is the "Moth Man" who chose 1966 to settle himself down in America. On September 1st, Mrs. James Ikart of Scott, Mississippi, phoned a local paper to report a man-shaped object fluttering about the sky. Reporters and photographers dashed to the scene but the winged being had flown. However, several other people said they had also seen it. John Hursh, a local meteorologist, solved the mystery by calling it a weather balloon.

Scott, Miss., is near the Mississippi River, not far from where it is joined by the Ohio. On November 15th, far to the northwest and less than a mile from the Ohio River, that weather balloon turned up again. This time it was seen at midnight by four young people who were driving through a local park, the McClintic Wildlife Station. They were astounded to see a tall, man-like figure with wings standing in front of an old abandoned power plant. Its eyes were a blazing red, some two inches in diameter, and it thoroughly terrified them before waddling into the deserted building. They went for the local police and their story launched the "Moth Man" saga. Within a few days the little town of Point Pleasant, W. Va., was in upheaval. Armed men searched the McClintic Wildlife Station and the adjoining TNT Area . . . a World War II ammunition dump which still contains igloos filled with high explosives. People were sharply divided on the "Moth Man" issue. There were the disbelievers, who scoffed, and there were the believers—who were mostly scared out of their wits after having seen the thing. Within a few weeks over one hundred people in the area had reported glimpsing the "Moth Man". Many were prominent business-men, teachers, and clergymen. All their descriptions were the same. The creature was taller and broader than a man, grey in colour, with luminous red eyes that had a hypnotic effect. It was seen both on the ground and in the air. When airborne, its wings, which had a ten foot span, were stationary and did not flap. On several occasions it was said to have pursued automobiles at speeds up to 100 miles per hour. Most of the sightings were either in the TNT Area, or very close by.

I first heard of this incident through Jim Moseley of *Saucer News* and I spent three weeks in Point Pleasant in December. The story of that visit is too involved and too bizarre to record here. But I quickly discovered that circular flying objects were being seen throughout the area and that most of these UFO sightings coincided with the dates of the creature reports and were always in the immediate vicinity. Oddly, everyone who had obtained a close look at the "Moth Man" later suffered from the same kind of eye ailment associated with UFOs. One woman, together with several other people, had a close encounter with the creature when it came up to within six feet of them after they got out of their car in the TNT area. The woman was so terrified that she actually dropped the baby she was holding in her arms. Her eyes were so swollen for two weeks afterwards.

Flying Saucer Review

A Gallup poll in 1966 disclosed that five million Americans had observed something they believed to be an unidentified flying object and that ten times as many - fifty million- thought there was a real phenomenon involved the the reported manifestations. When the percentages are broken down according to educational levels, the proportion of persons inclined to attribute the sightings to imagination and fraud is highest among the least educated strata of the population.

Jacques and Janine Vallee, 1966

In the topography of intellection, I should say that what we call knowledge is ignorance surrounded by laughter. Charles Fort

In 1955, Colonel Gernod Darnbyl of the Norwegian Air Force released information that a UFO had crashed near Spitzbergen, Norway.

'It has - this we wish to state emphatically - not been built by any country on this earth,' Colonel Darnbyl said. 'The materials used in its construction are completely unknown to all experts who participated in the investigation.'

The Colonel promised a complete report as soon as 'some sensational facts have been discussed with US and British experts. We should reveal what we have found out, as misplaced secrecy might lead to panic!'

No report on the analysis of the downed UFO was ever issued. Ufologists have charged that the Norwegians were silenced by threats of economic pressures.

Brad Steiger, 1967

The real tragedy is the laboratory. It is to these 'Magicians' that we owe technical progress. Technique, in our opinion, has nothing to do with the practical application of science. On the contrary it is moving against science. The eminent mathematician and astronomer Simon Newcomb demonstrated that a machine heavier than air could never fly. Rutherford & Millikan showed that it would never be possible to make use of the reserves of energy in the nucleus of the atom. Napolean III's experts proved that the dynamo could never function. Science erects barriers of impossibilities.

Louis Pacuwels/ Jack Bergier, 1960

While tracking Echo II on its course from North to South pole in November, 1964, Father Reyna (a Jesuit Priest, professor of mathematical physics, and director of three scientific centres/ observatories) and several other witnesses were curious and perplexed by a 'most wonderful and fantastic sight'. From the observatory at Adhara they picked up the man-made satellite at 8.37 p.m.

Eight minutes later, from the west, near Pegasus, came a UFO, following a right angle course to that of Echo II and continued east, where it descended to the horizon near Orion. The sighting lasted three minutes, during which time everybody inside and outside the observatory was alerted. Four minutes later, with Echo at its zenith, the UFO appeared again, but from the SW, near Centaurus, and performed much in the same fashion and descending to the horizon. The third sighting was at nine. This time it stopped briefly and again disappeared to the horizon at about the same time as Echo II was lost to sight. The object had been seen 'to perfection' when it was near the horizon, by everybody.

A stunning conclusion presents itself: the UFOs speed must have been at least 100,000 kms per hour, since the satellite was travelling at the known speed of 25,000 kms per hour. This was estimated by the observers using several different methods.

Joseph Goodavage 1967

. . . the earth's orbit changed more than once and with it the length of the year; that the geographical position of the terrestrial axis and its astronomical direction changed repeatedly, and that at a recent date the polar star was in the constellation of the Great Bear. The length of the day altered; the polar regions shifted; other regions moved into polar circles . . . electrical discharges took place between Venus, Mars and the earth when, in very close contacts, their atmospheres touched each other; that the magnetic poles of the earth became reversed only a few thousand years ago; and that with the change in the moon's orbit the length of the month changed too, and repeatedly so.

Immanuel Velikovsky, 1950

The secret of alchemy is this: there is a way of manipulating matter and energy so as to produce what modern scientists call a 'field of force'. This field acts on the observer and puts him in a privileged position vis-a-vis the Universe. From this position he has access to the realities which are ordinarily hidden from us by time and space, matter and energy. This is what we call the 'Great Work'.

Fulcanelli

19

SUDDENLY, OVERHEAD...

AIEEE!

ON A MISSION OF CONQUEST,

TRANSPORTER RAY ACTIVATED... MAXIMUM VELOCITY.

Anything that man is capable of imagining, other men will be capable of making a reality.

Jules Verne

So (HG) Wells plunged on . . . to try to envisage a new society, based upon this great knowledge-synthesis instead of on a religion. It had to begin with a world government, of course . . .

Colin Wilson, 1966

I am a firm believer in the existence of 'Angleas' or 'Higher Beings' whatever these terms may represent. But let me be free to point out that there seems to be something else in the woodpile too. Surely no greater disservice can be done to the Earth beings of our kind - and to our descendants too, if there are to be any - than is being done by the fatuous and insanely dangerous over simplification of the cultists and the crackpots who assure us so blindly that they are all benevolent, and that all is Sweetness and Light. Whence, we may ask, does this certainty spring?

Are brainwashings and mental manipulation already occurring? Has the great Take over already begun? If so, by what?

Gordon Creighton, 1967

Life can also be created. That particular problem was solved as long ago as 1836 by an English scientist named Andrew Crosse . . . It happened that Crosse was experimenting on the artificial formation of crystals by means of weak and prolonged electric currents, and found to his surprise that living creatures appeared in his chemical solutions. The creatures in question were insects of the type known as acari (mites), and they lived, moved, ate and bred. They first appeared when Crosse was trying to make crystals of silica by allowing fluids to seep through porous stone kept electrified by means of a battery. The fluid used was a mixture of hydrochloric acid and a solution of silicate of potash.

Cederic Allingham, 1954

Reference and Further reading:

Revelation for the New Age, by Anthony Brooke, published by the Regency Press

The Dawn of Magic, by Louis Pauuwels & Jack Bergier

The Prophet, by Kahil Gibran, published by Heinemann

The First and Last Freedom, by Krishnamurti, published by Victor Gollancz Ltd

Zen Flesh, Zen Bones, compiled by Paul Reps, a Doubleday Anchor Book

The Psychology of Man's Possible Evolution, by PD Ouspensky, published by Hodder & Stoughton

Planetary Influence and The Human Soul, by Manly P Hall, published by The Philosophical Research Society, Inc., Los Angeles

The Little Prince, by Antoine de Saint-Exupery, a Puffin book

Flying Saucer Review (bi-monthly) published by Flying Saucer Service Ltd, London

Worlds in Collision, by Velikovsky, published by Victor Gollancz Ltd

Flying Saucers, (quarterly) published by the Dell Publishing Co Inc, New York

The Humanist (monthly) published by the Rationalist Press Assoc Ltd

The UNESCO Courier (monthly), published by UNESCO

Flying Saucers, by Corale E Lorenzen, a Dell paperback

The Reference For Outstanding UFO Sighting Reports, published by the UFO Information Retrieval Centre Inc, USA

Secret Places of the Lion, by George Hunt Williamson, published by Neville Spearman

Fate Magazine (monthly) published by Athol Pubs. Ltd

The Flying Saucer Menace. Text: Brad Steiger, published by Universal - Tandem Ltd

The Story of Atlantis and The Lost Lemuria, by W Scott Elliot, published by The Theosophical Publishing House

The Letters of Vincent van Gogh, edited by Mark Roskill, published by the Fontana Library, (Collins)

Challenge to Science, by Jacques and Janine Vallee, published by Neville Spearman

The Warminster Mystery, by Arthur Shuttlewood, published by Neville Spearman

Flying Saucer from Mars, by Cederic Allingham, published by Frederick Muller Ltd

Digest compiled by Martin Sharp and Jon Goodchild. It is to be a continuing development, and comments, notes, contributions, thoughts, written and visual, within this theme are welcomed. Payment made for all pieces printed.

(OZ Digest, 38a Palace Gardens Terrace, London W 8)

'A healthy mind in a...'

Julian Manyon (17)

The last 20 years have seen a violent assault on the status of the public school. The response of many such schools has been to seek a new and progressive image to try and justify themselves in the eyes of the 20th century. St Paul's is to a large extent typical of these. It's abolition of the Army Cadet Corps; it's plans for ultra modern new buildings; even the calculated flirtation of it's headmaster with the Liberal Party; all serve to silence it's critics and to beguile another generation of 'progressive' parents into parting with £350 a year for the education of it's offspring. One has to experience St Paul's to realize that it's values and many of it's teaching methods are the residue of the 19th century.

Competition that began for me at the age of 7 and for years made life a continuous and pointless struggle as, with half a dozen other classical scholars, I fought and grabbed for marks and for the little silver emblems that were the symbols of academic success. It was a competition that left little room for anything else enforcing a kind of monastic discipline upon its participants. A competition whose objects stretched endlessly into the distance altering as the years went by from O to A level, to University scholarships and, ultimately, to a successful career with financial security.

I became aware of the compulsion inherent in St Paul's only as I reacted against the competition. It is a school with few written rules but dominated by established conservative values. 'Mens sana in corpore sano' is the maxim and to acheive this the traditional public school devotion to sport is fostered. Competitive sport is compulsory for all. Excellence at thumping assorted pieces of leather about the sole criterion for a prefectship; while to express a dislike of sport is to incur the wrath of a large section of the staff who are apparently capable of appreciating little else.

Prayers too are compulsory; objections on the grounds of atheism are not so much disapproved of, as totally disregarded. I have seen a senior boy who would not sing in prayers dragged violently by the scruff of the neck through assembly by a senior master, who told him outside that ... 'you do not deserve to be in this school, if you do not believe in God!'

There are few, however, who openly reject Christianity - ten years of compulsory religious instruction has its effect. I find it strange to reflect that I could say the Lord's Prayer in both Latin and English before I even knew what it meant.

This attitude is constantly defended by the claim that St Paul's is a Christian foundation. This is certainly true and there is even a statute limiting the number of Jews permitted in the school. The fact, however, that the authorities are prepared to employ random attendance checks, and even physical violence, to enforce their beliefs must belie their outwardly progressive attitude.

The true public school philosophy, however, was brought some to me in my experience as a boarder. For the first time in my life there was no escape from discipline and tyrannical regimentation. Every waking moment was controlled by bells . . . bells for getting up, bells for breakfast, bells for going to school and bells for coming back, bells for prayers and bells for lights-out at 9.30 p.m. Freedom of action rarely exists for boarders at St Paul's. The summary of their whole existence is contained in notice-boards and in the ridiculous regulations that surround them - you must queue for cocoa in order of seniority; you must not leave your slippers under the bed; you must have a hair-cut every two weeks. Above all I found that communication with most of my companions was almost impossible. Years of regimentation by masters - one of whom held, on his own admission, a puritan view of morality - and bullying by stupid and insensitive prefects had produced a kind of unquestioning apathy; a weak acceptance of their lot, yet an internal tension that erupted into unconscious cruelty and violence, as when, on one occasion,I was struck savagely from behind by a prefect for not making my bed properly - I broke a tooth; he subsequently became head of House.

The philosophy of a school such as St Paul's is indeed frightening, even more so, as Edmund Leach has noted, is the fact that much of the attitude I have described is held by the entire educational system of this country, and not just the public schools alone. Certainly, the horrors of boarding are almost non-existent in state schools, as is much of the Victorian paraphernalia to which I was subjected. But I think it is true to say that our entire educational system is dominated by the pursuit of disciplined mediocrity and the cultivation of an orthodox and standard intelligence. The highly organized national examination system results, not only in encouraging destructive and senseless competition, but also in elevating within our society those who possess only the particular talent and mental outlook catered for by the GCE.

In our educational system as well as in our society, success at jumping through a series of stereotyped hoops is all that really matters. For those who fall by the wayside or, more numerous still, for those who are never able to really enter the race, the future offers little more than a life of continual frustration and boredom made still worse by occasional glimpses of others' success.

Above all, by pre-selecting the rulers and the ruled by such means as the 11+ or the purchase of a public school education; by teaching some to compete and others, in the scores of sink schools littering the country, that they are incapable of competition; by training them for specific tasks rather than educating them in the widest sense; by indoctrinating them with the existing and moral prejudices of our age disguised as objective truths—we run the risk of creating an essentially split society where communication between the 'haves' and the 'have-nots', the 'educated' and the 'illiterate', is made almost impossible.

Perhaps we have already taken the first steps in this direction, for so few are even aware of this fundamental dilemma.

Ive got to get it together, man.
Ive got to get it together, man.
Ive got to get it together, man.
Ive got to get it together man
Ive got to get it together, man.
Ive got to get it together, man.
Ive got to get it together, man
Ive got to get it together, man
Ive got to get it together, man.
Ive got to get it together, man
Ive got to get it together, man
Ive got to get it together, man
Ive got to get it together, man.
Ive got to get it together, man.
Ive got to get it together, man
Ive got to get it together, man
Ive got to get it together, man.
Ive got to get it together, man.
Ive got to get it together, man
Ive got to get it together man
Ive got to

First time advertised in OZ, the best selling

Big O Posters

beautifully printed in
well selected colours on fine boards. 20" x 30".

Space allows only a small selection here,
and all prices include post & packing.

BO 7, Cannabis. 5/-d.
(Martin Sharp).2 col on gold.

BO2. Sex!. 5/-d.
(Martin Sharp).3 col on silver.

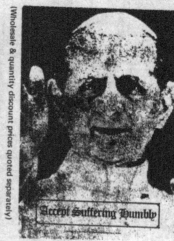

BO3. Pope. 5/-d.
(Bobby Davison). Purple.

(Wholesale & quantity discount prices quoted separately)

Big O Posters Ltd 49 Kensington High Street London W8 01-937 2613/4

BOP5. Buddha. 7/6d.
(David Vaughan). Black on silver.

BOP6. Max Ernst. 7/6d.
3 col on silver.

BOP7. Donovan, 7/6d.
(Martin Sharp).2 colour. SILVER

Reprinting:

BOPI. Dylan. 7/6d.
(Martin Sharp). 2 col on gold.

BOP2. Black Flower. 7/6d.
(Ivan Ripley). 4 colour.

Out Late January:

BO6. Bonnie Parker 'Original'.5/-d.

BOP8. Van Gogh. 7/6d.
(Martin Sharp).

BOPI2. General Custer.7/6d.

BOPI3. Wild Bill Hickock. 7/6d.

BOPI4. Annie Oakley. 7/6d.

BOPIO. Jagger (35"x45"). 7/6d.
(Larry Smart). 4 colour.

23

R. COBB

GEUVARA
G EU VARA
G EB VARA
G UEVARA
GUEVARA
GBELOARX
APOLOGY

DEVAL-UATION TRILO-GY !

I, Georg Buechner

Georg Buechner was a revolutionary German dramatist born in 1813. At the age of 19, he was forced to abandon his medical studies after publishing an address to the German peasantry. He lived and taught Natural Science in Austria on the royalties of his play 'Danton's Death'. There he wrote 'Leonie and Lena' and 'Woyseck'. He died aged 23 of Typhoid.

'The mayor coughs, the baby cries, the miner dies. The Poor follow the rubbish carts of prosperity and the Rich follow the Poor to fill their dustbins. For our land is split into two classes; those who own the land and the factories and the machinery and those who must daily sell their sweat as salt for the table of Capital. To serve at the Banquet are the Four Disciples. The *Police* and the blue fascists who ride in the middle of the road and use truncheons for their wives. The morgues and urinals of official *Art*, its practitioners and apologists fawning across the promise and the shame of each others buttocks. The *Universities* and the teachers with minds like bricks who shout from the classroom DEATH DEATH DEATH. The yellow *Press* owned by the purple monsters who swing from each others ears.

To defend their charnel house of freedom, the oligarchies must squad car the peasant and the negro who dare rise against their power. The groin smashers practice murder on plastic Andes erected in Fort Worth and the Pentagon telephones Death around the world. In the whiskey-bar, the cell and the barrack, the Congo Algeria and Vietnam, the Beast operates his electric torture machine. Professors in linen suits travel the Hiltons of the world talking of viable infrastructure. Radicals cry into their beer.

But the subversive passion of the revolutionary leans forward to free the present from the past; to the Revolution and the ultimate expression of all forms of human genius.'

2. An attitude of non-commitment in art can crystalise and become accepted only in a stabilised society where the foundations of national existence are generally taken for granted and where national conflict runs at a tension so low that it fails to communicate itself in art.'

Isaac Deutscher 'Ironies of History'

Since Johnson's second year of office, the dollar has been heavily overvalued on the international currency market. The Vietnam war until '65 acted as an economic stimulus, due to war-derived demand for materials and the creation of new jobs and spending power. But increasingly capital is scarce within the US and wage costs are rising at an accelerating rate, a typical war time phenomena. At the same time medium level technical skill is drained from industry especially because students either go to Vietnam or stay within the universities to avoid the Draft. The economy thus suffers the worst effects of both inflation of costs and deflation of value. But on the world market this inflation of US currency makes it easy for US capital to further penetrate W. European business by borrowing paper money out of the Federal Reserve Bank. US interests own 55% of the British car industry (Ford, Vauxhall and Rootes) and about 30% of the European car manufacturers. Despite the US's overall payments imbalance, in investments, she still takes more than she sends out; from '56-64, US corporations sent out 16 billion dollars for direct capital investment and the return as dividends, interest and branch profits was 23 billion dollars.

Faced with increased invasion of US capital and a relatively backward economy, France must either build supra national corporations which compete with the US or counter-attack on the dollar. De Gaulle tends to refuse the former in the name of national sovreignty and it is the logic of the latter which underpins the French attack on the Pound, the dollar's longstop. The attack is easier because British overseas arms spending distorts real trade performance and fiscal stability. The French and Swiss have accumulated gold by buying dollars cheap and cashing them expensive; an important source are the GI dollars draining through the brothels and bars of Saigon. French gold reserves may be directly strenthened by the Russians, who do not publish figures but may well be producing more gold than S. Africa, the other primary gold source. This is an article about politics because it uses words like flat irons. British devaluation then was forced by French based attack but carried out and timed on terms dictated by the US. France feels US attack most acutely but the same nationistic response to international capital is present in the business support for the NPD in Germany and Wilson's 'Britain First' devaluation speech.

In Europe, competition increases and isolated national recessions continue. So far partial measures have patched isolated problems (ie the protection of Italian autos and French refrigerators in '64), but a general recession will force European capital to shelter its industrial heart in the Paris/Amsterdam/Dortmund triangle, protected by a European currency (the eurofranc with which the decimal pound is meant to mesh) and supported by the appropriate organs of supra-national state power. Meanwhile the US war-demand speculation on internal money markets and the continued refusal of Congress to finance the expected 30,000 million dollars government deficit by June 68 makes the first major postwar monetary crisis look very likely. Certainly if the European assault on the dollar continues, while US interest rates increase, the alternatives are the revaluing of gold, devaluation of the dollar or the US abandonment of the Gold Standard, in that order. But in semi stagnant economies, the increasing profits necessary to continued international competitiveness can only come from decreasing the amount of capital going to shares and salaries. Working class wage levels must be held static while prices and rents increase, so that the working class sustains a loss of real wages which will never be recovered. In England this is accompanied by specific assaults on working class organisation by inducting the union beaurocracy into the state planning machinery at the top and isolating site level organisation by outlawing unofficial strikes (ie 93% of all strikes) where necessay, ie Barbican and Roberts-Arundel, the armed wing of the state will be used to break strikes. The increased aggressiveness of international competition will increase the level of class conflict within each nation.

3. Dr. Filth of 'Desolation Row'

'The Wipeout Gang buys, owns and operates the Insanity Factory - if you don't know where the Insanity Factory is located then you should hereby take two steps to the right; paint your teeth and go to sleep'. Bob Dylan 'Mysticism starts in mist and ends in schism' Cardinal Newman

Each man is his mystery. No reality is as interesting as the veil of my language and the marrow of thought. I need to celebrate being rather than becoming consumption rather than production, the silky fire of my mind before the paper skulls of their words. Poets suffer a fatigued anxiety about the meaning of their words but revolutionaries throw buckets at each other in the sandpit of the sentence. Oh Doctor Scholl, where are you now for these people who wear surgical shoes around their brains.

Socialism is the motto over the door of the prison which I notice as I pass from the sun to the moon. In my land everyone is like pious Buddists with pails of milk at the point where Beauty and Ignorance married each other in a ceremony served by Chinese Honey. The time for reflection is here. We turn from each other in disgust, weary of our puny exploits, weary of pretending to be able, of being able, of doing a little better than the same old thing. The time to relish and curl into the curves and find the world I miss, even when its here.

David Widgery

WHY IS THIS MAN LAUGHING?

A hand-out from
THE ANTIUNIVERSITY OF LONDON

Sorry that OZ 8 was over-priced and partly unintelligible . . . We can't seem to find an experienced, tenacious advertising pusher so we depend on sale revenue. This issue arrives courtesy of someone very kind, thank you, and if anyone else wants to help, subscribe, take an ad or send OZ a present.

Part of this OZ has been edited by Jon Goodchild and Martin Sharp. They think OZ is too amorphous and negative and have suggested we occasionally free a section for people to develop a world-view or to explore any subject they find important. Groups or individuals are invited to contribute material for up to 6–8 'I'll turn you on' pages.

Caroline Coon's piss may help change the law on pot. The Government pathologist, Professor Francis Camps, is researching cannabis resin and is unable to legally obtain it for his experiments. Hearing that Miss Coon, of Release, has a prescription for cannabis, Professor Camps has arranged for a taxi to collect a phial of her precious urine twice a week. He should be in for some surprises. Miss Coon is inviting friends to pee on her behalf.

Less colourful evidence was recently given by representatives of OZ and International Times to the sub-committee of the Standing Advisory Committee on Drug Dependence established by the Home Secretary and Health Minister. At one point the chairman, Baroness Wootton, told the OZ/IT men that they were 'too religious'.

Even more religious is Alex Lowsie-Akee, who gives the gospel on love communes in this issue and has prodded us into co-sponsoring a forum on communal living in March (speakers will include gypsies and Dominicans). His gay evangelicism is in ironic harmony with the current corruption of the London scene. Remember that busy week when the Beatles discovered God through acid (and others discovered acid through the Beatles), when this new generation had a new explanation, when Donovan said 'Pop is the perfect religious vehicle, it's as if God had come down to earth and seen all the ugliness that was being created, and had chosen pop to be the great force for love and beauty.

Pop stars were the golden hopes of the Underground because they could provide the capital, they could finance the revolution, they'd love to turn us on. In America, it is said that some pop groups have poured their money into constructive, radical enterprises. Here, the Beatles talk of launching a mini-cab service and sow the ludicrous 'Apple'. When George Harrison was recently asked to appear free at the Alpha Centaura Concert he reportedly replied, 'No, I've already given £10 to Oxfam'. All you need is love and short memory. God may have chosen pop, but pop chose Apple.

These days, in the Underground, the sound of lovemaking is drowned by the ricochetting of bouncing cheques. Hippie entrepreneurs open cool galleries, launch oracular magazines and acquire posters, vanishing as mysteriously as they came, laughing at their unhappy creditors (people who sell goods or services on trust). Sickening contempt for any financial obligations is now considered hip. The scene is crowded by a band of exhibitionistic hucksters whose disregard of responsibilities makes Dr. Savundra seem like St. Francis of Assisi. Watch OZ. We may soon, like 'People', name the guilty men.

Enjoying a traditional English breakfast in his Chelsea studios yesterday afternoon, Martin Sharp, OZ artiste, applauded the 'I'm backing Britain' movement. 'This is the spirit to get the country out of the horse & buggy era, into the Mini Moke era', he philosophised as he selected a caramel eclair from the tray offered by his Estonian housemaid. 'As my own personal contribution' said Sharp settling into an elegant plastic hammock, and unwrapping a luxury food parcel from Australia, 'I will endeavour to go to bed half an hour later'.

The Antiuniversity of London is to be where many of the original and radical artists, intellectuals, activists and workers in the London-Europe vicinity can meet with people and discuss their ideas and work. In addition, it is hoped that an increasing number of young people will be able to study at the Antiuniversity on a full time basis outside the usual institutional channels. The Antiuniversity is to provide a context for all of its members to find out 'what is going on' without being squeezed dry or turned into marionettes by the school system or the state.

Among those who will participate in the Antiuniversity are: David Cooper, Richard Hamilton, Stuart Montgomery, Allen Krebs, R.D. Laing, Ted Roszak, Alex Jensen, Joseph Berke, Jim Haynes, Asa Benveniste, Alex Trocchi, Juliet Mitchell, Calvin Hernton, Mike Horowitz, Roland Muldoon, Morty Schatzman, Malcolm Caldwell, Leon Redler, Jeff Nutall, Jesse Watkins, Francis Huxley, John Latham, Ed Dorn, Steve Abrams and Russ Stetler.

Subjects to be discussed include: 'Sound poetry poetry into music', 'The nature of vision, the importance of difficulty, the future of failure', 'Woman', 'The Sociology of Guerilla Warfare', 'The making of a counter-culture', 'The psychology of the family, of sex, of aggression, of the State', 'The fragmentation and violence effected by science and technology', 'From comic books to the dance of Shiva', 'Typography in Poetry' and 'Drugs and the mind'.

Meetings will be informal or not depending on the taste of those involved and will take place once a week or fortnight for a couple of hours. There will also be a wide variety of other activities and events.

The Antiuniversity is associated with the many 'Free Universities', 'Antiuniversities' and 'Antischools' that have sprung up in Europe and America during the past five years, among many more to come.

The Antiuniversity of London is located at 49, Rivington Street, London E.C.2 (a few minutes walk from the Old Street Underground, Northern Line). It will open the week of February 12th.

All who are interested are urged to write to the Antiuniversity for a catalogue.

Continuation of the HAMA Strip is held over for next issue. OZ No. 10.

1
4
5
6

27

The wonderful thing about London's more exclusive shops, as everyone knows, is their uncompromisingly personal service. Each customer is treated as an individual: evaluated, analyzed, and if necessary, reformed. Twelve years ago I was so rash as to present myself to a Dover Street tailor with a letter of introduction. It altered my whole way of life.

And now, catastrophically, I've been cut down in my prime by a pair of suede shoes. It all started innocently enough. They caught my eye while I was strolling through Harrod's just before Christmas (which is in itself a considerable achievement). They were tasteful, elegant, unique, unobtrusive – in short, all that a pair of shoes should be for a modest but impeccable chap such as myself. Ignoring the six guinea tag, I bought them forthwith.

Three months later they succumbed to their first heavy rain. The uppers stiffened and broke out in a white, scabrous rash. Fearing the worst, I hurried back to Harrod's Department of Polish and Shoe Repair for a diagnosis.

The attendant, a Harley Street specialist in grey coat and striped trousers, was gravely solicitous. "I'm afraid this is very serious, sir," he murmured. "You see how the leather has hardened and the pores have closed. And that white deposit – I don't know if we can get that out, but I can't be optimistic. I'll send them off to our factory, but I can't be optimistic. If only you'd caught them while they were still wet . . ." His voice trailed off into reproving silence.

I explained that I'd never had this sort of trouble with suede shoes before. Even cheap suede shoes. Entirely outside my experience. Caught me by surprise. Unexpected emergency.

He shook his head. "All sorts of factors could be involved in a condition of this sort." He lowered his voice discreetly. "Your feet, sir. Do they tend to be somewhat – ah – moist? I thought so. The rain could combine with the – ah – residue and bring it to the surface."

He paused for a moment, then leaned forward and spoke even more confidentially. "All sorts of factors, sir. For instance, you've probably never thought about it, sir, but very damaging things can happen to your shoes when you use a public urinal." I started to assure him that I always made a special point of not piddling on my feet, but he was well ahead of me. "Now I'm not suggesting that there's anything – ah – unhealthy about you, sir. But all kinds of people use those places. And water will splash, sir. And suede is so very – ah – absorbent."

Before continuing, he allowed me a few seconds to contemplate my urine-soaked extremities. "You may not believe this, sir, but when I worked at Lilywhite's, a gentleman returned a pair of bowling shoes. The uppers were in shocking condition — all checked and scaly they were, quite beyond repair. We sent them off to an independent factory for analysis. Sort of a second opinion from a specialist, you might say. We left it to them to determine who was to blame.

"Well, a few days later they sent me their report. You'll never guess what they found, sir. Had diabetes, he did. Very advanced case. Never even suspected it. I had to call in his wife and break the news to her so she could see to it that he went to a doctor right away. Caught it just in time, they did. You never know, sir. You never know . . ."

I left in a state of considerable agitation and came straight home to rest. Tomorrow I have an appointment with my doctor for a urinalysis. And if I'm found dead in bed, I've left a note for the coroner to examine my shoes.

John Whiting

28

LIBERATION NEWS SERVICE

WASHINGTON, D.C. (LNS) - In keeping with the fact that the Vietnam war is supported by and for America's big businesses, here is a way to take advantage of modern technology and to engage in simple but effective economic protest.

Anytime you find a business reply card or envelope, DON'T THROW IT AWAY.

If the postage is paid by the addressee, fill it out . . . with either the words STOP THE WAR or with a fictitious name and address (i.e. D. Rusk, III Main St., New York, N.Y.) Either way, it costs that company money, and sooner or later they'll know why.

Everytime you drop a card in a mail box - and it must be posted once you deposit it - it costs that corporation 4¢, 5¢ and more; and it costs the Post Office too. (Postal rates are already going up as a result of the war, and if this protest forces them up again, it may cause greater anti-war sentiment here.)

Order samples, encyclopedias, subscriptions to TIME, LIFE, Better Homes; join record clubs.

Even if they find out that the address doesn't exist, it will take them hours of time and paper work, costly fruitless effort, and valuable time in research.

Or, if you have just written STOP THE WAR, big and clear on the reply cards, even that costs plenty when you multiply the number of cards we can send in a week (with only the slightest bit of energy on our part), by the number of people who are slightly, very, or radically opposed to this war, by the numbers of companies that every day release hundreds of thousands of these otherwise useless communications.

We are asking all newspapers, magazines and radio stations to print, reprint or read this message to the nation. Let OUR reply to business be: STOP THE WAR!

A Thousand Days)

Will the World Bank offer its new president some obviously needed on-the-job training?

NEW YORK, N.Y. Dec. 15 (LNS) - Mrs. Eleanor Raskin, one of the lawyers currently involved in defending those arrested at Stop the Draft Week demonstrations here last week, adds this footnote:

'Last week one of the hippy . . . er. . . demonstrators came into court with shoulder length hair and an enormous, beautiful yellow balloon.

'The judge, nothing daunted I'm sure by the threat of guns, absolutely quailed at the sight of the big yellow balloon, and flew into an incredible rage when the lad wanted to take it with him when he went to stand before the judge for bail, arraignment, etc.

'The judge finally surrendered and yelled at the lawyers to get the guy out of court. Power of ridicule, to say nothing of love!

U.S. GIVES 7.1 MILLION DOLLARS IN PICKLES TO SOUTH KOREAN MILITARY

BALTIMORE, Md., Dec. 15 (LNS) - Beginning next month, South Koreans fighting in South Vietnam will be supplied with tasty tit-bits to boost their morale - highly spiced 'kimchi' pickles - courtesy of (you guessed it) Uncle Sam. 'We can live a whole year without meat,' Koreans say, 'but without kimchi, we can hardly live a week.'

The U.S., ever mindful of the needs of others, especially when they're the only really efficient pacification units in South Vietnam, is rising to this life-or-death crisis. Recognising the necessity of building Koreans' morale 'to an even higher level,' the U.S. agreed last month to finance a six-month supply of kimchi for its 47,000 freedom-loving allies.

WASHINGTON, D.C. (LNS) - Back in 1960, when Kennedy was assembling his Cabinet officers, McNamara was reportedly offered the choice of being either Secretary of the Treasury or Secretary of Defense.

He (McNamara) quickly declined the Treasury on the ground that he had had no experience in banking or fiscal affairs.' (Schlesinger,

By 'U.S.' we mean that Vice-President Humphrey, during his visit to Seoul last July, told General/President Park that the U.S. taxpayers would be more than happy to underwrite the cost of the six-month supply of kimchi - at a bargain, too - a mere 7.1 million dollars.

'Don't worry, Park,' Hubert probably said. 'You keep your troops in Vietnam and maybe send a few more; eh, and we'll see that your boys get their kimchi.' (Hubert is great pals with generals these days.)

The Koreans' kimchi rations will be prepared by the Korea General Foods Corporation in Seoul - quite a bonanza for the boys at Korea General Foods. We tried to look up this company, thinking it might be a subsidiary of the giant U.S. General Foods Corporation, but to no avail. There is no public record of the company, so it's probably privately owned. Someone's going to make a killing off this deal, but we don't know who. However, with South Korea having the type of government it does, the free enterprisers who own Korea General Foods may quite possibly be some of General Park's buddies. Such shenanigans are not entirely unheard of.

7,100,000 dollars worth of pickles started us to thinking about this little deal cooked up by Hubert and Park. The only parallel we can imagine to this might be if, during the American Revolution, King George III had sent a special shipload of wienerschnitzel to his Hessien mercenaries.

Of course, one way to save the U.S. taxpayers that 7.1 million dollars they're 'investing' in kimchi, plus the 2.1 million dollars in paychecks they're subsidising every month (part of the reported 83,655,000 dollars paid to Koreans or to Korea so far this year for their US role in Vietnam) would be to ship the 47,000 Koreans back to Korea and replace them in Vietnam with the 50,000 American GI's currently stationed Korea.

But that would make the Vietnam war even more 'American' than it already is, and, like Johnson said back when he was playing peacenik three years ago, we don't want American boys doing what Asian boys should be doing for themselves.

THE WORKERS AND THE MOVEMENT

STONY BROOK, N.Y., Dec. 15 (LNS) - The continued need for the movement to change the consciousness of the American working class became evident at a recent antiwar demonstration here.

Rain began falling as an antiwar rally was taking place on the campus of the State University of New York, so a janitor came out to take down the U.S. flag.

When a group of construction workers on a nearby job saw the flag being lowered, they assumed the students were taking it down. So they rushed to the scene, stomping on students, the janitor and even some school administrators.

THE MCCARTHY CAMPAIGN: A RADICAL POLITICAL CRITIQUE

WASHINGTON, Dec. II (LNS) - The crucial word in understanding the significance of the 'presidential campaign' of Sen. Eugene McCarthy is co-option.

In practice, co-option means neutralising political activists by removing them from a previously defined role and placing them in a new role while presumably, but not really, promoting the same goals.

There are many examples of people who are co-opted in America today: black militants who take high-paying jobs with government anti-poverty agencies; idealistic youths who join the Peace Corps to 'help' in underdeveloped countries; doctoral candidates interested in revolutionary social change who are required by their academic disciplines to remain aloof from their subject matter in the name of objectivity.

Now, as militant students are increasing the tempo of their attack on

the Vietnam war and the corporate elite that is behind the war, the McCarthy campaign emerges as a clear attempt to co-opt - to turn political activists into political moderates.

An editorial in the Dec. 8 issue of the University of Connecticut Daily Campus gets right to the point: 'By presenting a viable alternative to the war policies of the President, McCarthy will give many disaffected young dissenters a political home, giving them a chance to express their frustrations at the ballot box rather than in street demonstrations.'

One of McCarthy's primary aims, as he himself has admitted and shown by his actions, is to convince young radicals that they should use 'the system' rather than buck it.

McCarthy has so far directed himself to students, professors, clergymen, union leaders - another whole element already committed to opposition to the war in one form. If he were making a real effort to carry his antiwar message to the hundreds of thousands of Americans who support the war, McCarthy's efforts might be more worthy of support.

As it is, however, his is rather obvious attempt at co-option. Those who are associated with the McCarthy challenge are well known for playing this game. Senator Robert Kennedy, for example, has recently been very critical of students involved in free-wheeling street demonstrations, urging them to retain confidence in the system. Allard Lowenstein, one of McCarthy's top organisers, has frequently been described as a 'peacemaker for the establishment.' Lowenstein is a busy-body lawyer from New York who has appeared at virtually every National Student Association congress for the past 17 years. He has promoted a 'dialogue' between antiwar students and government officials, promoting the illusion that such conversations yield fruit.

The ultimate question, however, concerns McCarthy's belief that the electoral system does work as an outlet for radical ideas, and that liberal politicians like himself represent a viable alternative.

The answer to that question lies in the careers of Adlai Stevenson, Hubert J. Humphrey, and Arthur Goldberg - the McCarthy's of an earlier day. It should be quite clear to student activists that liberal boosters of the system are not the best allies in a principled, effective long-range struggle against the war and its causes.

In any case, McCarthy's antiwar views are vague and limited. They accept the concept of the United States as a worldwide police force.

MADRID (LNS - Canadian University Press) - Students at Madrid University celebrated Gen. Francisco Franco's 75th birthday Dec. 4 in a unique way. They staged a riot on campus.

The riot began as students returned to university after a three-day suspension of classes, ordered last week by the university's chancellor to quell similar rioting and student-police clashes.

The New Democratic Student Union voted to begin an indefinite strike in protest of arrests of Union delegates who were in town for a secret meeting.

Press reports said about 1,000 students were involved in the rioting.

...nert, beneath the ocean, drugged on dreams,
...n insect on the ceiling bathed in green
...at chance have crabs to taste the blooms of love
...ondle breasts of girls who sail above ?
...og, deep sleep dissolves, I AM my AM,
...ed by surprise, I stride across the sand,
...ing the rind, I stagger from the loam,
...ASH THROUGH SUN
...warmed billows of foam !

88888888

~~~~~~~~

eeeeeeeee
eeeeeeee

She naked, laughing, lithe,
            inrients her light,
spreading a lake which
ripples through my sight,
   wave by wave
        loud flash
           begin to burn

8888888888 88888888

88888888888888

88888888888888888

88888888 888888888888

eeeeeeeeeeeeeeeeeeee

as the wheat of my mind
is pounded into sperm.

I do not need to stagger clouds and trees
my butter heart is spread upon the breeze.

NEIL ORAM.

No 10

2/6

new
easy
to
read
for
over
thirties

OZ

THE PORNOGRAPHY OF VIOLENCE

the GREAT SOCIETY blows
another mind...

SHARP

Flight-Sgt. Noel Quesada, shot down on a bombing raid over Phuc Yen near Hanoi in a Republic F-105 Thunderchief fighter bomber. One of the devices provided for him by General John McConnell, U.S. Air Force Chief of Staff, from the £9,000,000,000 bombing budget was Incinderjell. Incinderjell is a liquid inflammable napalm jelly packed in 3000lb. aluminium containers. It is adhesive, can burn underwater, uses all available oxygen in confined spaces and is made by the DOW Chemical Company. For further particulars, write to the Public Relations Officer, Mr Shahin, The DOW Chemical Company, 2000, Main St, Midland, Michigan, U.S.A. Or telephone DOW Chemicals, U.K., 01-WEL-4441

London OZ is published
approximately monthly by
OZ Publications Ink Ltd,
38a Palace Gardens Terrace,
London W8. Phone:
BAY 4623 — 727 1042

Editor: Richard Neville

Deputy Editor: Paul Lawson

Design: Jon Goodchild assisted
by Virginia Clive-Smith

Research Consultant:
Andrew Fisher

Advertising: Louis Ferrier,
BAY 4623

Subscriptions: Louis Ferrier

Pusher: Felix Dennis

Photography: Keith Morris

Contributors: Martin Sharp,
David Widgery, David Reynolds,
Barry Craddock, Lynn Richards

Distribution: Moore-Harness Ltd,

OZ NO 10 March 1968

11 Levar Street, London EC1.
Phone: CLE 4882

Printing: Steel Bros (Carlisle) Ltd.
Phone: Carlisle 25181/4.
Printed Web Offset.

Typesetting: Big O Press Ltd,
49 Kensington High Street,
London W8. Phone: 937 2613/4

Dear Sir,

Your magazine is saturated with
totalitarian ideas. I disagree with
this, and, against my personal
point of view, decided to try and
convert you to my theories.

In anarchical society power is not
tolerated. Why? Because it inter-
feres with personal freedom. But
intellectual power is not thought
of though it is common knowledge that this mental prowess
corrupts as much as physical or
political power.

To be free from corruption our
minds must essentially be the same
as our fellows for mental power
corrupts (possibly not the one who
is so lucky as to have this prowess
but some helpful ignoramus, devoid
of intellect - rebuked - who now
becomes withdrawn and jealous).
Another example, God corrupted
Adam with his powers - for Adam
was jealous of God and wanted to
be one with God; this knowledge
prompted him to eat of the tree of
life, his jealousy was due to the
power of God. Of course this is
only a story yet it serves to illus-
trate a point.

John Wilcock and Alex Lowsiewkee
obviously desire a manifestation
of their own personalities in some
little project or other. They would
be better advised to follow Marxist
teaching; even that of Nietzche is
better than their own pathetic
warblings.

JM Skinner

Et cetera

---

continued   Et cetera

1. Farming is not Our Thing
I much prefer using my brain gainfully as a
computer exporter than to shovel cow-shit
from dawn to dusk. I suspect that most members of the Underground probably feel the
same way. Do you really think that The Exploding Galaxy and the Arts Lab would be appreciated as much in Little Paddlecombe on the Marsh
as in the centre of London?
2. Farming highly skilled and back breaking
and its difficulties are commensurate with the
rigours of the climate. It will be infinitely harder
to make an agricultural commune economically
self-sufficient in England than it would be in
Southern California.
3. Problems of Living Together
Alex Lowsiewkee states as a prequisite for living
in a Love Commune that 'Everyone has arrived
at that enlightened state of expanded awareness,
best described as freedom from possessive or
clinging attachment to things.' I wonder how many
members of the Underground have really reached
that stage. I know that I certainly have not.
But living together in an urban residential commune
would enable the members to help each other
expand their awareness faster, and overcome
their residual hang-ups, provided they can tune
in reasonably well to each other.

Dear Diggers and OZ,

My wife Gill and I have been interested in
community living for the last ten years, and
should welcome the opportunity of practising
it with congenial friends. We were thus very
interested in Alex Lowsiewkee's blueprint in
the latest OZ, but find this project too extreme
for our liking as well as — we fear — for it to
succeed. Rather than jump straight into the
overwhelming problems of an economically
self-sufficient rural commune, we feel
that the Diggers should start more modestly with
urban residential communes. May I state my
reasons briefly.

3

Dear Sir,

I was surprised to find, in Alex Lowsiewkee's article on Diggers, he advocates abolition of rules and regulations having just laid down a whole series of them (rather euphemistically termed 'points') — surely this invalidates most of his argument?

Yours sincerely,
David Graham
680 Lordship Lane,
Wood Green, N22.

Dear Sir,

Okay so UFOs exist, the evidence amassed over the past two decades is overwhelming. Craft displaying certain characteristics which set them way above the technology achieved on this planet clearly indicated a visiting race of extra-terrestrial beings. What is of real importance are the underlying implications behind the appearance of these aerial intruders.

The real question that intrigues UFO researchers throughout the world is 'Why are they here?' & 'What are their intentions towards mankind?' Obviously the answers to these questions are of paramount importance to the whole of the world. It doesn't take much thought to realise that UFOs, given that they exist, present a potential world revolution.

Personally, I believe that UFOs are here because of Man's present position. And Man's present position is in a hell of a mess. It is a highly significant fact that the UFOs arrived here en masse immediately following the nuclear explosions of 1954. Therefore, it is my belief that the intelligences behind the UFOs are highly regardful of Man's future progress. Seeing our state of affairs who could condemn the people who pilot the saucers from landing on this spinning time bomb planet of ours and making open contact? It seems that they realise we are rapidly approaching a cross-roads to our future advancement; a crossroads of decisions as to which path we will follow — the path of survival or death. It is up to we, and we alone, if we let them witness a nuclear holocaust or a peaceful revolution leading to a better world. If we manage to avoid total destruction and pursue a new course of world peace and radical amelioration of certain conditions prevalent through out the world, then we may well witness, in our lifetimes, the greatest event that has even occurred on this planet.

Yours sincerely,
Peter Coleman
7 Sleaford Road,
Hall Green,
Birmingham, 28.

Dear Sir,

I have a couple of contributions to make to your article on UFOs in OZ 9. The first is from a book called 'Flying Saucers From Outer Space' by Donald Keyhoe who, apparently, has acquired somewhat hush-hush information from the US Pentagon. On page 117 of his book is the following:

'Early that evening (Sept. 12, 1952) a glowing object was seen by thousands of people as it flashed over the state (W. Virginia). Among those who saw it, near Sutton, were Mrs. Kathleen May, her 3 young boys and a 17-year old National Guardsman, Gene Lemon. Though they couldn't be sure, they thought they saw something land on a nearby hill.

It was dark when they climbed the slope and Gene Lemon turned on his flashlight. The first thing they noticed was an unpleasant, suffocating odour. As they neared the spot where the object seemed to have landed, two shining eyes were reflected in the light. Thinking it was a racoon on a limb, young Lemon caught it in the beam.

'The light fell squarely on a huge figure, at least nine feet tall, with a sweaty red face and protruding eyes about a foot apart. As the light fell on it, the monster's body glowed a dull green, then with an odd hissing sound it started towards

---

The problems of living at close quarters with a large number of other people are much greater than those of tuning in to just one other person of the opposite sex with whom one also happens to be in here. I feel that the Diggers should concentrate on learning how to overcome these problems successfully, before the farming enthusiasts among them start tackling the problems of founding an economically self-sufficient farming commune in this cold, wet and overcrowded island.

Yours sincerely,
Fred Lamond

I am a Dominican interested in the hippie scene. I hope to be able to come to the forum if you let me know when it is happening. One gets so sick of being a Christian in a loveless Church — after all, love is what our whole thing is about. And religious communities are precisely there to demonstrate this. And what you're saying too, isn't it?
love,
Simon.
Brother Simon Tugwell O.P.

Dear Diggers,

Underground people living in London, (or elsewhere), presumably like to travel to various parts of the country from time to time, but find it a drag looking for places to sleep where it is both cheap, and where they are welcome.

Thus, to take a hypothetical journey from London to the Lake District or the Scottish Highlands. Keele University is about one mile from the Keele Service Area on the M6 Motorway, that is about half-way on the journey ie. a very useful location as a sort of North/South mid-way 'staging-point', especially for people who are hitching. If, therefore, it was desired to do the journey in two parts, the person could spend the night in a room at the university . . . free, of course, of course.

With about 12 people involved in the idea at Keele, it could be guaranteed that some of them would always be in and have floor space available for the night.

On this small scale, a duplicated sheet, distributed throughout the London Commune, and listing the location of the rooms available at Keele, would be all that was required as regards administration.

However, it would be very nice if this idea were extended throughout the country, so that whatever town you were in, you could always find a room where you were welcome.

Bryan P Roberts.

Dear all those involved in 'the Digger Thing',

I am from the U.S. and have lived in California for the past 4 years. Last June I started hitchhiking around the western states, staying at various communes.

Two of the communes I visited were located in Taus, New Mexico. One showed a great deal of progress as far as communal living was concerned as they had a few acres of cultivated land and were growing most all the food necessary to live on, for themselves and for trade. They had 2 or 3 houses on the property for all to live in.

The New Buffalo Reservation, in Taus, is another well-known commune, located right by an Indian reservation. Here the housing was typees as well as camp sites, and also seemed to be developing rather rapidly.

I lived for two months in Big Sur, a low mountain area on the coast of California, between L.A. and San Francisco. It's approximately a 60—80 mile range, with small

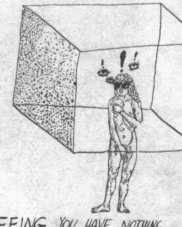

i Think I possess because i do not try to give......

in trying to give you see you have....

NOTHING.....

.... SEEING YOU HAVE NOTHING ..

4

em.
errified Mrs. May and the boys
ed down the hill. While Mrs. May
as phoning the sheriff, her moth-
noticed a queer oily substance
n the boys faces. Soon after this,
eir throats began to swell. Later
was suggested that the monster
ad sprayed the boys with some
nd of gas; but in the excitement
rs. May could not be certain.
When the sheriff arrived, a fog was
ttling over the hillside. Twice he
ied to get his dogs to lead him to
ne spot where the monster had been
en. Each time they ran away,
owling, and he gave up till morn-
ng.

During the night, the Lemon boy
ecame seriously ill, almost in con-
ulsions. His throat, like those of
ne May boys, was strangely inflamed
nd swollen. Later, a doctor com-
ared the effects with those of mus-
ard gas.

Just after sunrise, according to a
utton school-board member, a
trange machine took off from the
ill-top. When the sheriff and his
men searched the area they found
tracks on the ground, the grass
mashed flat, and bits of what looked like black plastic. There was no
trace of the fearful-looking creature
described.'

As a postscript, I would like to
draw your attention to a very vivid
passage concerning the appearance
of a UFO. The passage I am refer-
ring to is in the Bible, Revelations
4, i–viii, and also Daniel 7, ii–x. I
hope that you find this stimulating
reading. Many of the visions of
Daniel can, at a stretch of the
imagination, be interpreted in this
almost 'Rosicrucian' manner.

Yours faithfully,
Colin W Nibbs
10 Alexandra Road,
Leamington Spa.

MIDDLE EARTH
43 King Street, Covent Garden.
240-1327

Dear Sir,

I would like to congratulate Julian
Manyon on his article on St Paul's
School, (OZ 9(, I have only two
criticisms, 1) that it was not viru-
lent enough and 2) that it was not
extensive enough. It is well known
fact at the school that the headmaster owes his position to the
fact that he served as a captain under
Montgomery (himself an old Paul-
ine) in the Second World War, further
that various heads of departments
owe their positions to their acquain-
tance with the headmaster. I would
like to point out though, that it is
not the headmaster who runs the
school, but a certain 'senior master',
who missed his vocation in the army.
Through the 'old school tie' system
which I have described above, the
school manages to lose all its most
talented masters, it is a fact that
since I came to St. Paul's, at least
25 masters have left out of a total
of about 70. An incredible figure
for a school of this repute.

I could continue indefinitely but . . .

Yours lovingly,
ANON
(St Paul's School)

Sir,
Judging by Julian Manyon's sentiments in 'A healthy mind in a . . .'
St Paul's public school is a remarkably nasty place. This may be the
case. But the plight of those at
St Paul's should not be vaguely
extended to 'the entire educational
system of the country' nor, for that
matter, is it remotely similar to
conditions at other public schools.

I would like if I may to describe
some facts of another public school
of which very few of you will have
heard. Perhaps its only claim to
fame is that its Old Boys are highly
represented on the staff of 'Private
Eye'; another Old Boy is the late
Judge Jeffreys. The school is
Shrewsbury, 400 years old, 550
pupils of whom over ¾ are boarders.
I wouldn't pretend that Shrewsbury
is any more representative of
English Public Schools than St

Et cetera ➤➤

communities every 7 miles or so. The land
we lived on was owned by an elderly woman
who was pleased to let her property be used
by people who truly appreciated its beauty.
We had only one main structure, a large stone
house used for cooking, for those people
who stopped for only a few days. The rest
of us made camp sites. Because this particular place had been started by those people
who worked for an underground newspaper
from San Francisco, they helped support it
by taking up food and other necessities. We
also had begun to grow vegetables for ourselves as well as make handicrafts to be sold
in the head shops in L.A. and S.F.
It was very loosely organized, and because of
its location much of the pop. was made up
of people traveling up to San Francisco or
down to Los Angeles. Of course we had many
problems — e.g. leadership, people adjust-
ments, forest rangers (patrols), surrounding
communities; we also found out we would
have to incorporate for a variety of reasons.

The most outstanding problems that I can
remember were: 1. supporting ourselves,
2. adjusting to the idea of communal living,
that is everyone is a part, and everyone must
take part to make it complete and workable.

3. the acceptance of all those who wanted
to experience this — this became a problem
when someone would join, or enter and did
not abide by basic rules (e.g. on the mountain
no one was allowed to cut trees for fires —
we had a sufficient amount of dried dead
wood; no soap in the water — others lived
down stream).
I know these are specific items that you will
not become involved with. I point them out
as every situation has its own particular problems that must be understood, with all com-
plying to the solution. Being a love community it seems hypocritical to turn people out,
to tell someone what to do, to have any form
of leadership but when a large number of
people join a commune, such problems arise.
I must say that the experience was one of
tremendous growth of learning regarding myself and my relationship with others. I am
hoping that you will be able to get people
together with the attitude that this is a truly
beautiful and beneficial thing.
I would be very pleased if you would let me
know when your meeting is going to be, and
if there is anything I can do to help put your
ideas through. Go well.
My love, Judy Slottour

TRY TO GIVE OF YOURSELF.

TRYING TO
GIVE OF
YOURSELF
...YOU... YOU... YOU...YOU...You...You...

SEE

THAT YOU
ARE NOTHING......O....

Paul's is, but I think it is much nearer the norm than the fascist-type repression which Julian Manyon claims to have suffered.

Shrewsbury, like St Paul's, has just voluntarised the CCF; it has also built new buildings just in time for the Public Schools Commission visitors including a symbolic Pentagon HQ for the headmaster. A Bursary scheme for poorer, would be Salopians, is in its third year, launched with great and favourable publicity. But beneath these surface changes, the school's system has not greatly altered. Games are compulsory for 3 years but, and I speak as one of this planet's most unco-ordinated spastics, there is no unpleasantness to those who fail to be Georgie Beste in miniature and the demand for sports amongst those in their fourth year, whom one might expect to be glad of a rest, has forced further games facilities to be organised.

Julian's 'discipline' seemed to consist mainly of bells and seniority in the cocoa queue. Naturally

a bell first thing in the morning is highly annoying, but if failure to hear the bell means lateness for a lesson etc. anyone who abolished this means of regulating the day would soon regret it. As a prefect last term, my time was largely taken up by people complaining that the bell wasn't loud enough, or was late, or early, or too nerve-jarring . . . There were many ingenuous suggestions including using a drum (we tried it and nearly brought in the local army depot) but no one wanted to do without bells, all realising that some means had to exist of making the school run smoothly.

It isn't as if prefects were nazis; anyone may complain about any rule to his contemporaries, prefects, housemaster or head. If Julian has ever been a prefect I'm very surprised he hasn't gripped on to this. If he isn't a prefect I wonder why.

Public schools are not savage mind-disciplining-to-mediocrity places — the image put across in Julian's article. The 'savage and tyrannical regimentations' that give him so

much pain are merely necessities for a free and smooth-running society such as is to be found at Shrewsbury. Within the framework of these rules boys can complain, criticise, suggest, and express themselves (cliché again, I fear). I ran two societies (inviting national figures to speak), and a newspaper which constantly landed me in trouble but never caused a breakdown in the reasonableness of the authorities. (I also helped with a magzine rather superior to 'OZ', if you'll forgive me.) This was by no means outstanding, other boys occupying themselves with a large variety of different interests and many doing very well at them. There was no 'enforced mediocrity' and the numerous and varied facilities lessened competition by widening the fields available.

Sincerely

Martin Wainwright (17)
Editor 'Sixth Form Opinion'.

Onward And Upward And Onward And—

When Dick Gregory landed in London a few weeks ago he explained to prying immigration officials that he was on his way to South Africa to collect a white heart. And while he was here, he took time off to convert a few black ones. He gave a lengthy, passionate speech to a West Indian student congress. They were Uncle Toms when Gregory mounted the dais to speak. Hours later they seemed ready to form the black klu klux of Earls Court. He told them that the negro's biggest mistake in America was to begin desegregating washrooms. It ruined the greatest thing they had going for them. The giant cock myth. Desegregated washrooms gave whitey his first chance to spy the unremarkable black membrane. The myth probably arose, said Gregory, when Southern slave owners were selling broken-down old niggers. 'This here grandaddy, probably looks old and useless, folks, but he can do twenty women a day . . . The price stayed firm in the stud-farm market.
Gregory also told how slave mothers and fathers would pray that their children

would be born deformed so they wouldn't be sold as slaves.
Some extracts from his speech:
'When whitey sent missionaries to Africa, the missionaries had the Bible and the Africans had the land. By the time they were finished, the Africans had the Bible and the missionaries had the land . . .
If there's any story in the Bible that makes a lot of sense to me, it's Judas. And Judas is better off than many of us are here today. When they offered him 30 pieces of silver he had the choice of whether to take it or not. Usually in the system as we know it, we get our thirty pieces of silver at birth.
We marched down the street and we got shot at because we were black. And for some reason we felt ashamed because we were aggravating the situation to make white folk shoot black folk. To get rid of some of the shame we went to the police station and prayed for the sherrif . . .
So now, when we march down the street, we have a bit more confidence in the black man. We try and walk awkward if we can just to prove we don't have rhythm . . .
We know that if we take the country over tomorrow and gave whitey the same treat-

6

Dear Sirs,

I tend to agree that in the last twenty years there has been a 'violent assault' on the whole standing and workings of the Public school. But also in the last twenty years the Public school has rapidly changed from the shrouded snob school to a progressive educational institution. For example, Eton, regarded as one of the hierarchy of the Public schools, is most probably the most forward school in the country. It does not lack new working ideas, and always keeps an open mind on ideas of improvement.

Mr Manyon goes on to tell us about the minor ordeals he had to go through while being a boarder at St Pauls. This seems to be the main attack on any boarding school. Whereas we find the same in all the Services or anywhere where men are gathered in communal life. It has always been a case of the strong versus the weak and will always be. Such is human nature.

The cross that the Public schools is carrying is heavy enough without Julian Manyon trying to make it heavier with his rather drab experiences of Spartan hardship he seems now to enjoy telling us about.

Yours faithfully,

K M Kraunsoe
87/95 Battlebridge House,
London, SE1.

ARTS LABORATORY,
182 DRURY LANE, WC2.

THEATRE and DANCE THEATRE,
CINEMA, GALLERY, FOOD, ETC.

Open 6 days a week.

ARTS LAB, 242-3407/8
phone for details

Dear Sir,

May I add my stick to the camel's load? I am an Australian living in London. Here is an excerpt from a letter I received from my brother who was conscripted and is currently serving with the AIF in Vietnam.

'One time we were following a track along a creek.. The forward scout spotted a few heads looking at us through the scrub. He immediately fired a burst of rounds into the scrub, then there was a sudden panic and the machine-gunner ran forward and fired burst after burst.

The platoon sergeant organized a sweep through the area. Doing this we found four bodies — a woman, two kids and a bloke in black pyjamas. We had run into a family of Cong. We found three rifles which had been fired at us. The platoon sergeant had by this time called for a helicopter to pick up the wounded (only one of our blokes was wounded). The woman had been shot pretty badly through the leg and as they loaded her onto the chopper her leg fell off, so they threw it in with her. We buried the other three bodies — the two kids aged about ten and twelve, with the old man in the same hole.

Later on that night we were mortared . . .

To prove authenticity I enclose my brother's name, rank, identification No etc. Please withold this information (along with my own name). I have reason to believe that already some of my brother's letters to me have been stopped — and vice versa.

Yours in good faith,

Dear Sir,

I am writing to you, or rather to all John Peel supporters on an extremely important matter. Radio Luxembourg is planning to completely change its line-up of DJ's giving them much longer shows.

Anyone who has ever experienced the ecstatic joy of existing with the **Perfumed Garden** will, of course, immediately realise the possible mind-blowing con-

ment he's given us for the last 100 years, he'd burn the country down. After all, he's burning Vietnam down to the ground. And that's to free a foreigner. You know what he would do to free his mammy! Ha! To guarantee a foreigner instant freedom. Well, dig this — my six black kids in Chicago are still getting theirs on the installment plan . . .

During World War Two they brought German soldiers back to America and all the prison camps were located in the South. When those troop trains pulled up to feed the German soldiers they were permitted to go to the front of the restaurant and sit down and eat like human beings. THE BLACK AMERICAN SOLDIERS HAD TO GO TO THE BACK. Now my father told me this story and I told him, man you've got a gun and you're fighting a war and you can't let them do this to you. That's why the niggers in Vietnam tonight are hoping that the Vietcong will kill them before they kill the white boys . . .'

Dick Gregory has vowed that he will not have a haircut or shave or wear anything but work clothes till the war is over in Vietnam. Let me record that both beard and hair are as trim and respectable as the cutest

National Provincial Bank clerk's. And as for the work clothes . . . they're crisp, clean and tightly tailored over a button-down Madison Avenue shirt and ties and elegant boots. He is also fasting: 'In America, a country where we lose more people from overeating than under-eating, where doctors make more money on people overweight than underweight, well, I figure that our conscience is probably in our stomach.'

This year Dick Gregory is running for President as an independent write-in candidate. 'I won't get elected but enough people will write my name in to have an impact. (In US elections there is a blank space on the ballot paper for people to record any non-listed preferences).

'After the elections I am going to declare myself the elected write-in President of the United States in exile, and I will go to all the countries that don't recognise the United States and ask them to accept me as the President in exile. I also plan to establish an office in Washington near the White House where I will conduct the business of the write-in President.'

Q: Do you see black people in America . . . continued

Et cete

sequences of this. Every single person who supports John Peel must write to: Geoffrey Everett, c/o Radio Luxembourg, London W1; asking, begging, pleading or demanding John Peel has a regular late night spot, and if all the beloved are faithful to the Perfumed Garden and write, Geoffrey will have to sit up and take notice, and we may well see the return of the Perfumed Garden to the radio!! The importance of writing cannot be sufficiently stressed. The **Perfumed Garden** must return.

Love,

John Powers
Ramsgate,
Kent.

Get Peace News every Friday: order it from your newsagent

If you believe that treatment which you have received at the hands of the authorities is unjust, call Civil Liberties:
National Council for Civil Liberties, 4 Camden High Street, London NW1. EUSton 2544.

Dear Sir,

I'm interested in obtaining what might be called 'coital calendars'. These are simply the records, over a considerable period of time (say at least a year) kept by women (married legally or consensually) of the days on which they menstruate and those on which they have sexual intercourse with their husbands.

Ideally they would be women
1. who were virgins at the time of marriage, and
2. who have had no extramarital affairs, and
3. whose calendar starts at the time of marriage.

I should emphasise that I'm not interested in identifying the women who keep the records: neither am I interested in whether the records indicate a high or low coital frequency.

Alternatively, if none of your readers has such data now, may I appeal to any of your female readers (preferably virgins) who a are contemplating marriage, to keep such a calendar for a year after marriage?

Yours faithfully,

William H James PhD
18 B Monmouth Road,
London W2.

ANTIUNIVERSITY OF LONDON

Music, Art, Poetry, Black Power, Madness, Revolution.

Opens 12 Feb 1968.

49 Rivington Street, Shoreditch, London EC2. 01-739 6952. Membership £8. No formal requirements. Write for catalogue.

---

participating more in the electoral process?

A: No. I hope not. Because the electoral system has not satisfied our needs. They have played a number of games with us you know, and . . . I don't want to ride on your car while you're TRYING to get it fixed. It has left us cold. We have got more done with the brick in the street than we have with the ballot box. And now America understands that she's got a choice now – it's either going to be ballots or bricks.

You know Henry Ford just hired 6000 Negroes in two days without their even taking the tests. And that did not come from political muscles; the fire got too close to the mustangs, this summer in Detroit, and this is what got it, you know.

When democracy works right, we don't have to go all over the world shoving it down people's throats with a gun. It's this fact that we've got armies all over the world with a gun, shoving this system down peoples throats which is proof that there's something wrong with it. You know? And the day that we stop backing dictators in every country . . . Where were we when democracy fell in Greece? Mmm? Always looking the other

way. But I don't think that the Negro's problem is answered in politics at all. None whatsoever.

Q: Do you see any hope for the sane elements in America getting together in some k kind of coalition that will build throughout the country . . .?

A: No. Because we are about eighteen months away from open revolt in America. Everybody's getting ready to turn their backs on the political machine anyway. I think this coming election might be the last election we will have. And that's why the people who don't want to see America blow – like it's headed – will have to get together. But there's more to politics than just electing a politician.

If we don't elect statesmen, no politician's going to solve the problems. This is the dilemma. And I think, more and more, the whole peace movement and the freedom movement is losing people to the revolt. And I think this is what it's coming to. There is revolt in the air! And people are reacting to it.

And the kids demonstrated in Washington, DC at the Pentagon. It was a very honorable

demonstration. They told them two months in advance, 'We will be in Washington, DC and we will hold a demonstration, and then we will go and we will try to float away the Pentagon.

So they didn't surprise anybody. They knew they were coming. They said the kids were violent! How do you bring out your army with the guns and the nightsticks, and then say that the demonstrators, who didn't have any weapons, were violent? Well, the reason they were called violent is that this is the first time in America that a gun doesn't stop anybody. And that's a very violent action when The Man puts a pistol on you and tells you, 'Don't keep movin', and you keep moving.

And just that action alone makes you violent—the fact that we run and control this country with guns. And for the first time in the history of America, the gun doesn't control anymore.

●

Biometrics researchers have established that the chances of getting a girl pregnant when screwing (a) in between periods, and (b) without contraceptives, are 1 in 32.

here is no reason to emulate, and every reason to ignore, the staid formalised forties hang-up of the conventional shop front. The Urban street scene is dreary enough as it is with all its inspired non-design. Attempts are constantly being made to enliven this environment in their ones and twos but they seldom match the shop frontage shown here for economy, effect and sincerity. Striking subtle-coloured, it is designed to catch the sun and street light and impart its own 'message'. It shows the Godhead in the form of a dragon, making the supreme sacrifice by descending to earth as inspiration to the 'earthly Dragon' (realised as a flower with roots reaching to the pavement). The 'heavenly' dragon weeps tears that crown the flower, giving understanding; as rain falls to the natural flower providing a life source. The Lotus, opening behind the 'head of the Flower Dragon' symbolises this realisation. The flower has grown to the exact height necessary to receive the tears the amount of effort required to receive the 'understanding'. Fire from the God Dragon, at almost ground level, incorporates the only areas of unpainted glass by which to see into the equally impressive interior. Designed and Painted by Omtentacle, the Shop, in Worlds End, SW10, is open for meals etc all day

THE MEN WHO BAN OZ

Safe behind their anonymity, little men inflict their prejudices upon the reading public. These are the men who purchase magazines on behalf of newsagents or wholesale distribution companies. Such a man is Mr Scott of Abel Heywood & Sons Ltd, Manchester; who, despite brisk demand refuses to let his firm farm out OZ to provincial retailers. Why? 'We don't deal in dirt', he told an astonished OZ secretary.

If you can't get OZ in Exeter, blame Mr B Doust from Surridge Dawson & Co, 24 Gandy Street, who was outraged that OZ gave space to Michael Malik. ('Life' gave **more** space to Michael Malik, but little men are not susceptible to argument). The man from Exeter was so angry he warned his head office not to handle OZ. Head office retaliated with puritannical bravado by instructing their chain of wholesalers to cancel all orders. Thank you Mr Durance at Surridge Dawson HQ, 133 New Kent

his is
spector Lambrou.
e maims people.
ee Page 16.

Et cetera

... continued ⟹

The **Last Exit to Brooklyn** decision had a lot of publishers blue-pencilling their own dirty books. Amongst these was Blond, at work cutting out detailed descriptions of cunnelingus, buggery, and jolly scenes with dildos from Gore Vidal's new novel **Myra Breckinridge**. This was published (intact) in the States without publicity because Mr Vidal was 'afraid that the critics might give away the surprise twist which would spoil the fun for the reader.' The real reason is that it's such a bad book: Mr Vidal feels badly treated by the Establishment after his bitchy attack on the Kennedys and is sensitive about American reviewers. The 'surprise twist' concerns Myra's dubious sex, and is a peg on which to hang all Mr Vidal's own fantasies.

As part of their spreading **Apple** empire, run by the 2-year-old ex-road manager who doesn't know from beans the things 'cultural', **The Beatles** are proposing to start a series of Sergeant Pepper Clubs across America. These are to be art centres like Jim Haynes's, only they'll be run strictly for profit, professionally, with discotheques in case. Expensively mounted productions from the Establishment avant-garde — psychedelic plays, happenings, and what-have-you — will be imported from the

Old Coutnry, though how they will stand up to the native product, vastly superior in this field to anything Europe can manage, is difficult to foretell. The Beatles are great on 'the experimental' as long as it's commercial, and such is their standing they can make a hit out of any old thing. However, with the heavyweight critics climbing on their backs like Ned Rorem in the New York Review and Deryck Cooke in The Listener, they may never survive the excruciating pain.

File

BECAUSE I'M ONE LITTLE WEB-SPINNER WHO LIKES TO KEEP BUSY!

Et cetera ⟹

Continued

9

by Andrew Fisher

OH, WHAT A LAWFUL WAR!

Justice & Violence in 'Armed Conflict'

As countries go on national alert, reserves are called up, revolutionaries prepare, power groups get ready for the summer and the street fighting goes on, you may be feeling left out of it all. Everyone has his own scene going - so why not you? But some problems will present themselves as you mobilise for your own war.

First: war has been abolished for some time now. What we have instead is armed conflict. War as an instrument of national policy (that's how Clausewitz saw it) was abolished by the Treaty of Versailles (ending World War 1 in 1919). It was abolished again by the Pact of Paris in 1926. You may remember after that war sprang up again — in Spain, for example, and later on, in certain other places. So at Yalta in 1945 three old men sat down and reabolished war. One was sick, another was dying and the third was thinking about something else. Churchill, Roosevelt and Stalin. 'We three shall be the policemen of the world' they said and they created the United Nations with the Security Council as their Scotland Yard. It didn't work. They had also created the veto which stopped the Security Council from offending anyone. Under the United Nations Charter members undertook never to use force or the threat of it in their international relations. Since that moment war has raged every day somewhere or other in the world — usually between members of the United Nations — and under the strangest of names. 'Police action, opposing aggression,

---

Road, SE1 — we now sell 2,000 less OZ per month.

A few months ago we negotiated sales of OZ with a large Paris wholesaler. He was keen but wanted us to export through an English firm; 'Continental Publishers & Distributors Ltd'. This bustling, hustling, back-Britain organ-

nation had never heard of OZ. Thundering silence followed various phone calls, letters, samples etc. Finally, their manager, Mr Dick, was prodded into regretting that OZ was 'too risque' to be bundled up with Penthouse and Mayfair. Goodbye Paris.

Lastly, acknowledgements to Mr HA Baron, Manager of WH Smith's and Mr PG Redwood of John Menzies Limited for their persistent firm refusals to accomodate OZ. If they ever did; we should probably lose heart.

● A hand-out from:
WORLD YOUTH FESTIVAL
Sofia, Bulgaria. July 28th - August 6th.

One thousand young people will be going from Britain to the World Youth

Festival in Sofia, Bulgaria, this Summer. The Festival will be the ninth since the war, and will be the largest and the most representative ever held. Over 30,000 young people will be there, from 110 different countries.

The first Festival was held in Prague twenty years ago, the latest in Helsinki four years ago. With large delegations expected from France, the United States and West Germany as well as Cuba, Russia and Vietnam, some lively debates are expected. The Conferences on the Vietnam war, world disarmament, the cold war and apartheid should prove particularly exciting.

The massive organisational task of sending so many people to Bulgaria next July is being shouldered by the 'British Preparatory Committee' from its office at 54, Rochester Row, London SW1. The committee which employs one organiser is made up of officials from the fourteen organisations that have so far decided to send delegates to the Festival.

The British Preparatory Committee hopes that between now and next July 28th many more youth organisations decide to

---

San Francisco cops, determined to prevent a repetition of last year's pilgrimage to Haigh-Ashbury, have instituted hourly harassment patrols. The fuzz sit in patrol cars on the side streets off Haight, emerge several times a night to sweep almost everybody in sight into paddy wagons . . . Most of the Oracle staff have split for the country — circulation is down from a one-time high of 60,000 to about 30,000 — and the office is closed more often than not . . . Max Scherer's Berkeley Barb, now with yellow wraparound pages, varies from 35,000 to 50,000 weekly with almost half that sold on SF streets . . . During the daily paper strike Ramparts has been putting out an 'interim' daily which is just about as cornily amateurish as was Sunday Ramparts. Supported mostly by Roos-Atkin department store ads (which has nowhere else to go) it has given away for a while and now sells about 17,000 daily at a dime. Listed as publisher is Howard Gossage, owner of a SF agency.

MOSTLY NAMES: Paul Krassner invited Boris Karloff to write about the heart transplant operations for the Realist . . . 'It's not conscience that shapes a man's life - life shapes his conscience' (Jean Luc God-

ard) . . . 'Leonard Cohen's political temperament is revolutionary. But, like Camus, he is starkly aware of the paradoxes of rebellion. He is frozen in an anarchist's posture but unable to throw the bomb' (William Kloman) . . . David Amram, his autobiog at Putnam and a tour in the offing in which he'll play only his own music (half classics/half jazz), will undoubtedly be promoted by the mass media as the younger (36) Leonard Berstein . . . The Diggers' Emmett Grogan conned 500 bux out of the Village Voice's Ed Fancher who was then told that it hadn't been Grogan after all . . . 'McLuhan is in danger of becoming to electronics what Norman Vincent Peale is to capitalism' (Neil Compton in The Nation) . . . With a 23-film showing, NYC's Museum of Modern Art is about to turn Charlie Chan into a classic . . . EVO'S Walter (Get-the-Money) Bowart got an advance on a book, turned the paper over to Allen Katzman . . . Playboy is now promoting (for a mere $ 15), 'the pipe that Hef smokes' . . . Pink or baby-blue are the colors of the new button, Dr Spock Brought Me Up, I Won't Go.

Why is Howard Hughes buying up Las Vegas?

Writing in a Nevada magazine, Roland Hill explains: 'Southern Nevada is the only logical spot from which we can defend our country . . . and (it) will be turned into a vast arsenal and war plant territory as the last ditch in our defense against all of Asia . . . Great things are in store for Las Vegas and Southern Nevada and by 1975 or before well over a million people will be living here working frantically to save our country from destructive invaders' . . . Jerry Hopkins' 'end-your-paranoia' list of 39 things you can do with cigarette papers (in LA's Open City) concludes with 'use as toilet paper for tiny shits' . . . If you want a free guest card for the Osaka Trade Fair (April 9—29) including free invitation to a garden party amidst the cherry blossoms, write to Secretariat, Honmachibashi, Higashi-ku, Osaka, Japan . . . 'The hippest place to be is inside the Trojan horse' (Ron Shepherd).

● There is a perverse streak in most people that will urge them to see the worst film, read the worst book, or vote for the worst politician if they are assured that standards cannot fall any lower. It is important, therefore, to avoid saying that The Mercenaries is the worst film ever made. What matters

assisting in a country's internal affairs, counter insurgency' and above all, 'self defence'. Because the big let-out clause in the UN Charter was Clause 51. 'Nothing shall affect each member's inherent right of self defence'. NATO, SEATO, The Warsaw Pact are all treaties of 'mutual self defence'. Not aggression, oh no. What happens is that if, for example, someone attacks Greece, then Canada, 5,000 miles away but another member of NATO, can say —'the territorial security of Greece is so closely connected with that of Canada, that we, in exercise of our right of self defence under Article 51, are automatically entitled to attack the country attacking Greece.' Ludicrous you might say. But that's the theory behind our defence policy. NATO is for the Western North Atlantic countries, The Warsaw Pact for the Eastern European and Asian Communist countries and SEATO for the pro Western South East Asian countries. America's presence in Vietnam incidentally is based on a far less sophisticated fiction. It is the age old right of one power to call on another for assistance in its internal affairs. When one power is represented by Messrs Thieu and Ky you understand America's desire to make the result of South Vietnamese elections look truly popular.

So whenever I say war, you'll know I mean armed conflict.

Second: To make war you have to be a state. Or a prince. War was a public affair and was waged between princes. Principality against principality. If it was public the comatants had certain rights and privileges — as soldiers — in an old and honourable profession. It was public if it was between princes. If it was between private citizens it was called brigandry or banditry. Same product, different labelling. If you were caught at it you were

killed quickly, nastily and indifferently. Unlike soldiers. Then states took the place of princes. Rousseau in his *Contrat Social* (1762) said:

War is not a relation between man and man but a relation between state and state in which individuals are enemies only incidentally, not as men, nor even as citizens, but as soldiers.

This dehumanising view was then premature, but now forms the basis of the international law of war. It lends itself ideally to the distancing effect of modern weaponry where the gap, emotional and physical, between the killer and killed increases. It is also irrelevant because most fighting in the last twenty years has been revolutionary — between despotic rulers of a state and a popular insurgency within that state.

Third: You must therefore use soldiers. In uniform or they might be called spies. The definition of a spy is one who 'acting clandestinely or on false pretences obtains or endeavours to obtain information in the zone of operations of a belligerent with the intention of communicating it to a hostile party.' (Hague Rules 1907) If a spy is caught he is not to be punished without trial. Hague Rules again. Unfortunately they forgot to say what sort of trial. Hence in Korea, when a US pilot was shot down and captured by North Korean soldiers, an officer on some of these occasions would line up the platoon and shout 'Members of the peoples court of the Korean Peoples Army is this man a spy?' And they would all shout 'yes'. And shoot the pilot. Obeying the laws of war is not always a problem. But one should try so . . .

Et cetera

Fourth: You must obey the international law of war. Distingu-

---

Dated 9th Jan 1968

Dear Sir.

We submit that:
1. This issue was folded and displayed so that it appeared in the form of a magazine and was sold as such. The words OZ Special surprise issue! on the cover being in conformity with the previous issues and the normal magazine price of 2s.6d. was printed in the upper left hand corner.
2. The issue was number five in the series of OZ magazines. It was sold as such, posted to subscribers as such and intended as such. The issue before it was numbered 4, the one after 6. The ommision of the number 5 on the cover does not alter the character of this issue as a magazine.
3. The issue was accepted, sold and distributed as a magazine by our distributors Moore-Harness Ltd who passed it on to the retail outlets in exactly the same fashion as every other issue of OZ. Prints or posters are never, to our knowledge, passed on to retail outlets in this way.
4. Any examination of this particular

Et cetera

---

is that the perverse public who care about films, let alone politics, stay away from this abuse of the medium, in the way that anti-apartheid aficionados boycott things South African. To see it is not only to reward MGM and the director, Jack Cardiff, for an appalling piece of film-making, but also for the most degraded, reprehensible, gimcrack gallimaufry of prostituted commercialism and amoral sentimentality that has every brutalised Technicolor.

It has as its core the philosophy that violence is the only real form of communication, and accordingly uses a setting, the 'strife-torn' Congo, that can justify fascism, murder, rape, torture, carnage, riot, killing for greed, pleasure, and revenge, and of course a native massacre. There are no redeeming technical features.

The abysmal dialogue is one reason why verbal communication is secondary to action, but you can't just bemoan the portentous philosophising (which incidentally is always handed to the good Negroes to deliver). This is a racist, Uncle Tom film, yes, but there is worse to it than that. It is emphatically on the side of capitalism (the Government backed by the diamond-mine owner) against the rebels depicted, naturally, in

primitive war-paint and feathers, but one would hardly expect MGM to go Left-wing. What is significant about this nonsense lies in the assumptions of those who made it, that this concatenation of evil distortions is justified by the gusto of violence, that platitudinous characters are given heroic substance by their readiness to kill and be killed, that the only way to answer questions is in blood, and, by no means least, that this is what the public most appreciate. The lump that rises in the gorge is not sentiment, but nausea.

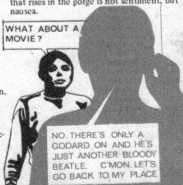

WHAT ABOUT A MOVIE ?

NO, THERE'S ONLY A GODARD ON AND HE'S JUST ANOTHER BLOODY BEATLE. C'MON, LET'S GO BACK TO MY PLACE

English television programmes are often shown in Australia. Here an Australian MP comments on one of them:

Mr. Turnbull (Country Party, Victoria) told the House that 'While on this subject I might mention that I watched a television programme the other night which was called 'The Frost Report'. I was attracted to it by a strange coincidence. As honourable members know, I represent 78% of the dried fruit pack of Australia. People in my area are troubled with frosts. When I saw the title of this television programme I thought that it was about frosts. However, I was soon disillusioned. I soon found out that the programme was by a man named Frost who makes a report. I am surprised that the Australian Broadcasting Commission would put a programme on like this. It went as far as to ridicule the Ten Commandments. Once this happens I think a programme should be put off the air.'

Et cetera

continued: 13

ish between the laws which govern states resorting to war (Point 1) and the laws which govern the conduct of war once it has started. And these are a joke. But they shouldn't be. The law of war is humanitarian. It is a restriction placed on the most illogical enterprise a human being can undertake. The supreme anti-human relationship. Any restraint on it must be humanitarian. But it is also stunningly obsolete. The law of war is fit only to deal with the technology available in a mid 19th century battle.

It started with codes of chivalry, of which the fundamental rule is that no more force should be used than necessary to obtain the military objective. Rousseau again had his say:

. . . the object of war being the destruction of the enemy state, one has the right to kill its defenders only when they have weapons in their hands; but immediately they put them down and surrender, thus ceasing to be enemies or agents of the enemy they once again become ordinary men and one no longer has right to their life. Sometimes one can extinguish a state without killing a single member of it; moreover, war confers no right other than that which is necessary for its purpose. These principles are not those of Grotius, they are not founded on the authority of poets, but they flow from the nature of things and are founded on reason.

Which was very turned on. But how, you may ask as the ICBM curves away into the sunset, will it distinguish between those who have put down their arms and those who still carry them. And mere civilians for that matter. The answer is that it is no longer important because the rule was effectively abolished in World War 11 when the British High Command issued a directive that bombing of German cities would take place, as Lord Cranbourne put it, to

'bring the whole life of the cities in which they are situated to a standstill, making it quite impossible for the workmen to carry on their work.' Or as *The Times* said in 1945:

. . . to burn down the house with all its contents in order to roast the pig.

It is because of this that it is probably legal to use nuclear weapons. The target saturation bombing (complete destruction of all property and personnel, civilian or military within a given area) practised by the allies against Hamburg Dresden and Cologne was new in that it attacked civilians to destroy enemy morale. It was supposed to be in reprisal for the blitz. But the right of reprisal is narrow and only allows normally illegal acts as long as they are to stop an enemy who is at that moment carrying out illegal acts. The blitz had stopped long before Hamburg, Dresden and Cologne. All were by the existing law illegal. In war you only get punished if you lose. And the allies won. The right to kill private citizens as part of the destruction of national morale became an accepted custom of war — like so many other customs — simply because everyone did it.

The law of war built up in the 19th century as custom. It was found in governments instructions to their troops in Military Manuals. In 1907 at The Hague the customary rules of armed warfare were gathered together by an international convention. Annexed to it were the rules that still govern the conduct of war. They made sad reading in the light of what happened in World War 1. They make even sadder reading today. The emphasis is on things like the number of drummers, trumpeters and buglers that should accompany a flag of truce. Or the number of attendants who

could follow a parlementaire and the honours with which he should be received by the enemy. The drummers, trumpeters and buglers are to warn the enemy of the approach of the flag of truce. No one in 1907 considered the possibility of amagnetic telephone or a valve radio. Yet these are the rules for today. There's nothing in them about aeroplanes. Only balloons. *'Persons sent in balloons for the purpose of carrying despatches . . .'* are not to be regarded as spies. That's all the rules say about people travelling through the air. There was a separate declaration at The Hague in 1907 prohibiting the discharge of projectiles and explosives from balloons or 'by other means of a similar nature'. However no state ever bothered to obey it — the 'other means of a similar nature' were proving too useful. Again a prohibition lapsed because everyone broke it.

Before both World War 1 and World War 11 there were laws which provided that submarines before attacking should surface, warn the ship it proposed attacking, take off crew and passengers and only then, sink it. No one really tried to obey it although a lot of reprisals were said to be based on the practice of unrestricted submarine warfare. Both sides did it and the prohibition passed into history.

The only thing that everyone has always been able to agree on is the use of poison — and by extension poison-gas. In the old days it wasn't liked because:
(a) It was a woman's weapon — it killed by deceit and stealth — and was therefore unchivalrous.
(b) The all powerful church was frightened someone might get at the communion wine and wipe out the faithful.

So it was banned. It still is. The Americans gave up poisoning the Vietcong rice stores because of international pressure. They came across huge piles of rice in the jungle, sprayed them with poison and then with green dye to warn the Vietcong of the contamination. But in 1915, in a famous case, some poor German soldier found a stream in West Africa that might have been useful to the enemy and poisoned it. He meticulously put up signs saying 'Achtung!' or whatever. The verdict was that it didn't matter about the signs, he shouldn't have used poison in the first place.

He was shot. The Americans now burn the rice with napalm and everyone is happy. No one thought of napalm in the 19th century so you can use it in the 20th century. Along with most other horror weapons far worse than the now militarily ineffective poison. In Malaysia a few years ago the British War Office advised its officers against employing certain tribesmen in the Malayan jungles because of the War Office's sensitivity to the tribesmen's poison dart blow pipes. This is about the only level that realistic discussion of the law of war in combat can take place. Arguements on the illegality of nuclear weapons seem to depend on analogies between fallout and poison or on a recent cultural convention which prohibits the destruction of works of art — the bomb might get the Picassos too. The genocide convention is no use — it only applies to ethnic groups — not humans en masse. No one, of course, can agree on a simple banning of nuclear weapons.

The Law of War is now found in the Hague Rules, some customary law, the judgment of the Nuremburg Tribunal (unanimously approved by the members of the UN), a few miscellaneous conventions mostly on things like Dum Dum bullets and exploding projectiles and the Geneva Conventions of 1949.

The four Geneva Conventions are the most advanced of all war legislation — mainly because they deal with non-combatants (prisoners of war, shipwrecked at sea, sick and wounded and civilians). States lose interest in people once they can't fight. Therefore they can afford to let others be humanitarian about them. The conventions are the product of the work of the International Red Cross and not of the efforts of any country.

It all started in 1859 when a man called Henri Dunant saw 38,000 killed and wounded in five hourse at the Battle of Solferino. Later in the Battle of Gettysberg in 1862 'the flower of Virginia' was wiped out. Both events led to the creation of the Red Cross movement. They culminated in the Geneva Conventions of 1949. Four conventions signed by — for all purposes — every power in the world today.

More than any other enactment these conventions could act as a brake on the horrors of war today. The law cannot do anything about the methods of combat — the scientists and computers control that. What it can do something about is those who are not doing the fighting — civilians, people who have surrendered, sick and wounded. The conventions, not surprisingly, are out of date. But less so than most.
The problem is to get them to apply to the different situations. Once they apply, and all sides recognise them, then their protection is very good indeed. Although a neutral power or the Red Cross is needed to enforce them.

So, when do they apply?

(1) In a straight out war between countries (as recently abolished) there is no problem. Nearly every country in the world is a signatory to the Convention and non signatories would quickly accede. But in a straight out war there would probably be no one left to enforce the conventions or receive the benefit of them.

(2) In Vietnam type situations where neither side will admit there is a war', or armed conflict between two or more of the high contracting parties going on, but there obviously is. What should happen theoretically is that each side maintains the non war fiction but agrees to apply the conventions. This should also happen in a major revolutionary situation between the revolutionaries and the government. But a true revolution is one in which no government would dare agree to apply the conventions for fear of being taken to have 'recognised' the revolutionary force and therefore allowing the possibility of international recognition of an alternate government.

In Vietnam what happened is that the US claims to have ordered its troops to observe a standard of conduct higher than that demanded by the Geneva Conventions (without admitting that the conventions automatically apply). The North Vietnamese Government in response to an appeal by the International Committee of the Red Cross for the observance of the Prisoners of War Convention said that it was not bound by them as it *'contained provisions which correspond neither with its action nor with the organisation of its armed forces'* and went on to declare it was observing a 'humane and charitable policy toward the prisoners who fell into its hands.' The reasons are not hard to find. A common provision of the Conventions states that, apart from obvious members

Et cetera

of regular armies, militias etc. it would only apply to volunteer corps and other militias if they fulfil the following conditions:

(a) that of being commanded by a person responsible for his subordinates;
(b) that of having a fixed distinctive sign recognisable at a distance;
(c) that of carrying arms openly;
(d) that of conducting their operations in accordance with the laws and customs of the war;

Does that sound like the Viet Cong? Dr Castro's Guerillas? No one can afford to fight that way anymore unless he happens to be the United States.

What's left is a clause which has to serve for situations ranging from the attack of the Great Train Robbers, an Arkansas Prison revolt, civil wars and Vietnam itself. It is a terrifyingly important clause. It is the last frontier of humanity.

This is it:

Article 3. In the case of armed conflict not of an international character occurring in the territory of one of the High Contracting Parties, each Party to the conflict shall be bound to apply, as a minimum, the following provisions:

1. Persons taking no active part in the hostilities, including members of armed forces who have laid down their arms and those placed hors de combat by sickness, wounds, detention, or any other cause, shall in all circumstances be treated humanely, without any adverse distinction founded on race, colour, religion or faith, sex, birth or wealth, or any other similar criteria.

To this end the following acts are and shall remain prohibited at any time and in any place whatsoever with respect to the abovementioned persons:

(a) Violence to life and person, in particular murder of all kinds, mutilation, cruel treatment and torture;
(b) Taking of hostages;
(c) Outrages upon personal dignity, in particular humiliating and degrading treatment;
(d) The passing of sentences and the carrying out of executions without previous judgment pronounced by a regularly constituted court affording all the judicial guarantees which are recognised as indispensable by civilised peoples.

2. The wounded and sick shall be cared for.

The lawyers can cut it to ribbons of course.

But for all human beings it must be a minimum standard of conduct. It is a clause common to all four Geneva Conventions, subscribed to by over 100 countries including Britain. Another common clause is this:

Article 127. The High Contracting Parties undertake in time of peace as in time of war, to disseminate the text of the present Convention as widely as possible in their respective countries, and in particular, to include the study thereof in their programmes of military and, if possible, civil instruction, so that the principles thereof may become known to all their armed forces and to the entire population.

When were you last instructed in the principles of the Geneva Conventions?

VIOLENCE

JUSTICE AND VIOLENCE IN ATHENS, 1968
Report by Amnesty International on Greece

TORTURE

The following account presents in summary form the evidence the Amnesty International Delegation took from the 16 people they saw who reported that they had been tortured, and from the 32 people still in prison about whose cases they received second-hand evidence which they found convincing because it was in many cases corroborated.

Techniques of Torture
A. Physical Torture

1. The standard initial torture reported from every Asphalia station is the so-called falanga. The prisoner is tied to a bench and the soles of his feet are beaten with a stick or pipe. Between beatings the prisoner is usually made to run around the bench under a heavy rain of blows. We examined the feet of a person who suffered this treatment four months before and his sole was covered with thick scar tissue. One prisoner now in Averoff prison had his foot broken under this torture. As he went without medical attention the bones have not set properly and he is crippled. The next step in this method is to strike the prisoner on the sternum. Prisoners vomiting blood from the lungs have generally undergone this treatment. Falanga is almost always accompanied by other inflictions of pain on the prisoner. In general five or six men are engaged in the torture of one prisoner. Common methods accompanying falanga are: pouring water down the mouth and nose while the prisoner is screaming from pain; putting 'Tide' soap in the eyes, mouth

and nose; banging the head on a bench or on the floor; beating on other parts of the body, etc.

2. Numerous incidents of sexually-oriented torture were reported. In the case of women, the torturers shove as many fingers as possible, or an object, into the vagina and twist and tear brutally. This is also done with the anus. A tube is inserted into the anus and water driven into the prisoner under very high pressure. In the case of men, beatings on the genitals with long, thin sand-bags have frequently been reported. One trade unionist was beaten so much that a testicle was driven up into his body.

3. Techniques of gagging are frequently reported. The throat is grasped in such a way that the windpipe is cut off, or a filthy rag (often soaked in urine) is shoved down the throat. Suffocation is prevented only at the last moment.

4. Beating on the head with sand-bags or beating the head against the wall or floor are standard procedure. Many cases of concussion have been reported.

5. Beating naked flesh with wires

THE COMIC WAS PUBLISHED A YEAR AGO.
THE GREEN BERETS WON - COMIC STRIP
HEROES USUALLY DO - BUT AS THE 1968
SAIGON SHOW PROVED, THE MEDIUM
WAS'NT THE MESSAGE:

knotted together into a whip.

6. Prisoners have been hung up for long periods of time. Usually the wrists are tied behind the back and the prisoner is suspended from the wrists.

7. Jumping on the stomach.

8. Tearing out the hair from the head and from the pubic region.

9. Rubbing pepper on sensitive areas of the body, such as the genitals, underarms, eyes, nose, etc.

10. Pulling-out toe-nails and finger-nails.

11. Different methods of inflicting burns, including putting-out cigarettes on parts of the body.

12. The use of electric shock. This is done at Military Hospital 401 and unconfirmed reports state that it is done at the Asphalia Station at Bouboulinas.

Physical beatings by the army and police as a method of intimidation and interrogation are general. Physical beating can be classified as torture if it is done in a systematic way. One man of over sixty

contacted by the Delegation was beaten at regular intervals for more than 12 hours. He suffered broken ribs but reported that young people were beaten steadily for periods of up to five days. Generally from four to six men beat a prisoner with their fists and kick with their booted feet, or use instruments such as planks, pipes, canes etc. At the Dionysos camp, which houses Greece's elite soldiers, prisoners are made to run a gauntlet. A reliable second-hand report from this camp is that a man literally had his eye knocked out of his head. The Amnesty International Delegation spoke with others who had broken ribs, noses, eardrums, etc.

B. Non-Physical Torture

Many informants who have under-gone torture consider that the non-physical methods were more difficult to bear.

1. Certain prisoners are intentionally moved to cells within earshot of other prisonors who are being violently interrogated. This has caused a number of nervous break-downs. One informant said that listening to the cries of the others was worse than undergoing the torture,

RANGER FORCES SOUTH VIETNAMESE PRISONER INTO A MUDHOLE:

MAKE HIM TALK, KSOR! I DON'T CARE HOW YOU DO IT! THERE'S TOO MUCH RIDING ON WHAT HE KNOWS! I'LL WAIT OUTSIDE...

one wanted to run in and be beaten rather than listen to the sufferings of another. It is reported that Mikis Theodorakis, the composer, who was never physically tortured, suffered a nervous collapse under this method.

2. Conditions of detention in some places are particularly bad. One technique is to leave the prisoner in a tiny, dark cell without food, water or blankets, for some days. The cells at Dionysos, which are cut into the side of Mount Pendelli, have 10 centimetres of water in them all the time. There is an iron bench in the cell. As prisoners held are not allowed to go out of the cells, the water is filled with their own excrement. The cells in the basement of Bouboulinas used for solitary confinement are full of vermin.

3. Threats to kill, maim and rape. People who had been tortured were often told that it would be repeated at a certain hour in the night, and were kept in constant terror by threats that they would have to undergo again what they had just experienced.

4. Stripping prisoners naked is partic-

ularly effective in Greece, where the association of nakedness with shame is very strong in the culture.

5. Mock executions were frequently reported. The prisoner faces a firing squad, is blind-folded and the rifles are fired. Some prisoners experienced this more than once. It is often done at Kesaryni, in the place where war-time executions took place.

6. Signing Declarations is considered by many to be the most inhuman technique of the regime. Compulsion to sign a paper denouncing parents, wife or political beliefs particularly affects a person of highly developed conscience and ideals. This is used in a deliberate way to break down the spirit of the prisoner. The expert in these matters is Mr Tournas, promoted to be Director of Greek Prisons under the regime. He begins by getting the prisoner to sign something innocuous, then tears up the paper, and makes the prisoner renounce more and more that he holds sacred. The Delegation interviewed people who had signed under this pressure, and all were in some sense broken. One part-

icularly moving case was that of a man who signed in order to be free to see his daughter who was dying of cancer. She died before he was released and he has had a nervous breakdown.

The Security Police and the Military Police are un-restricted today in Greece. Since, in Mr Pattakos's words, 'the laws sleep', the police may arrest anyone, in any place, at any time, with no obligation to charge him or inform anyone of his arrest. Believing that their own position is threatened by opposition to the Government, they have reacted brutally to those engaged in opposition. Those who have particularly suffered at the hands of the security forces are the young people those who are not known abroad, and those believed to be of the left.

Organisations, Places and Persons Engaged in Torture

Torture as a deliberate practice is carried out by the Security Police (Asphalia) and the Military Police (Ethniki Stratiotiki Astinomia). The Delegation heard first-hand evidence that the army and the gendarmerie also carried out torture, but it was diffi-

VIETNAM ☮

One of our chief problems is to keep repeating that one word till it becomes inescapable for everyone, especially those who have as yet, never questioned our alliance with the USA. Lets talk about 1968.

There should be reminders of the war, everywhere. Simply writing or painting that one word – VIETNAM – in as many places as possible would help. We should go out and splash patches of red paint on streets, roads, highways and pavements; on buildings which have anything to do with the conduct of the alliance.

Why red paint? It is the obvious symbol of blood and fire, which has already been used with some success in various ways in American, British and Australian demonstrations. Red paint, synonymous with destruction, is not itself destructive.

The Red Paint campaign needs no central organisation, it can be spread by example and by word of mouth. It will take time to spread, but that can't remove the dramatic impact of more and more of these patches appearing. Newspaper and T.V. will have to investigate what it's all about.

We will tell anyone that asks: 'RED PAINT is simply a protest against the Vietnam War, and a reminder of the pornography of such violence, period.

Because the paint is red they'll say we are communists. They'll say that anyway. The paint is RED because human blood is RED.

Begin Now – let the red paint spread . . .

ADRIAN MITCHELL,
PEACE NEWS, (UPS)

FAMILY IMMOLATED WITH FLAME-THROWER DURING CONG VENGEANCE RAID: DAK SON.

BUT WHILE THE YANKS WERE MAKING THE REDS SEE RED...THE CONG WERE PLOTTING A FEW NEW WRINKLES IN THE DEADLY GAME OF KILL-OR-BE-KILLED! AT A SECRET HIDEOUT IN CONG TERRITORY, VC GENERAL TU LIN... ALSO KNOWN AS THE *VIET CONG VIPER* WAS HATCHING A TERROR PLOT...

WE WILL BRING THE *JUNGLE* TO THE *CITIES*...AND WE BEGIN WITH SAIGON! WE WILL CRIPPLE THAT CITY WITH *FIRE*...*PANIC*... *SABOTAGE*...MAKE THE YANKEE CURSE THE DAY HE SET FOOT ON OUR LAND! THE PLAN IS SET...THE TIME-TABLE TICKING AWAY LIKE A TIME BOMB...

AND I....WITH MY PICKED INFILTRATORS....WILL TAKE AN AMERICAN SPECIAL FORCES OUTPOST BY SURPRISE...TURN IT INTO AN INFERNO OF DEATH...WIPE OUT THE GARRISON TO THE LAST MAN!

UPI. 7.12.67.

cult to determine if these were isolated cases or standard procedure.

Those whose names are most frequently mentioned as directing and carrying out torture are: Inspector Lambrou, the Director of the Security Police Headquarters, in Athens at Bouboulinas Street, and the following officers — Mallios, Babalis, Karapanayiotis, Kravaritis, Spanos, Yannicopoulus, all the same office; Major Theophiloyaiannakos of the Military Police located at the Dionysos Camp outside Athens. Others mentioned frequently were Zagouras at Dionysos, Lt. Kapoglou, Director of Asphalia at Aigeleo, and Kouvas of the Asphalia in Pireus.

The places where the most serious torture was reported in the Athens area are the Bouboulinas Asphalia, Military Hospital 401, and the Dionysos camp.

27 January 1968. Amnesty International, Turnagain Lane, Farringdon Street, London, EC4.

JUSTICE AND VIOLENCE IN ARKANSAS, 1968

This is part of a transcript of a documentary about Arkansas State Penitentiary, Cummins. It was shown on BBC's '24 Hours' on February 6th. Murton is the new Superintendent at Cummins.

MURTON: We have around 200 inmates who are sentenced under the felony courts to prison and yet when they come here they are given a gun and given life and death control over the rest of the inmates. It's the only place that exists in the United States and I suspect probably anywhere in the world . . . We have a closed society of exploitation and well the nearest thing I can think to it in the free world would be the general situation in Chicago in the thirties whereby you had bosses and operators and every system of justice and everything else was controlled by the association, the organisation and those who deviated from the plan were eliminated. And the

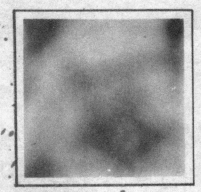

Et cetera ⟶

...RE ARE A CHANGING ALL THE TIME ALL THE TIME THE TIME IS

RANGER STOMPING ON S.VIETNAMESE FARMER SUSPECTED OF SUPPLYING INCORRECT INF-
ORMATION TO GOV. TROOPS...

same thing has happened here . . .
Those who tried to talk about the brutality and the torture were eliminated. And
the system — when you have a system
that's operated by fear and oppression
then you must back that up with brutality, and it's been the custom here in the
past that men were beaten with a strap
which was about five feet long and five
inches wide; an inmate would be spread
out on the floor naked and another
inmate or staff man use the strap on him.
It was such a brutal thing that the man's
body would convulse and he would lift
off the floor six or eight inches. They'd
have to have inmates sitting on the
extremities, the arms and the legs, to
keep him from coming up . . .
I mean I inherited a system of inmate
guards which is antithetical to what we're
trying to do. You see, in the past the
inmate guards, which are called trustees
here, have been in complete control of
the prison . . . They've made the job
assignments, they've decided which detail
a man worked on; they shook down the
incoming prisoners to take radios and
watches away from them; they charged —
the yard men charged a dollar for a man

to get a bed the first night he came in.
They assigned people to lucrative positions where they could make money.
They decided who would become a
trustee, who would carry guns, who
would be in charge of the commissary.
This was the system as it was. They know
here at Cummins that it has to change.
And when I came here there was no way
to tell how many prisoners there were —
which is really another subject — but
there is an inventory of guns and there
are some 22 guns missing off the official
state inventory. There are some indica-
tions that in December there were three
rifles and four pistols in one of the barracks here. We think they are still there.
We do not have the capability at this time
to shake the place down and there are
no doubt knives — we've taken knives
off people all the time. And whisky,
there has been free wheel whisky coming
in. So, I don't know exactly what the
right criteria or the time is but when I
feel it's the proper moment and I have
support enough from the trustees I will
shake down the other barracks and get
those illegal guns and weapons away
from the inmates. But then I have to

devise a method to shake down the
trustee barracks. There's been no shake-
down for ten years.
COMMENTATOR: Everything is incredible in this prison without walls. Last
year alone 69 escaped. Mr Murton says
that is more than escaped from all other
American gaols. Equally incredible have
been the state authorities. In recent years
they have openly boasted about the
unique way in which they made a profit
from a prison farm. The explanation is
simple . . . this was the ultimate in slave
labour violently enforced with the Tucker
telephone.
MURTON: The Tucker telephone was a
device used to extract information, to
discipline and to torture the inmates at
the Tucker prison farm. It did not have a
dial it had a crank — in America similar
to the army field phone, you crank it
and the battery generates power and
rings across the line. This was used
at Tucker as a torture device and the
general procedure was that the subject
was brought into the hospital, taken
into the surgical room and strapped naked
to a bed, a surgical table, and there was
a positive and negative control — anode

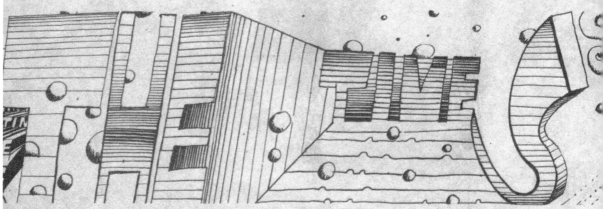

20

Tales of the Green Beret 'discovered by BBC's 'Eleventh Hour'

and cathode — and one was run from the anode to his penis and other from the cathode to his big toe and then somebody would sit at his feet and crank this machine and send a current through his body. This literally drove some of them out of their mind; it certainly destroyed some of them physically as a man, and it was excruciating torture, I have never heard of before. It's probably one of the most effective devices that could be used. And I've talked to inmates and have seen them and it's a horrible thing.

COMMENTATOR: These are not just the superintendent's personal views. This police report documents the way in which dangerous prisoners had keys to their cells, food crawled with bugs and maggots and brutality and corruption are daily occurences. But how could it happen here? — especially in the midst of such an apparent — ly ordinary American community? The answer is that it's not ordinary. This is the Bible belt of the South where puritanical standards still rule. The name of the capital, Little Rock, is itself synonymous with racial prejudice. In Arkansas justice is so fierce that a man may legally be given ten lashes a day, each day of the week. Inside Cummins, there's one man serving a forty-five year sentence. He's completed twenty years, it was his first offence; it was a theft. Judges will send boys of 14 to a place like this where there is a proven history of forty years of sadism. Of course the local people knew what was going on. In these agricultural communities where strangers are regarded with suspicion, secrets are impossible to keep. It's just that in the past nobody saw any cause for protest. Now the facts are officially known there is still no sense of public outrage — except, that is, for criticism of the Superintendent and threats against his life, because he has dared to tell what goes on inside Cummins Prison.

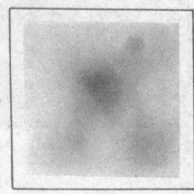

A Wild New Magazine Is About To Happen!

YOU are about to witness the birth of a crusading new bimonthly. **The Running Man Magazine** will report on every aspect of the ebullient new life-style now emerging in Britain, exercising the right of Free Speech on politics, literature, the avant garde and the New Morality, down to the very last syllable.

The editors hope to give this country its first completely uninhibited magazine, providing a forum for the most exciting new writing of this generation.

THE RUNNING MAN

A new, fiercely libertarian, magazine

Indecent Exposure — A damning indictment of the unscrupulous methods used by sensation-seeking newspapers to probe the intimate details of people's lives.

President Bobby Kennedy: The First 100 Days—The most intimate and informed appraisal of Kennedy ever to appear in print.

IN summation, The Running Man is a fearless magazine of uncompromising independence, edited for open-minded readers. Begin your subscription with Volume 1, Number 1, simply by sending in the coupon together with 35s, and you will receive your copy of the inaugural issue *free* . . . but please act at once, since first issues of high-quality magazines invariably become collectors' items.

The Running Man, 28 Rocks Lane, London S.W.13

I enclose 35s for a one-year subscription to The Running Man Magazine. I understand that I will receive *free* a copy of The Running Man's inaugural issue.

NAME

ADDRESS

OZ

The Permissive Society is in Fact Hypocritical and Furtive — Peter Fryer demonstrates how censorship is a bigger potential danger than pornography.

Preparing for the Worst— Mordecai Richler's scathing send-up of U.S. anti-brainwashing courses for Vietnam.

Eros and the Mechanical Brides — Raymond Durgnat's report on the wildly hedonistic cinema of the Sixties.

Vengeance, Baby — The Black Power pow-wow as observed by William Rushton.

The Book Nobody Dares Review—An absorbing profile of the most lubricious Englishman who ever lived.

Beatle Power—An inside look at the growing financial empire maintained by the Four Lads from Liverpool.

Thoughts After Prosecution—John Calder, publisher of the banned *Last Exit to Brooklyn* reports on the dangerous erosions of our freedoms.

Will Brecht's Theatre Survive Socialism?

Leather Pants — Fiction. **Contributors include:** Paul Ableman, J. G. Ballard, Saul Bellow, John Bird, Barry Fantoni, Paul Foot, Allen Ginsberg, B. S. Johnson, Norman Mailer, Spike Milligan, Jack Newfield, Dennis Norden, Ralph Steadman. *Edited by:* Christopher Kypreos and Charles Marowitz.

OZ SUBSCRIPTION

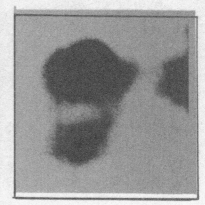

smalls

PIN BOARD

OZ ADVERTISING WORKS
BRILLIANTLY
(Circulation: 21,000 guaranteed,
print order: 25,000)
Smalls: 1s per word,
1/6 semi-display,
2/6 box no.
Display: £65 per page,
£35 half page,
£20 quarter page,
£2.10s per col inch.
Bookings to OZ,
38a, Palace Gardens Terrace, W8.
Smalls must be paid in advance.

DUREX GOSSAMER 7/6 per dox
POST FREE

Tit-bits, 709 Fulham Road, SW6.

SHORTCOMINGS ?

Prolong the pleasure of intercourse
with Suifan's 'Kwang Tze' Solution.
This Chinese preparation is specially beneficial to men who suffer
from premature ejaculation and is
guaranteed to end mutual frustration and bring satisfaction to both
partners.
The Suifan's 'Kwang Tze' Solution
is completely safe and reliable, as
stated in Government certificates
supplied with each bottle.

Special Offer
To prove our claim we will send
you by return and in complete
confidence — a bottle of the
'Kwang Tze' Solution for only
2gns.

Order Direct from Sole Distributors

Blacks International,
Suite A,
24 Cranbourne Street,
Leicester Square, W.C.2.

Please Cross Cheques & P.O.s &
make payable to: Blacks International

Liverpool Poet, 40's, desperately
frustrated would love to hear from
intelligent, sexy women, any age,
who can help him relax. Meetings
later. Photos appreciated, returned. OZ Box No:

Photographer, seeks interesting m
model for week-end. Own town
flat, E'Type, etc.
OZ Box No: 10

RELEASE office at 52, Princedale
Road, W.11. Holland Park Tube.
Office 229 7753 - Emergency
,603 8654. We sell OZ, I.T. Peace
News and Posters. Come and see
us for legal or other advice. We
need information about busts and
irregular police behaviour etc. Ring
us if have, or want a room or flat to
let.
RELEASE needs your help -
support us if you can.

Conture (Form-fitting)	15/- doz
Durex Fetherlite	15/- doz
Durex Gossamer	10/- doz
Crest Naturac	10/- doz
Silver Tex	6/-
Conture (Form-fitting)	15/- doz
Durex Fetherlite	15/- doz
Durex Gossamer	10/- doz
Crest Naturac	10/- doz
Silver Tex	6/- doz
Fifteen Assorted	14/-

Booklet Free, Return Post,
Double-packed, Plain Wrapper.
SUREX LTD, 8 Edward Street,
Blackpool

FOR ALL PROBLEMS,
REMOVALS, DELIVERIES, ETC
DORMOBILES WITH HELPFUL
WORKING DRIVERS.
TAXIMOVES GULiver 8923.

PREGNANCY TEST £2. Inquiries
BELL JENKINS LABORATORIES
Charlotte St. Portsmouth (23366)

MEN! End disappointment now.
New method of increasing virility
and vital dimensions.
100% safe: no drugs etc.
Money back guarantee.
NEWAN PRODUCTS
76 Shaftesbury Avenue,
London W1.

JOIN THE BADGE SET
Kiss Me . . . LSD not LBJ . . .
UNITE all QUEERS . . .
SMILE if you had SEX last night . . .
etc. All badges 1½" diameter.
Dayglow colours. 1/6 each, 6 for
8/-. 12 for 15/- plus 6d for post-
age. Free catalogue available.
New titles regularly.
Badges & Novelty Co. (London),
21 Fitzroy Street, London W1.

A JACK FOR EVERY JILL
OR JOE. 5/-d Each introduction,
no extra charge whatever:
Write INTROBOUTIQUE,
709 Fulham Road, SW6.
736 2871

CONFIDENTIAL ADVICE ON
THE PILL FOR ALL WOMEN
EVERYWHERE.
WRITE STEP ONE LTD,
(0) 93 Regent Street, W1. s.a.e.
or telephone 01-622 7815.

24

... continued from 24

*Splash Poster, UFo over Vietnam,
to be published March 1968.
See page 34.*

The Digger Thing must be **your** thing!
OZ has been *inundated* with letters from readers respond-
ing to the article in OZ 9. All letters are being answered
now.

Meantime, an interim group of London Diggers have been
going ahead with the arrangements for staging the Forum,
and setting up the contacts necessary to get a successful
community into action straight after.

The Forum will be held over the weekend beginning
Mar 23 or Mar 30, depending on just when we can get a
site. The hang-ups in getting a hall for anything are unbelievable! If anyone thinks they can help please contact us
at OZ. Final arrangements will be announced in the next
OZ, out mid-March, and also in IT.

We will be announcing a program for the Forum and the
guest list. Invitations are going out at the moment and we
expect representatives from experiments in Community
living, including delegates from Holland and from the West
Coast Communities.

Why is
this
man
laughing?
Who was Werty
anyway?

CONTINUED PAGE 28

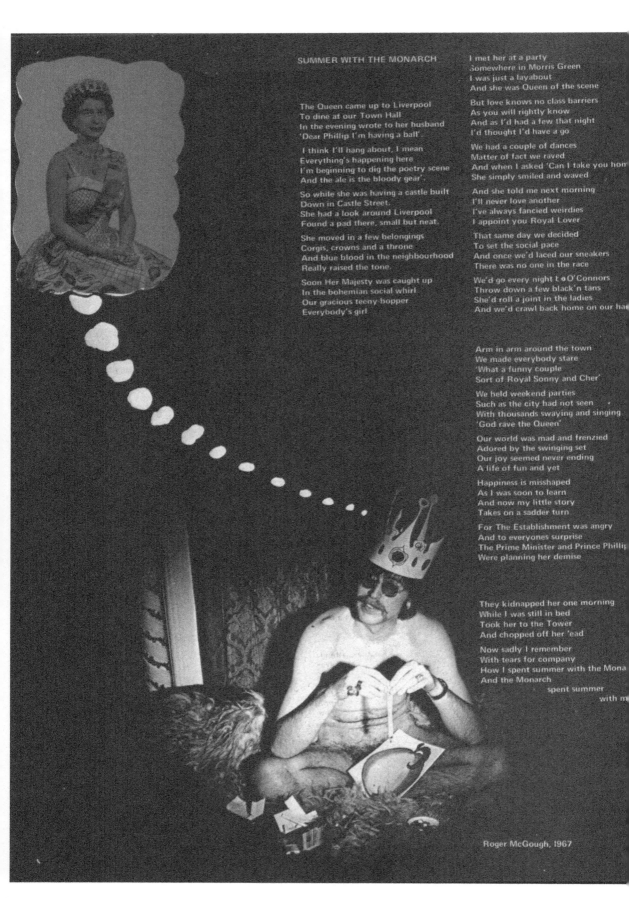

SUMMER WITH THE MONARCH

The Queen came up to Liverpool
To dine at our Town Hall
In the evening wrote to her husband
'Dear Phillip I'm having a ball'.

I think I'll hang about, I mean
Everything's happening here
I'm beginning to dig the poetry scene
And the ale is the bloody gear'.

So while she was having a castle built
Down in Castle Street.
She had a look around Liverpool
Found a pad there, small but neat.

She moved in a few belongings
Corgis, crowns and a throne
And blue blood in the neighbourhood
Really raised the tone.

Soon Her Majesty was caught up
In the bohemian social whirl.
Our gracious teeny-bopper
Everybody's girl

I met her at a party
Somewhere in Morris Green
I was just a layabout
And she was Queen of the scene

But love knows no class barriers
As you will rightly know
And as I'd had a few that night
I'd thought I'd have a go

We had a couple of dances
Matter of fact we raved
And when I asked 'Can I take you hom'
She simply smiled and waved

And she told me next morning
I'll never love another
I've always fancied weirdies
I appoint you Royal Lover

That same day we decided
To set the social pace
And once we'd laced our sneakers
There was no one in the race

We'd go every night t o O'Connors
Throw down a few black 'n tans
She'd roll a joint in the ladies
And we'd crawl back home on our ha

Arm in arm around the town
We made everybody stare
'What a funny couple
Sort of Royal Sonny and Cher'

We held weekend parties
Such as the city had not seen
With thousands swaying and singing
'God rave the Queen'

Our world was mad and frenzied
Adored by the swinging set
Our joy seemed never ending
A life of fun and yet

Happiness is misshaped
As I was soon to learn
And now my little story
Takes on a sadder turn

For The Establishment was angry
And to everyones surprise
The Prime Minister and Prince Phillip
Were planning her demise

They kidnapped her one morning
While I was still in bed
Took her to the Tower
And chopped off her 'ead

Now sadly I remember
With tears for company
How I spent summer with the Mona
And the Monarch
                    spent summer
                              with m

Roger McGough, 1967

I don't know how many people here regard themselves as members of the underground or how extreme is this vision that some of us have for an alternative kind of society. How far are we prepared to accept the consequences of the kind of insights people have? Most people are compromising their notions in this respect particularly when they move towards political activities. For instance, the International Times in aligning itself with the Black Power Movement and talking about the Coming seems to me a compromise of an inward looking, simpler approach to existence that Hippies have been talking about and that we felt rather excited by. It seems that once you move into politics, like Dick Gregory has . . .

Yes, in between all this talk about crushing a system Dick Gregory is standing as a write-in presidential candidate. He always throws the American constitution at you, which of course was not exactly written by black power. Screw politics. What sort of future has a drop out philosophy in this country? . . .

There's an experiment going on here in the Tribe of the Sacred Mushroom . . . Many people are talking about it but these seem to be the first people who have gone out and done it, who have gone to estate agents and found a place outside London. And they've lasted the winter. If they can last the winter outside London with no income, it seems they've made it.

But isn't the point that the size and structure of these communes is very limited and merely parasitic on the existing framework — what's going to happen next? . . . if you're going to try and replace the whole system and advocate an alternative, then itdoesn't seem likely that it's going to exist as a small series of these small communes.

You're going to have a network of alternative systems — the purists in tribes, hippie minded people who sell things, and plastic parachutists, but actually you're going to need all 3 groups of people . . .

• •

But aren't we talking about a few religious eccentrics . . . Can communes have real meaning for anyone here?

Robert Tasher has what seems to be the most viable idea of setting up in London. He's done a demographic survey of England and projected population growth and what areas the population will grow and he has found that as you know the population is increasing in south east England and decreasing in north England and in about 10 years time 60% of the population will be in south east England. Hereford county has lost population in the last 10 years from 170 thousand to 130 thousand and with this increased velocity of the population moving to south east England it will even lose more. He's planning to go to Hereford to gauge the planning commission to find out which bit of land they feel least strongly about — not to argue with them — you go there to buy land as an outsider you're immediately looked on with suspicion, so he's going to do it from the inside, find a piece of land, build tidal generators, put up geodesic domes, buy more land and set up a fortress commune . . he's going to have his piece of England and he plans to buy more and more of it . . . he has enough money to make it feasible.

The Americans seem to have got it much better than us, because when they drop out they go and live in the country and do things . . . they paint and sell their paintings — they can survive by making money. All the people I know in England when they drop out they go on a horse and cart, but they don't try to do anything except survive and cadge food. They don't read books they don't do anything — I don't see how they can survive unless they do something other than just living in the country . . .

But once you start being productive and active in these things you start playing the old game . . .

But aren't they playing the old game in the States by doing their posters etc?

You're gaining creative energy . . . poster design or jewellery making is really trade; exporting and importing rather than playing the old game. The creative energy is generated by the community itself.

There have been communities in the past that have come about in similar ways and have had in mind similar ideals . . . Owenites, Ammans and the Mormons of course.

Don't they usually come to grief through boredom?

The fortress commune seems to be an excellent mechanical way of being non parasitical.

It's also a way of not denying a couple of hundred years of technical advance.

The underground as a community still has a balance of trade deficit which mainly comes through payment of rent and

• •

food. My interest right now is in making it happen in urban areas rather than making it happen agriculturally. One way it might be done is using housing cooperatives — 3 or 4 getting together with a minimum amount of resources — a couple of hundred quid perhaps to form a housing cooperative — we can go for all sorts of GLC and borough facilities. Then we can divide the house into 3,4 or 6 flats. We own the house as a corporation. We're living in the flats and that's one way of alleviating the balance of payment.

You're still getting on the tubes every day.

You wouldn't just be growing cabbages, everyone would be doing something they find interesting, and the fact that everyone was together and they weren't having to work for the Government or pay taxes or involve themselves in a society which they didn't believe in, and could involve themselves in something in which they were interested, the motives for working would be completely changed.

It seems to me that the underground really is a church, and a fortress community is a free generation monastery - you have your plain clothes people - necessarily part of the system although it's based against the system. There's interplay between the system and the church. Now that sort of interplay that there is, is going to be between the underground and the overground — therefore the underground is bound to be riddled with hypocrisy, but fortunately we can riddle the overground with hypocrisy too.

One of the reasons why you have vigorous drop out communities in the States is because of the extreme conditions in the States especially in the cities, which you don't have here. We had our car stolen last week and I was surprised more than anything . . . car stolen in London? Whereas in New York if you leave your car in the streets 3 days you find it completely stripped and come back to find 8 Puerto Rican children playing in it because that's their only playground. Tyres off, motor out . . . you expect it.

This discussion about a changed society, an alternative type of existence seems to run parallel to the idea of a changed state of mind — that seems to be crucial and I think the whole of the idea of setting up communes and the whole idea of getting out of the existing situation is not necessarily relevant nor is it necessarily the thing which strikes you when you are in that kind of mind from acid or pot or just through being lucky . . . for instance I am, in a way, the product of a community because my father dropped out in the 30s in Australia. He's a painter, and he went off to the hills, bought up a lot of property which his friends helped him purchase. The binding force there , was not psychedelia or emotional alternative societies but the idea that art was to come before possessiveness — man possessing a woman, all these sort of ego kind of activities, and that anybody who was concerned with painting, sculpture, writing and so on took some precedence. 27

And somehow we did manage in that situation — my parents grew their own food, had a lot of people in like plumbers, electricians etc, who didn't pay rent, but lived there as well, and contributed their services of one kind or another. And that ground to a halt finally 20 years later, which seems quite a period, because people were just getting too old, I think, and too bored. But the two things it had, were a terrifically dictatorial figure at the top, and this binding unifying kind of faith in a certain notion of art. Now the thing I think that the underground has to articulate in a much stronger sense, is a binding philosophy — like the Ten Commandments you were talking of, and I really don't think it's got anything like that yet. It's far too diverse and confused . . .

Well, I think that moral chaos is stimulating. We ought not to force the Ten Commandments upon us. Maybe a manifesto, rather than the Ten Commandments. Nothing can be achieved by having rules and regulations.

What you need is some people going round saying thou shalt not and other people, also within the movement, saying what's all this rubbish about thou shalt not, and form the dialogue between the two, people would, with any luck, know what it was all about and at the same time not take it too seriously.

There are hippie underground people working in the BBC and bookshops, teaching in schools, etc and — I often wonder what can ever unify them.

There's one thing that probably all these people agree on, and that's legalised pot . . . I can't think of any other specific issue.

You're not actually selling pot are you? You're selling a state of mind.

No it's just an extension of freedom to do what you want to do, an issue of civil liberty.

Well, I've got freedom to do what I like with my own body, but there's nothing I like doing with it . . .

Don't you think that it will take 50 years of absolute wisdom to get anywhere? . . . I think the state of mind that people are onto now and are aware of, is still so affected by other kinds of consciousness . . . and the articulate and slightly extrovert members of the underground are putting out their philosophies and their poems — all great entertainment, but not of any grand signigicance.

Because they're still employing establishment media it's still part of the establishment because they are clever enough to ••

keep a few new voices in for a while, anyone who comes with radical ideas sooner or later becomes successful and then the demands of their social life, the city and the people moving in TV or in the art world and galleries — they become very much absorbed and part of it. What they might be saying is completely different, but in the context, in the form it's in, it is no longer discernable from anything else. It's presented in the same way, same pace, same pressure and same rhythm. It's got to be something which is distinctly outside this. A voice in the wilderness is never really joined by other people because it's . . . in the wilderness. Pop music established an international relationship between young people all over the world in a very primitive way, but it has established something and everthing that has gone with pop has spread this . . . but you hear a song by one of the underground groups next to a song on the radio by Humperdink. It just doesn't sort of have anything anymore . . . it becomes weakened, diluted . . . ➤➤

ON THE PATH TOWARDS . . . ON THE PATH TOWARDS . . . . TOWARDS THE EVOLUTION OF THE COSMOS. TOWARDS THE ANSWER TO THE QUESTION.

But it's still important to communicate underground ideas on overground media.

Not if it's only ideas. Like the humanist kind of trouble, because in the end it was only words they were sending out, they weren't asking people to come for sustenance only meetings. They weren't teaching people how to build houses, they weren't teaching people a trade. When the apocalypse comes, and the universities and the media closes, I'm lost. All these things . . . trades, sustenance . . . we have to establish natural demonstrations for our arguments . . . arguments are no longer useful,worthwhile except as a call to arms and then you need natural demonstrations to keep the people that you have stirred up.

We need a new form to house the new content. . .we're still trying to fit it into the old form, and the old form is the old form and it comes across the same way.

What is the situation in American now? In 20 years time the poeple who are now dropping out . . . by simple statistics, must take over all sources of power.

No, I don't think they will.

Who else?

This will happen if they become part of the establishment — at the moment I certainly don't think that will happen in 20 years time . . . there's still all those other young people.

A friend of mine who said she had taken so much acid she could no longer hallucinate isn't going to be part of the establishment.

Because of sheer numbers they come to a position where they will elect the establishment if necessary.

But in that framework they will be absorbed back in by that time because at the age of 19 one can still feel young and healthy enough to drift. You haven't got family obligation or anything else. Remember that monologue in US 2. That girl, 'how we were young and . . . ' a perfect example of how age creeps up on you — if you remain within the framework and create a new form. The world is in such a desperate situation that anything that is any good is created in art — if someone does a fantastic visual work of art, within a year and a half it will be used for advertising soap perhaps . . . the fact that everything that is produced is absorbed into selling in a matter of years, no matter how good it is, everything. This is the terrifying thing, that it is gobbled up so quickly by this commercial thing, depending on how many goods are sold and what your numerical rating on TV is. Quantity is the thing now, not quality. The worst magazine, newspaper, TV sells the most.

. . . .

evolution is gradual. You have to start preparing it 30 years earlier.

Isn't this too much team spirit again? Now it's entirely individual, and the one revolution that can be achieved overnight is by you — you don't have to worry who is going to go with you. Have your own barricade.

es, but individuals can never fight against the establishment.

hy fight?

think individualists have had it. What the underground is emerging out of is the fact that progressively every kind of link, family links nd so on, are all being atrophied and this has made life so unbearable . . . the grow up mass media of art is simply because nobody can e anything to anybody, not that they ever could. But given the fact that a lot of other constraints have been removed, mal-constraints, ractical constraints, the only thing left which isn't void is trying to fulfil this sort of personal contact. If we let everybody have his wn personal barricade, it is actually leaving people so much on their own. One needs a kind of combination of getting people away om a lot of dreadful ties to which they are attached (having a career, a job and so on). Perhaps a combination of acid and a communal fe, access to a fantasy world, to an emotional world which is nonetheless more or less viable or sharable.

n my case I like what I do, teaching and writing. If I contracted out into a community I'd be leaving these best things behind . . . What I ally want to do is to get away in the evenings or the weekends or a nice holiday somewhere where one's ego can totally dissolve and if ould shift between an everyday life and something totally different then this would make me quite happy and this is hypocritical.

it?

ell it might be hypocritical in that if I'm getting my daily dose of respiritualisation then I go back to the system and in fact, remain a isoner of the system. On the other hand I might be so changed by the break that even in the system I might be a different person. herefore, I might be able to link up. In every pin-striped fellow there is 25% of rebellion sitting there, and it can't think, can't talk, n't recognise itself. With other people it's more.

hat are we going to do with that 25%? In a sense this is what the Underground is about, how to get that 25%, how to get him to burn s draft card to pull out of IBM and this comes back to whether John Peel should be playing records on the BBC, ending up promoting ngelbert Humperdink. The alternative is just putting out underground publications and using underground methods but in that way e are not going to get the guy in the pin-striped suit. It is worthwhile taking the risk of modifying and diluting our message in order to ach a wider number of people.

Et cetera

I SUPPOSE IN A FEW THOUSAND OF THEIR YEARS THEY'LL DEVELOP SPACE TRAVEL OF THEIR OWN... AND SUDDENLY THEY'LL REALISE THEY'RE NOT ALONE... THAT THEY ARE PART OF A MUCH LARGER PLAN... THAT THOSE GODS AND ANGELS IN FIRERY CHARIOTS ARE US... IF THEY LAST THAT LONG... JUDGING ON PAST RECORDS WE MUSTN'T BE TOO OPTIMISTIC...

AN ADOLESCENT PLANET... BIG PROBLEMS... CONFUSED... SPOTTY... I WONDER WHERE THE FIRST BUDS OF REALISATION WILL BREAK THROUGH? THE FIRST EYES OPEN?

THE SAME PATTERNS AS USUAL, I IMAGINE... A FEW "DISREPUTABLE" BOOKS BY "CRANKS", A MUCH SCOFFED AT LECTURE OR TWO... SOME CRUDELY SCRAWED PICTURES ACCOMPANIED BY NIGH ILLEGIBLE, BADLY SPELT TEXT IN SOME QUAINT LITTLE PSEUDO-RADICAL MAGAZINE... ... WHO KNOWS.

COMING COMING

...AND SO IT CAME TO PASS.....

it gets around

This movement is not going to come from a political platform or anything, it's going to come very naturally; probably the influence of drugs has taken people away a step from society, so they can see it more clearly . . . we still find that isn't enough, we still seek a new society we still start getting involved in the games of the old society . . . one has got to physically remove oneself as well as mentally.

world birth earth  death mother open

All this discussion is futile. It's like Isadora Duncan trying to change the world by teaching people a new dance routine.

IN OUR SPECTAC-
ULAR SOCIETY
WHERE ALL YOU
CAN SEE IS
THINGS AND
THEIR PRICE ...

THERE'S NOTHING
THEY WON'T DO TO
RAISE THE STANDARD
OF BOREDOM

Mystery solved? These panels from
the strangely disturbing cartoon
poster being pasted all over
town are rumoured to be the
latest guide to an alternative
society offered by Black Power —
merchant banked by James Baldwin.

FROM FEB 24, THERE'S A CORN
of SE9 that will be forever foreign. Malco
Ross and the South London Diggers are
beating the Scots Nats to the punch. The
are declaring BLACKHEATH an Indepen
ent Free State.

Immigration Policy sounds remarkably
liberal.

'Dadaists, existentialists, sensitors, imagis
intentionalists, New Apple Apocalypticis
concrete poets, phallic symbolists, surrea
ists, etc.,' are invited to 'get off their
intellectual arses' abandon their 'isolate
frustrated dream states' and become cit
of independent Blackheath.

'Your mystical force can be brought to
bear in the Magical rebirth of South Lon
don and reconstruction of people's awar
ness,' declares the New State's slightly
chauvinist Manifesto of Independence.

The Exploding Galaxy and the Northern
Open Workshop will perform at the
independence 'Festival of Everything'
but the Manifesto warns, 'PS. This is no
an electric technology experiment. Brin
your creativity with you and do it.'

30

It is Year Zero. We are on the 39th Step of the Kahn Excallation Ladder — Slow-Motion Countercity War . . . Industrial spy, the red-headed transvestite, Morel, is relaxing between routine assassinations when Top-Priority Orders are encoded into his cocktail-hour musak. Report to —

Et cetera

Rare Eye-Witness Account: How We "Pacify" Them and Brutalize Ourselves

Xuan Dai, South Vietnam—Little fires were still burning in the ruins. Frightened baby chicks chirped frantically in search of their mothers. From the charred entry of one of the buildings, a middle-aged peasant woman tentatively poked her head, then emerged with a puzzled-looking little boy. Quickly another much older looking woman followed her and then several more children.

"Hey you, get over there," a tow-headed Marine, barely 20, shouted at the women and children. Slowly they padded silently where he pointed. American jet bombers demolished this village with tons of bombs and napalm. The Communist troops had stolen away before dawn. Only the women and children were left.

"We should have killed them all," said the young Marine, jabbing his M16 rifle in the direction of the crowd of women and children. "There's eight Marine bodies lying on the landing zone across the rice paddies."

An old man with a dirty gray beard clinging to a little boy with large burn blisters on the back of his neck, extended a tin can and pleaded for water. "Don't give him

any," the Marine shouted to his buddy. "Let them starve, let them die." Wordlessly another Marine extended his canteen and filled the man's cup.

Communist troops, firing from entrenchments on the tree line in front of the village, killed or wounded an entire Marine platoon on Thursday as it advanced across the rice paddies. It was not until Friday, right after the air strikes, that Marines dared enter the village.

Marines counted the spoils—two malaria-ridden men, blindfolded and shaking, held on suspicion, and several "captured" weapons, all of them rusted. As night fell women and children started crying. The intelligence sergeant asked what was wrong, and the interpreter reported they were "starving."

"Won't anyone feed these people?" the Sergeant asked. An officer, assigned to both calling in air strikes and directing civil affairs, said he'd see what he could do. "First I annihilate them and then I rehabilitate them," he said, laughing at his own joke.

—*Donald Kirk in the* Washington Star *Dec. 31. (Abr.)*

'BETTER THAT THE WHOLE WORLD SHOULD BE DESTROYED AND PERISH UTTERLY THAN THAT A FREE MAN SHOULD REFRAIN FROM ONE ACT TO WHICH HIS NATURE MOVES HIM' (K. MARX)

The whole event is under the patronage of Alan Ginsberg — the Underground's Duke of Edinburgh.

In the face of this latest crumbling of Empire, the Home Office are maintaining a superb stiff upper lip, *'The Ministry of Housing know nothing about it — it's just a flash in the pan.'*

WE HAVE BEGUN A CONSUMER
Survey of the products advertising in OZ. Perhaps predictably enough the first report back is from our intrepid tester of Suifan's 'Kwang Tze' solution, the 'Chinese preparation . . . guaranteed to end mutual frustration and bring satisfaction to both partners.' Our man among the 'sexies' reports:

'Twenty minutes after taking the stuff, what James Baldwin laughingly calls my 'sex', went bright red and I had a large and painful erection, which cold spoons and showers notwithstanding, refused to vanish for an hour. My girlfriend was already fast asleep.'

FORD'S THEATRE ::E—OPENED
Jan 30 in Washington for the first performance since Lincoln's Assassination. Conspicuous by his absence Lyndon Johnson.

Et cetera

KHATMANDU — Chicago of the East!
Home of the Mobs and the Meat-plants...
Khatmandu, where the Intergalactic
Security Corps is locked in gruesome
conflict with ... The Perils of the Flesh!

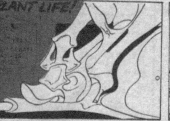

It began down at the **Protoplaxon Plant** as surgically-improved human workers can the fabricated meats . . . Was it a rogue cell? A pseudo-divine orgasm, an obscene Second Coming? The Word is Made Flesh, and flesh CRAWLS. Protoplaxoid people slither corruptly into seats of power . . . (**Tell-tale signs**. Protoplaxon is grey, fungoid. Harold Wilson was protoplaxoid).

But General Zuk of Intergalactic Security counter-attacks. In the nick of time, he collects the fact, and prepares to meet the Machiavelian Morel. BUT THEN . . .

Et cetera ⟫

TON. (LNS) THE NORTH KOREAN GOVERNMENT
een protesting intrusions into territorial waters by American
s with electronic spying devices for over a month prior to the
e of the U.S.S. Pueblo.

Christian Science Monitor reported a formal demand to cease
esist issue Jan 20 by the North Koreans. The Pueblo was seized
2.

FRANCISCO (LNS) 12 STUDENTS CHARGED WITH
rbing the peace' in a mill-in at San Francisco State College mana
avoid arrest for some weeks by holing up in an art gallery on
us. Not so audio-tactile, John Gerassi, the Professor of Internat
Relations turned himself in.

CINATTI. (LNS) 18 YEAR OLD MARY DECOURCY
e is in her 2nd day of total fast in quaintly named Cincinatti
house.

has been taking only water and vitamins since her arrest Dec 7
anti-draft demonstration. 'By fasting, I want to say, human
s do not belong locked up in cages,' she says.

ANA (LNS) CUBA HAS BEEN PUBLISHING
y works written by U.S. authors without paying royalties on
ound that 'developing countries should have free access to the
al and technical advances of the industrialized countries.'

al advances 1 & 2. Truman Capote's **In Cold Blood** & Edward
s **Who's Afraid of Virginia Woolf?**

PHILADELPHIA (LNS) THE U.S. AND CANADIAN
military are two of the most important buyers of those scale model
soldiers that come in the bottoms of Kelloggs packets.

Associated Hobby Manufacturers which produced or imported over
26 million scale model tanks, guns, trucks and men in 1967, revealed
in **Toys** and **Novelty** that the US and Canadian military were major
customers.

Assistant to the President, Peter Van Dore, confirmed that, 'We ship
20 or 30 'combat teams' a week to military posts.'

MILLBROOK (LNS) UBIQUITOUS ARTHUR KLEPS
(OZ 8 & 9) founder and Chief Boo Hoo of the Neo American Church
has been arrested with four of his followers and charged with conspiracy to distribute psychedelic substances on the premises of the church's
headquarters at Millbrook, also the site of Timothy Leary's League
for Spiritual Discovery.

'The Dutchess County Sheriff came upon the sanctuary for all living
things, smashed sacred shrines in our places of worship, absconded
with money, and forced the High Priest of the Sri Ram Ashram,
William Haines, Guruji, to his knees on the ice,' said one of the
arrested.

Five members of Leary's League, who have chosen to spend winter
in a circle of five teepees in the woods at Millbrook have also been
harassed.

Liberation News Service

the evening was a tribute to Lincoln,
er Harry Belafonte, in a letter to the
s, the US Department of the Interior,
ned to withdraw should the President
y Bird enter the theatre. The Presi-
ayed home and the show went on.

rudent, Lynd ird and husband,
Chuck Robb, who, attending the
e of John Wilson's anti-war play, 'No
nd', at the Washington Theatre Club,

were harassed and embarrassed all evening by
LNS' own correspondent Ray Mungo and
friend 'Verandah' Porche, who providentially
found themselves sitting beside the Robb's in
the tiny theatre. Mungo reports he spent the
whole evening **pointing** at Lynda and Chuck,
'who attempted to hide their faces in the
playbill, but couldn't resist peeking out to
see if somehow we had gone away. the rest
of the audience knew we were pointing and

the air was alive with electric tension'. Mungo
also reports he managed to whisper 'execut-
tioner' in Robb's ear as he left the theatre.
Lynda came off a little better, though perhaps
because Mungo found her, 'erotic, fragile,
skinny . . . caresses her calves and thighs in
public.'

Paul Lawson

33

Norman Rubington/Anthony Haden-Guest

TO BE CONTINUED

Love Me This Year

34

Flight-Sgt. Noel Quesada, shot down on a bombing raid over Phuc Yen near Hanoi in a Republic F-105 Thunderchief fighter bomber. One of the devices provided for him by General John McConnell, U.S. Air Force Chief of Staff, from the £9,000,000,000 bombing budget was Incinderjell. Incinderjell is a liquid inflammable napalm jelly packed in 3000lb. aluminium containers. It is adhesive, can burn underwater, uses all available oxygen in confined spaces and is made by the DOW Chemical Company. For further particulars, write to the Public Relations Officer, Mr Shahin, The DOW Chemical Company, 2000, Main St., Midland, Michigan, U.S.A. Or telephone DOW Chemicals, U.K., 01-WEL-4441

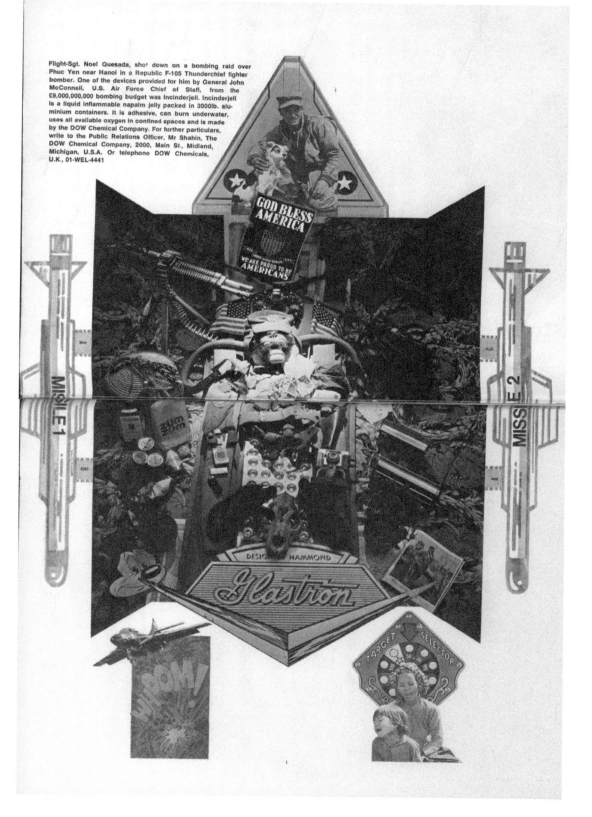

the meat pack

Anthony Haden-Guest   Norman Rubington

It is Year Zero. Morel, the transvestite industrial spy, has been summoned by General Zuk of Inter-Galactic Security to the Chicago of the Orient — Khatmandu! Menace lurks at the Protoplaxon Plant where the canned artificial meats begin to swell with alien life... but, even as Morel arrives, General Zuk is struck down by the Flying Lobotomy. Now read on...

Morel checks out Khatmandu...
7.30 am, time for Kelloggs, and the rituals of Baptist-Yoga, guru naked, except for his hat which is a personal relic of J Edgar Hoover IV, and comes equipped with a Strontium-count, an instant abortive, and a sensitivity to

many common plague bacilli.
10.30 am. A touch of the fingertips at the Holy Water stoop, and Morel insinuates himself with the Maharanee of Nairobi & Dover (who is, in fact, an agent for Shell Chemicals)... Under the guise of deep-trance sexplay, Morel submits the Maharanee to brain surgery, in which he took a degree by post... HER PALPITATING MEDULA POINTS DIRECTLY TO PROTOPLAXON!

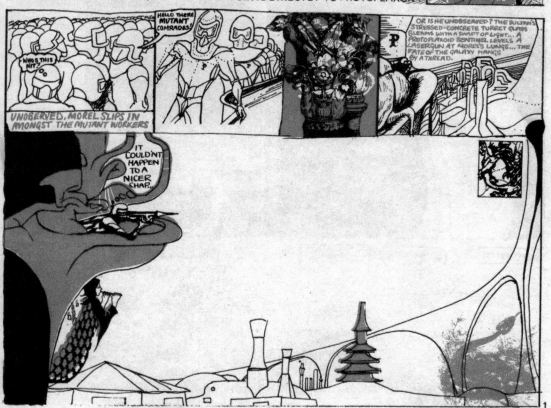

1

MEANWHILE IN PARIS . . . a mult-iple suburb where glitters a two-mile Eiffel Tower passed in 18 carat gold, and Maurice Chevalier is kept in suspended animation by a quart of blood a month . . . wanders SYLVAN !

SYLVAN is on a quest . . . It leads him through decaying drug stores and discoteques, crumbling art factories and compulsory orgies given for the bourgoisie . . . What is SYLVAN'S quest?

In the foyer of Maxim's he meets a decrepit super-woman . . . buys a packet of matches . . . she whispers an electric message !

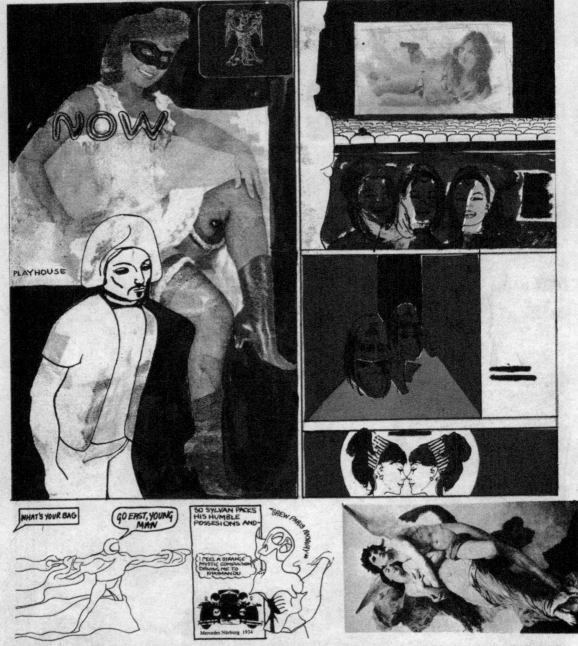

TO KHATMANDU, WHERE SYLVAN WILL FIND HIS LONG-LOST TRANSVESTITE ELDER BROTHER ... YES, MOREL !!!

2

(Continued. Very Copyright.).

London OZ is published
approximately monthly by
OZ Publications Ink Ltd,
38a Palace Gardens Terrace,
London W8.   Phone:
229 4623 . . . 603 4205.

Editor: Richard Neville

Deputy Editor: Paul Lawson

Design: Jon Goodchild assisted
by Virginia Clive-Smith

Advertising: John Leaver c/o OZ

Art: Martin Sharp

Writers: Andrew Fisher, David
Widgery, Angelo Quattrocchi

Subscriptions: Louise Ferrier

Pusher: Felix Dennis

Distribution: (Britain) Moore-
Harness Ltd, 11 Lever Street,
London EC1. Phone: CLE 4882
(Holland) Thomas Rap,
Regulierdwarstraat 91, Amsterdam.
Telefoon: 020-227065.
(Denmark) George Streeton,
The Underground, Larsbjørnstraede
13, Copenhagen K.

Printing: Steel Bros (Carlisle) Ltd,
Phone 0228-25181. Printed
Web Offset.

Typesetting: Jacky Ephgrave,
Big O Press Ltd, 49 Kensington
High Street, London W8. Phone:
937-2613/4.

Dear Sir,

I was interested to see in issue
number 10 of OZ that you are
having problems with the
Commissioners of Customs and
Excise.

You appear to be approaching
this from a common sense point
of view. This is the last approach
to succeed with the purchase tax
authorities.

They are however sensitive about
being embarrassed or faced with
the possibility of having to do
some work. I have found that in
negotiating with them it is useful to show examples of similar
situations where tax is not being
charged. If you can claim that
you are being discriminated against unfairly, their grounds for
argument seem to shift. If you
tell them that you are willing to
take the matter to court, they are
more likely to back down.

I am sending to you with this
letter, copy of a magazine published by Evans Brothers, the
entire format of which makes it
suitable only for display on the
wall of a classroom. It cannot be
argued by the Commissioners
that the educational connection
has any significance since they
steadfastly maintained for years
that educational apparatus is
liable to tax as a toy.

I hope you win this fight. You
probably realise that the civil
servants attempting to exercise
their rather spurious authority are
hollow men susceptible to deflation by a sharp prick.

Yours sincerely,
T B von Hohenheim

Dear Sir,

With much reluctance and fore-
thought, I feel the need to write
to you in connection with the
London Diggers Love Commune.
(OZ No 9.)

It is an admirable idea, but it
would obviously become the
retreat for sex-starved male, yellow bellied cowards: men who
want security from life, without
all the responsibilities that it entails. They feel the need to be
wanted by the opposite sex and to
cement this need with a child but
they will not accept the responsibilities resulting from these actions
In fact they can not face up to
this 'modern world'.

Yours,
C F Eaton-Hall

13 Uxbridge Street,
London W8.

Dear Sir,

amici N A Megson (optimist)
wrote before on many issues and
is to be congratulated on raising
his head above the money-coloured
urine that drowns this peaceful
slumbering middle-class Solihull
place. With approx. (v.approx.)
population of 25,000 one new-
agent manages to sell 8 copies of
OZ; i know 4 of the people who
buy it so well i mean once in a

dirty article (Wog Beach Shock)
quattrochi (sorry Quattrochi as
in God) wrote about how all good
true 'hippies' should invade the
black Italy place . . . * . . . could we
have a few pleasant peasant diggers come blow our/their minds.
Even if you dont pubically publish
this could you do something, tell
or send someonebody. We have
pleasant green-bladed parks,

Yours . . .
anun.

the main thing is COME BUM IN
SOLIHULL.

Dear Sir,

The OZ No 10 'Pornography of
Violence' impressed me very
much with the horror of violence,
but it left me more confused than
ever.

What confuses me is this; on the
'Guevara' poster of OZ No 8 was
written 'Guevara is dead. Long
Live Guevara.' Wondering who
Guevara was I forgot about it
until I read in 'Radio Times' Sunday 11 February (3rd Programme)
'Che Guevara, who died last November, has left behind a reputation comparable to that of the
legendary heroes of the past. In
this talk, Peter Calvert discusses
the theory and practice of
guerrilla warfare and assesses the
achievements of Guevara as a
guerrilla leader.'

Does this mean that the producers
of OZ condemn all violence provided it is anti-communist and
support violence which is pro-
communist?

Do they love the socialists and
hate the 'capitalists'?

Do the people behind OZ have a
batch of machine guns hidden
behind those innocent looking
flowers?

If this what 'Flower Power' is
all about, count me out

Sincerely,
Colin Connaughton
(ex-hippie?)
68, University Street,
Belfast, 7.

PS: I will be very surprised if
you publish this letter but if you
don't I suppose I'll have to try
'International Times'.

Dear Sir,

Julian Manyon's critics have
rightly picked him up on the question of the necessity of rules and
regulations for the running of any
community. But I think he was
trying to say that the whole ethos,
ie. the emphasis on competitiveness
in games (both athletic *and* academic) is fundamentally anti-educa-
tional. It is a hindrance to the
growth of intelligence and sensitivity. Nevertheless he seems to
have a pretty bad chip.

My earlier experience was that,
with notable exceptions, teachers
at St Paul's saw the image of
themselves as benevolent dictators.
The prefect system (ostensibly
democratic) was *their* system — not
ours. For the crime of being found
out by a prefect for pissing into a
convenient milk-bottle at prep, I
was called before the High Master.
He obviously thought I had done
something else — maybe I had, I
can't quite remember ! He was
sweetly understanding and, to my
utter astonishment, confessed to
a somewhat similar school-boy
error himself. Was I really happy
there, he inquired? The next scene
is the sportsfield with the solicitous prefect giving me encouraging
smiles as I worked off my energies
in the proper way.

This incident surely suggests that
a real conflict of values has been
going on for some time; and all it
symbolizes is the new psychological, open-ended approach to the
business of education. I had hoped
psychology was winning.

Yours sincerely, R N Parkhurst (42)

Friends,

April 21st, 1968, marks the black anniversary of the military junta's takeover in Greece. The regime has spent the last ten months tightening its grip on the country; by appointing its own men to key positions in all areas of public administration, and by making the "oath of loyalty" a pre-requisite to the right to work.

In the recent report of Amnesty International it stated, (OZ 10—Ed) "The Security Police and Military Police are unrestricted today in Greece. Since, in Mr Pattakos's words, "the law sleeps", the police may arrest anyone, in any place, at any time, with no obligation to charge him or inform anyone of his arrest". From the details given in this report, it is no exaggeration to state that the methods employed by the Greek security police, including torture, sadism, and blackmail, have not been parallelled in the Western world since the heyday of Nazism.

Resistance to the regime within Greece grows stronger. Two major resistance movements, Democratic Defence and Patriotic Front, organised by representatives of all political parties, outlawed since last April, are working together for a common aim . . . the establishment once and for all of true democratic government in Greece. The hope for Greece rests at the moment with D.D. and P.F., but they must be able to rely on support from democrats all over the world.

All those in this country who are outraged by the military regime's very existence, let alone their barbarous methods, and who wish to express their support for the Greek resistance movement, will have the opportunity to do so at a Rally to be held at Trafalgar Square on Sunday, April 21st, at 2.30 pm. This will be followed by a march via Downing Street to the Greek Embassy — letters of protest will be delivered at both.

The actress Melina Mercouri will be coming from New York specially for this demonstration, and will speak at Trafalgar Square; together with Greek Democratic Movement leaders, and invited representatives of the political, trade-union, religious, academic, and artistic worlds. It is hoped that the BBC Greek Service will record the voiced approval of all those present for a resolution condemning the military regime and expressing solidarity with the Greek resistance movement. This will later be broadcast to Greece.

Yours sincerely,

Raphael Papadopoulos, Ph.D. for April 21 Greek Freedom Rally Committee.

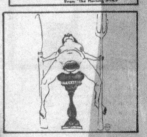

● With the sponsorship of the second issue of the SHINJUKU SUTRA, carrying 12 pages of his material, John Wilcock finishes his first year of publishing OTHER SCENES, a subscription-only newsletter which grew out of his column of the same name. The 800 subscribers to OS have received 20 mailings during 1967: five small issues from Los Angeles in the spring; a 16-page tabloid, prepared as four issues from New York in May; a 32-page color magazine prepared in collaboration with Oz in London during the summer; a full-size poster filled on one side with stories and pictures from Greece in September; a four-page tabloid from New York in October; the 24-page Sutra from Tokyo in December. In addition to these 13 newsletters, subscribers received the Los Angeles Free Press, the San Francisco Oracle, LA's Open City, New York's Books and Downtown, California's Nude Living and two copies of OZ from London. (Eight years ago Wilcock offered subscribers to his Surprise Club ten mailings per year; now they get

LISTEN

Anyone who lost marbles, pepper, glass cutters or any other belongings at Trafalgar Square recently can claim them from surprisingly friendly police at West End Central.

What ever happened to Tony Bennett? According to an interview in the latest Rank Showguide, He's doing better than ever. When asked about his income he reported coyly: "There are an awful lot of people not making as much as me and I don't want to offend them. Let's just say my income is enormous and leave it at that". Bennett regards pop as "mumble jumble . . . " "I get up on stage, tune in to how the audience is, what sort of people they are, how they swing and I sing accordingly. I try to make myself a sensitive instrument". A prick?

Dial 160 and Engelbert Humperdink will tell you how to help Britain and help yourself.

That totalitarian institution, Private Eye, labours incessantly to stamp out its rivals — especially indigent newcomers. When OZ appeared, Eye editor Richard Ingrams lurched through Soho boasting it wouldn't last three issues. He did his best to guarantee this prediction with a gauche attempt to blackmail our mutal distributors. And Christopher Booker's witty retaliation to our little magazine was to publicly tear it up. Their OZphobia has since jellied into a blanket warning from Ingrams that he will dissociate himself from anyone who contributes. Meanwhile, that "affectionate lampoon" of Whitehall continues to delight young Tory audiences at the Criterion and the Eye's nervous attacks on projected magazines continues. Both the Running Man and the Black Dwarf have been singled out for continued abuse. Perhaps this will be justified, but why not wait for them to appear? There's a shortage of good little magazines.

Not that OZ holds any brief for the Running Man. Their promotional advertisements (see OZ 10) claim it will be available on subscription only. In fact, arrangements have already been made for its national retail distribution.

Sinclair Eustace, "the hippy candidate" pulled few votes in the South Kensington by-election despite his 3½ page advertise-ment in IT, paid for in advance (yes, yes, we're jealous). His cozy press party was crawling with sympathetic Tories and Eustace himself was amiably evasive. His attitude on Vietnam and pot legalisation was aggressively equivocal, or rather, allegorical: "If you try and cross a big river in a little boat and you pack too much luggage in your little boat, then it will sink." His little boat never got floated in the first place.

Nomadic underground newspaper editor, John Wilcock, is now co-producing a new "truly international" paper, the SEER. Twenty thousand copies of the first issue have been printed to sell in New York, Boston, Chicago, San Francisco, Los Angeles and London. It will appear as often as necessary. Enquiries: Oliver Johnson, 26 Perry Street, NYC 10014.

So you think the most fascinating and exciting man of the century, dead or alive, is the Duke of Edinburgh; that his wife is the second most glamorous woman; that Australia is your home away from Ongar? Please try again. I can't believe it. Send us your answers, addressed to OZ Quiz, 38a Palace Gardens Terrace, W8.

1. Who do you think is the century's most glamorous woman?

. . . .

2. What profession or occupation, in your estimation, carries the most prestige?

. . . .

3. If you were not British, to which nation would you most like to belong?

. . . .

4. Who do you think is the most fascinating and exciting man of the 20th century, dead or alive?

. . . .

The Free Bookshop exists to serve all; is not a charity and wants to see more things for free. Send unwanted books, magazines and children to The Free Bookshop, Coleherne Mews, Wharfedale Street, Earls Court, SW10. phone PAD 2409 and they'll come and collect. Open 6 to 10 pm weekdays; 10 am to 6 pm Saturdays.

Frankie Dynon (known as "Y" to his friends at 'the Times') is off to Paris next week to 'negotiate arms'. When he returns he'll be playing a black power leader in a new film for Paramount. He fills this month's OZ hand-out section:

R.A.A.S.

BLACK POWER

Message to My Brothers and Sisters All Over England and The World !

Brothers and Sisters !
We are faced with many problems in this Western society, where we are the only ones who can liberate ourselves.

1. We must recognise what we are and never be anything else but proud of being black.
2. We must stop imitating the White man and meet him on our terms. (b) If he continues to use violence towards us we must use it in turn towards him.
3. We have waited for over 400 years for our freedom, we can wait no more.

4. We must liberate ourselves now for the benefit of our children. Their legacy must be a better one than the one we have got.
5. Our unity is being challenged by white mans power structure in forms like:
(a) Arrests of our leaders and people.
(b) Denial of halls for public meetings.
(c) Our communications system interrupted.
(d) Laws against us entering his country where we are citizens.

We must defy it and do it now. Your part is important, for without you we are not full strength.

6. Our brothers and sisters in South Africa are being killed by Whites, we must help them.

There are 3 million whites who are taking advantage of over 14 million blacks. We cannot leave them alone.

Our brothers in America are doing things, so must we.

If you feel that you don't know what to do or you want to do something, please write to us. We will also tell you what we are doing and you can tell us how you can participate.

Our address is:—
58, Compayne Gdns.
London NW6.

RAAS,
25 Bearing Street,
London N1.

Your Brother:
Frankie Dynon "Y"

The most important short film festival in the world took place in Tours, France, at the end of January. It received no English coverage, except a small and slightly snotty piece in that well-known cineaste's bible, The Financial Times. All right, it's only the wogs, but as a matter of fact the Grand Prix was won by an Englishman (the prize was an original sculpture by Jean Arp, worth £700). Not a Froggie was placed.

This particular prize-winning Englishman has never had the public recognition he deserves, despite heavyweight critical encomia that are a blurb-writer's dream. Undoubtedly he is one of the most talented and adventurous polymaths English culture has produced since the War, and if certainty is a virture, he sets an even higher valuation on his own work than do the critics. He doesn't progress from book to book, but produces something different each time. His achievment is to force senses into play other than those expected to be employed in reading a book, so that the reader is brought into an involvment, or a participation, in the act of creation and reaction that has been usurped by the theatre. This does no not involve off-putting stylistic tricks, but engaging experiments with form, like pages with see-through holes or a grey, op-art fog. By staying with the familiar, but tripping us over the expected, he induces the imagination to work differently. In the way' in which Beckett has altered the form of the play and Godard has tinkered with the form of the film so that both media are capable of achieving effects, and eliciting responses, they couldn't before, the author of Travelling People, Albert Angelo, Trawl, and now a new book to be sold in a box, its sections unsewn, so that apart from the first and last chapters it can be read in any order, has shown how the novel can be revolutionary without taking off into incomprehensibility. He's even the subject of a half-hour radio programme called "Novelists of the 60s".

His Grand Prix-winning   m You're Human Like the Rest of Them is written entirely in decasyllables. It's central character is a schoolmaster whose lesson is simply that we must make it as difficult as possible for us to be destroyed. To even make this attempt to describe the film is to risk making it seem portentous. It isn't. Though the language is extra-ordinary it is totally familiar: to make sense and Beauty out of the obvious is the film's original achievment. The British Film Institute backed the project: at the same meeting at which its winning of the Tours prize was announced, they turned down his request for £800 to finance another film, to be about three minutes long. Perhaps this was because the script is to be, in the author's words, gibberish. No progression, you see – you never know where you are with him. That is the fate of an author who has to appear in a borrowed dinner jacket to receive the short film maker's highest award, who has won the Somerset Maugham Award, been called "one of the best writers we have got" by the Sunday Times, and who won't stay in one furrow long enough to build that popular following of beloved publishers. His name is B S Johnson.

Now that April's almost on us the big city dailies are starting to run their usual con game stories about how the eyes and ears of the Internal Revenue service are everywhere. All about the all-seeing robots who can spot tax-evaders and brainwashing pieces about how generous the government is to allow you to keep anything at all. It's always amazing to me how few people question these obviously planted stories . . . A GI named Andy Stapp is trying to organize soldiers into a union with such common human rights as democratic election of officers by their troops, an end to saluting, seats on court martial boards for enlisted men, the right to join political groups and the right to refuse illegal orders such as being sent to Vietnam etc. Supporting Andy Stapp is the Comm. for GI Rights (PO Box 76, Old Chelsea Station, NYC 100100) . . . Howard Hughes' phone number is (702) 735-1122 . . . Right after word got out that Andy Warhol had been sending a substitute to impersonate him at bookings on college campuses came the word from Rome that Warhol's old friend, poet Ger-

ard Malanga, had not only forged a Warhol painting but actually had a buyer for it (for $3000). Answering Gerard's frantic call to authenticate the picture, Warhol outfoxed Gerard by sending a letter agreeing it was his but belonged to his private collection and couldn't be sold . . . The Underground Press Syndicate, finally out of EVO's clutches, now operates out of its own independent address: Box 26, Village Post Office, New York 10014. List of papers, information etc on receipt of a stamped self-addressed envelope . . .

. . . Aspen magazine (a quarterly that offers a batch of assorted goodies in a box) included a reel of film in its current issue and most its subscribers are still looking for a friendly projector . . .

The National Theatre has come up with another brilliant idea. Why not 4 playlets about 4 aspects of Woman, all starring the Boss's wife, Joan Plowright? And, even more scintillating, why not commission 4 women to write them – even if they all bitterly resent the label "Woman Writer". So, over dinners with the Oliviers, Shena Mackay, Maureen Duffy, Margaret Drabble, and Gillian Freeman were all asked in a vague sort of way if they would produce an outline, a sort of synopsis, for which a sort of fee might be paid. Penelope Mortimer was also approached, but felt she was "too old" for that sort of thing. The whole project however, may come to nothing, firstly because the National are so vague about things like contracts, the authoresses are getting a bit wary, secondly because the history of multi-authored evenings is universally disastrous. Remember Peter Brook's US with its casualty roll of writers? Perhaps managers in despair at the "new" playwrights, are looking to novelists for drama, but scared of the possible results want a lucky dip to spread talent and blame thinly and evenly.

We can't afford advertising. Please help us by sticking up your OZ cover-sticker.

The smuggest industry in the country – publishing – held its annual National Book Awards in New York's Lincoln Centre last week. Poet Robert Bly and author Jona than Kozol mildly reprimanded the industr for its lack of action against the Vietnam War. They were met with some boos, mostly indifference. It takes an occasion like this to remind us that there's nothing courageous, adventurous or even civilized about most publishing – a big business tha gains more from the continuance of the wa than its ending . . . Calling Playboy's Jazz and Pop poll 'insipid' and its audience 'mu ically retarded', Soul's jazz editor, Leroy Robinson, expresses surprise that Nat Hentoff "who cut a good deal of his teeth with the raw, real jazz artistes and their music should lend his authoratative name and writing craftsmanship to such a big joke as the Playboy poll" . . . Graphics: New York magazine says that the city's new subway map (totally incomprehensibl was "apparently designed by a taxi industr lobbyist"

For one lovely week there will be no neces sity to watch underground movies lying fu length on a rubber floor at the Arts Lab. From 22–28th April the National Film Theatre is running an 'underground' week which will include works by such notable anti-film makers as Warhol, Markopolous, Bruce Connor, Stan Brakage, Harry Smith and Ron Rice. Don't miss 'The Match Girl by New Yorker, Andrew Mayer.

The feature film 'Charley Bubbles', directe by Albert Finney (who now wears a 10 gallon hat and spurs) is not quite the smas success the publicity boys here would hav us believe. In fact, no New York distribute would touch it unless Mr Finney played th lead on Broadway in 'A Day in the Death of Joe Egg' so they could cash in by publi sing the great presence.

'Spike File' is just that. A hotchpotch of editorial and outside contributions. Writers this month include, John Wilcock (Other Scenes), Bruce Beresford and Pete Buckman.

OZ/AntiUniversity
FORUM ON COMMUNAL LIVING
26–28 April 1968

The Digger Forum will be held at the AntiUniversity, 49 Rivington Street, London EC2, over the weekend, Friday to Sunday, 26–28 April.

OZ is pleased to welcome the AntiUniversity as co-sponsor.

The Forum is planned as a working, creative event. Represen tatives of Communities as diverse as Dominicans and Gypsies German Left Radicals and Welsh Quakers will contribute their experience of the commune in action. But the Forum is not planned as a long lecture with the audience sitting statically in their seats. It will be a genuine dialectic. Every single person attending will contribute to the shape of the Community expected to emerge. If the Community is your bag, you will be at the Forum.

Further information will be posted in OZ and IT.

6

A CALL TO ARMS FROM:

Mobilization for an
International
Mock Election (MIME)
46 Leckford Road,
Oxford,
England.

International Mock Election

On November 11, 1968, the United States will choose its next President. That man will effectively determine the foreign policies of every nation in the world; his decisions will affect the lives of virtually every person in the world. In the technological age, domestic politics are in fact foreign politics, and national politics are in fact international politics. The United States, because of its overwhelming power and presence, has assumed, consciously or by default, the role of structuring the shape of international politics, to which every nation must react either in conformity or opposition. In a very real sense, this man is the President of the World.

And how is this extraordinary power delegated to this one man? The Americans hold an election. This is the first point. The entire world, except for America, is disenfranchised from the democratic process; the world's peoples have no voice in the selection of the men who exercise power over their lives.

But that may be a moot point, for American democracy disenfranchises most Americans as well. Democracy is the form of government wherein the people control the body politic. The central tenet of democratic politics is that periodically the people will exercise their prerogatives and choices by an election. The 'free' election has become the sacred trademark of Western democracy: having an election means having a democracy; ie. the holding of elections in South Vietnam means that there is a democracy there! But, in fact, elections in themselves mean nothing; they are only the climax of the democratic process. The real significance of democracy lies in the way the system generates the alternatives from which the people choose the way they will live and be governed.

The Proposal

We propose that an International Election be held concurrent with the US Presidential election: an **International Mock Election.**

The project, in itself, makes the two major points: that all politics is world politics and that the established system is an unacceptable form of democracy. The first point is made precisely because we are conducting an INTERNATIONAL election, pointing to the realities of power and politics and asserting that national boundaries are in fact imaginary. Secondly because it is a MOCK election, we are beginning to say that the normal procedures of western democracy are inadequate (to say the least) to cope with the problems we consider crucial to the survival of humanity — survival in spiritual and moral terms as well as physical. These points may be emphasised to a greater or lesser degree, expanded upon or not, but they cannot be avoided completely.

Apart from demonstrating these themes, the election project is conceived to answer two basic needs: 1) to be a common form of action that can serve as a focus for the amorphous international movement that is directed to a redefinition of Western society in sympathy with the realities and the ideals of a non-Western world; and 2) to be a new vehicle for protest.

There is in fact an international movement growing out of a common fundamental disaffection among the young for Western society. There is an increasing consciousness of the perverse values of the formal structure, resulting in an almost instinctive reaction to the mindless way our social and political institutions impose their values on the world and ourselves. We all react in common to manifestations of gross colonialism, acquisitiveness, nationalism, and hold a belief that war is an evil, at the very least because it is an anachronism in the nuclear age. We want men over machines, and at the same time assert the capacity of the computer to free men if properly used. We suspect a drift to technological totalitarianism in Western civilization; yet we know the creative age looms in the midst of the great Grey. This and much more. It is, then, our belief that our instinctive reaction is closer to the realities of the world than are the values of the established system, a contention that, if true, is the reality on which the international movement will crystalize.

But a genuine movement cannot be formed by words; it is a product of action, action linked to words and words linked to actions. And since our actions are generally labelled protest, so the election project must be conceived as a vehicle for protest. To this end, the structure of the project precludes no particular issue, no mode of protest. Generally, however, the form of the project implies that the actions will be creative rather than nihilistic. This project may generate alternatives to the system, provoke experimentation in humanistic democracy, and enable us to learn creatively from our opposition.

The following outline is intended to give some of the positions that might be developed by the election project. But since the most fundamental rule of the project must be its openness, making the campaign framework available to all modes of expression and protest, then any part of, or all of, the following explanation may be ignored. In essence, a mock election will be held and a hypothetical candidate announced. Beyond that, the entire content of the project must be filled by the initiative of the participating groups — national, local, or international.

Our intention is to hold a MOCK election. It is mock because we are in no way playing the power game. This is not a third party attempt; this is not a disguised way to gain power, nor is it really even an attempt to influence policy in

the sense that we therein commit ourselves to measuring our success by their rules. We want to play with the real world, so we must ignore the false game the politicians play. Holding a mock election is not doing the establishment thing, because the sickness in the Western policy does not lie in its holding elections, but rather in the way it contorts the choices and options into one sort of mold. And that is the crux of our problem: how to articulate issues so as to make them relevant to the system, how to make them relevant to the people who are to vote, and then how to make the political act and these issues significant to everyday life — not as impositions but as possibilities.

Our operational set for this project — for ourselves and others — ought to be that **participation** is the real point of the mock election.

The Candidate

We will run an election, the whole circus. We will have our own buttons, rallies, speeches, platforms, manifestos, petitions, conventions, parades, door-to-door canvassing — all in our own style. And, of course, we will have our own candidate. But our candidate will not be a real person, he will be a symbolic candidate. The candidate must be hypothetical because his speeches, his platform, his views will be the views of all the groups and all the people using him as their expression of what the world ought to be and what a political figure ought to be saying.

Our election is really to be used as a means to test two different world views in a political arena, and therefore the exact makeup of the candidate is not a big thing — ie. we do not need a perfectly identifiable alternative to the personalities on the other side — but what we do need is a means to confront the established political system. Established candidates per se are quite irrelevant because they are all representative of basically the same mentality and value-structure — the differences that they imagine to exist between one another having little substance in a world that has moved far beyond them. The real point is that our **election** confronts their **election**, not that our candidate is confronting their candidate; the candidates are merely symbols of respective world outlooks. Since we reject their rules as having produced an undemocratic system, then we must begin to experiment, devise our own rules or play by as few restrictions as possible. And since we are not tied to either party or man, and certainly not to a hope of gaining power, then we can keep the notion of the candidate wide open. Our candidate can speak in a dozen places on the same night, give a dozen different kinds of speeches, give a dozen different press conferences. Rather than have a candidate that is the lowest common denominator of many pressures, our candidate can be open to definition by anyone who wants to play our game.

8

By Jerry Rubin
LIBERATION News Service

Consistency, why? What we must generate is wide experimentation, wide participation, provide a constant dynamic and interaction of our own ideas. We are ready neither for power nor for ideology, so why be bound by that pretension?

The end of the project, on or around November 11 — assuming that we have carried the drama this far — will probably culminate in a ballot. The ballot should be kept simple. We might just present the American non-alternatives against our own hypothetical candidate. Or perhaps the American choice of Johnson and Nixon (or anyone else) could actually be made one choice so our ballot really becomes a choice between world perspectives. The polling itself might take place in polling stations that we would set up, or it could be newspaper balloting, or perhaps ballots passed out on street corners.

As the campaign progresses, the technical questions of an end ballot will be decided, but the important thing now is to remove the concern about the vote itself — the emphasis remaining on participation, doing the election, not on having a vote.

An Attitude

This mock-election is presented as a serious endeavour. We are declaring the bankruptcy of the present style of Western democracy and our intent is to face it and its problems on an active, involved level. Our effort is deadly serious in that we assume the eventual disintegration of the present structure and are committed to evolving a conception of what shall replace it. Yet, as we act, we must incorporate the characteristics of the world we envision — of beauty, love, and openness — rather than the visage of the taut, intensely serious, humourless revolutionary of a by-gone era. To break the patterns of the past, both the institutions and the mentality will require wide experimentation in bizarre forms of action.

The End is only the Beginning

Conducting a free-swinging, open experiment — itself serving as a tremendous medium of expression, for dissent, for zapping people — will initiate thousands of different individual experiments with the election form, experiments in resolving all the questions we ask. Many attempts will be interesting and a few might yield genuine clues about new alternatives, new forms and notions about how the political can be made more responsive and more like the human.

The possibilities inherent in the election medium are infinite. It can serve both the short-run goals of particular protest on Vietnam and other contemporary issues, and it can begin the long process of evolving a world-order that will not accomodate Vietnams, imperialisms, cultural distortions, and the debasement of human dignity

in an age that can afford freedom for all men. To all these ends the mock election is an experiment that hopefully will lead to many other forms of action. Finally, we really don't want to try to predict specific goals for this project, or to decide now just what will have made it valuable, but give it some room to expand, to move, to teach us where to go next.

YIPPEES ARE COMING, COMING, COMING TO CHICAGO!

NEW YORK, March 1 (LNS) - 1968 is the year of the "yippees".

A yippee is anyone who wants to be. A yippee! sounds like the name. Say it loud, and you'll see what I mean. Yippee! Yippee!

The yippees will be in Chicago this August for the youth festival, or Youth International Party, YIP.

The yippees were born at the Pentagon last October, although they have been developing in the womb of Mother America since the late 1950's.

The yippees are the children of the middle class, children who refuse to 'grow up', refuse to accept the world their parents created. The yippees have had white middle class America, and they didn't like it.

A yippee is a stoned-idealist, moved by a vision of a future utopia. He is a romantic. It is not fear which moves the yippee; it is faith and hope.

The yippees are fighting for their own freedom. The yippees know in their bones what America has done — rivers of blood, man against man, death of spirit, denial of dignity. The yippee is free because he is engaged and committed to change.

The yippee sees America as a huge prison, with her institutions (bureaucracies, office building, armies, universities, schools) as bars. The yippees are drop-outs from that world. They were raised on horror stories of Eichmann, the bureaucratic cop-out.

The yippees are with the Vietnamese, peasant guerrillas wherever they are, and the black and other struggling people of America in this mid-20th century saga of the battle of Man vs. Machine.

To America's insanity, the yippees ask: 'Why?' Yippees are naive.

The answers?

'You're freaky-looking.'

'The Chinese are coming.'

'Watch out for the commies.'

'Get a bath.'

The yippee is not busy working within the system or trying to explain his actions to the Establishment or the middle-class mentality. He is too concerned with creating a clear alternative, an underground, an opposition. He is involved in a cultural revolution. In the process he is seducing the 10 year olds with happenings, community, youth power, dignity, underground media,

music, legends, marijuana, action, myth, excitement, a new style.

You don't agree with this description of yippee. That's because you are a yippee, and you have your own fantasy.

The New Left created the teach-in, the hippy created the be-in, and the yippee is creating the do-in or live-in. America's first youth festival will be a do-in and it will take place Aug 25 to Aug 30 in Chicago in Grant Park.

That's the same time the National Death Party meets to crown LBJ. Quite a coincidence! The world will see what the youth of America thinks of the Death Party and its war games. Our youth festival will be a living alternative. Take your choice.

Imagine the sight: thousands upon thousands of yippees, from 200,000 and beyond, making their way to Chicago by thumb, Magical Mystery Tour Bus, bicycle, car, truck, foot — from big town to small hamlet — carrying sleeping bags, guitars, blankets, food — and coming together in the middle of the country at the end of the summer for a super-creative synthesis, energy explosion, information exchange.

It will be a total multi-media experience. For six days we will be together sharing and learning. Every morning all our money is thrown into big barrels to buy enough food to feed everyone. Our own Alice's Restaurant! And that tells America how we think the needs of human beings should be solved — everything free.

The music will be free. The performers will be playing for their community. Definite already are Country Joe and the Fish, the Fugs, Arlo Guthrie, Phil Ochs, the United States of America band, Pageant Players, Bread and Puppet Theatre, Allen Ginsberg, Timothy Leary, Paul Krassner, Steve Miller Blues Band; invitations are now going out to Dylan, Eric Burdon and the Animals, the Monkees, the Jefferson Airplane, Richie Havens, Simon and Garfunkel, the Doors, the Who, the Blues Project, the Beatles, Mothers of Invention, Mamas and Papas, Janis Ian, the Cream, and Smothers Brothers, to name just a few.

Walk across Grant Park at any time during the youth festival and you'll find:

1. Free mikes and soapboxes for anyone who wants to rap.
2. Free mimeo for anyone who has something to pass out.
3. The underground papers will come from all over the country to Grant Park to publish a daily paper for the festival. They'll do it right in the park and teach people how to start and do a paper.
4. Film-makers will hold workshops on the film, and they will show at night what they film during the day.
5. Continuous workshops will be

offered on the draft, and how to end it. A real school for the dropouts. Art of the streets, art for and from the people. You name it. You do it. Everyone participates — every man a creator.

6. We'll have yippees dressed like Vietcong walking the streets and shaking hands like ordinary American politicians. We'll infiltrate right-wing crowds with short-hair yippee veterans who at the proper moment will blow minds with speeches like: 'Now, these yippees have something to say . . .'

7. Guerrilla theatre groups from all over the country will be there. The day before LBJ arrives in Chicago we will announce to the overground press that LBJ will arrive at 2 pm at O'Hara Airport. And it will be our own LBJ who will be greeted enthusiastically by the yippees, honored by a motorcade through Chicago, and then on to a hotel for a press conference to announce America's withdrawl from from Vietnam. You are there!

8. Yippees plan to paint their cars like cabs, pick up delegates, and drop them off in Wisconsin. We are infiltrating the hotels with bellboys, cooks. We are also infiltrating the press.

9. We'll also have our own theatre convention. We'll nominate Bancroft P Hogg, a pig made out of vegetables, for President and LBJ for Vice-President. After Hogg is nominated, we will kill him and eat him. And we will say to America: 'You nominate a President and he eats the people. At our convention we nominate a President, and we eat him!'

10. The youth festival will dramatize the nation's most massive collective and individual acts of resistance. One night 100,000 people will burn draft cards at the same moment, with the fires spelling out 'Beat Army'. The next day all the pyromaniacs will send signed letters to the government confessing their act, and will encourage more young men to follow them.

This do-in will be unique in that it must be a bottom-up revolution to succeed. Heavy preparations are naturally needed. You are needed to work on it and to make it happen. It will not be done for you. We have opened up a coordinating office at YIP, Room 607, 32 Union Square East, New York, New York 10003, Phone (212) 982-5090, and we are there coordinating information.

At the same time as the American Youth Festival (YIP), youth festivals may take place all over the world, dramatizing the youth international revolution.

The Chicago power structure, especially Mayor Daley, is not going to be thrilled about our using Grant Park. But with hundreds and thousands of us, what are they going to do? It is our human right. We are confident of receiving a permit to use Grant Park.

That week in Chicago will be a living theatre of America. King will be there, also Gregory, also Spock and the peace movement. The Cemocrats will probably have to travel from hotel to convention hall by helicopter. Johnson will be nominated under military guard, under the protection of bayonets and the Army. Even if Chicago does not burn, the paranoia and guilt of the government will force them to bring thousands of troops, and the more troops, the better the theatre.

A lot of troops will have to stay and watch us (long hair freaks them out), diverting troops from the black community. And the yippees, being wanderers, will be all over the city.

Lyndon Johnson and his Democratic Party gang cannot rule this country — it is becoming clearer every day. The choice is between the life of American youth or of the American Establishment. For those who don't see that now, Chicago will be an eye-opener.

Yippee!

(prepared cooperatively with the *Berkeley Barb*.)

smalls

EXHIBITION
3rd APRIL
EWAN PHILLIPS GALLERY.
22, MADDOX ST., W1.
629 4204.

YOUNG TOUGH ENGLISHMAN
needs partner/friend — with some
capital to co-op in Carribean Club
of ill repute.
S.A.E. to
K Gurry, c/o Wilfred Went,
238-240 Ballards Lane,
Finchley, N3.

FLYING SAUCER REVIEW

Costs: (see form below). 2d per
unit. 31 units per line. (The dot
indicates new line). A unit is a
letter/space/numeral/punctuation.
Indicate capitals as required.

Semi-display words: 1/6d each.
Box-numbers: 2/6d.
Display: £2.10s per col inch.

ATHLETIC YOUNG ENGLISH-
MAN & Attractive Coloured
girl friend seek part-time remun-
erative work, anything considered,
have own car. S.A.E. No time
wasters please.
K Gurry,
c/o Wilfred Went,
238-240 Ballards Lane,
Finchley, N3.

TAKE A TRIP
3 weeks Instanbul (£45), 2 wks
Greece (£35) or 10 wks India
(150): all round trips. Mixed
groups. Write HAL, 125 Park Rd,
Beckenham, Kent.

RELEASE 603-8654 (24 hours).
Call us if you are busted for drugs
or need legal advice.

BACHELOR 38. Artist/Craftsman.
Shy. Hypersensitive — seeks
Sophisticated Cultured Older
Woman.
Box No 16.

'VOICE' projected male homo-
sexual magazine needs: Finance,
Sponsers, Patrons, Subscribers,
Contributors, Advertisers, Mailing
Lists Etc.
Box No 17.

Rare OZ first issues. £1 to:
38a Palace Gdns Terrace,
London W8.

Angelo Quattrocchi is preparing an
anthology of underground writing.
He's looking for long pieces already
published by the underground
press. Most needed are reprints in
English of foreign underground
material. Any suggestions. Write to
him c/o OZ, 38a Palace Gardens
Terrace, London W8.

OZ needs a talented, beautiful,
energetic secretary who can
TYPE, RESEARCH, INTERVIEW,
WRITE and who is capable of
enduring mundane clerical work
(eg handling subscriptions). She
should be able to sell advertising.
SHORTHAND is not essential,
but would help. Salary by negotia-
tion. Only applications in WRIT-
ING will be considered. Do not
apply if such things as SECURITY
and SUPERANNUATION are
important. OZ Girl, 38a Palace
Gardens Terrace, London W8.

Use this form for your small Ads,
(see above). Mail to: OZ Smalls, 38a Palace Gdns Terrace, London W8.

Name: _____ I enclose postal order/cheque for £   s.   d

Address:

11

The Anglo American Pumice Factory

Richard Meltzer will be writing regularly on pop for OZ. He is a staff writer for "Crawdaddy", (the magazine of rock) and about 10 thousand light-years ahead of London's free-lance pop hacks.

Geographic reinforcement of distance is amazing.

Two major hunks of land where **English Language** is the public window & window shade and sand mold and force-fed billiards game and black-on-white curved & pointed sound picture jamboree. Mm-hmm. What am I babbling about? (What, no ??) Okay, you now see or don't see the language-meaning-distance-interpretability-distance picture on just a simple you/me level, right? Do you or don't you? Add to that all, and some of, the standard and personal personal-transitory-topical-tedium & interest-through-linguistic-expression (-and-all-that) variables and you're either bored or not bored (and/or both and/or neither), in addition to being confused or not confused (and/or etc.)... And it's still just you-me of sorts. language qua language plus **concrete reference**. But now more.

Just imagine a far-reaching **physical** intensifier of things. Then think about the same intensifier in-principle as an intensifier for **everybody**. Right? Here it is: (North) America & Britain. America: you don't get the first *Traffic* album until three months later (how could you live without it, only you also got the under-ritualized who-even-knows-about-that-sort-of-thing so you live somehow), you don't even know if anybody outside of Mick & his boys over in Britain have really ever heard of/heard Arthur Lee and his boys (*Love*), you don't even consider Australia just because you read somewhere that Mick considered Australians a pack of hicky farmers. There's New York & San Francisco & there's London & Liverpool and all that, but just dig: USA & ENGLAND!

Have a lot of fun with Beatle-Zombie English accents and English apparent enunciative and referential localisms in their foreignness (and their extensions to total foreignness with 'Komm Gib Mir Deine Hand') and (who can tell?) New Jersey, USA, nasality by the *Knickerbockers*, **but this is black on white paper**, man!

Well, the *Stones' Satanic Majesties* is *Simon & Garfunkel* 'Dangling Conversation' focused in on itself overstatedly enough via the modification of 'Is the theatre really dead' into 'Are the Stones really dead' as sung by the Stones themselves: such a degree of infinite-regress world self-referential unity after-it's-too-late (?) that it really cuts through layers and layers of universal bone. That bit about how *S & G*, by being really almost scarey for a second, are really scarey by the fact of being scarey at all, like, how can *Simon & Garfunkel* be scarey? And with the *Stones*, death-dead and over-under-over-musicality, never awkward, until finally, when it's just finally, or something like that. And 'All you Need Is Love' is all about *Arthur Lee* and **his** boys stateside, isn't it? Argh!

Comic books too: 2 major conceptual comic realities in US (*Marvel, DC* just to make sure you ...) comic metaphor of total explicitness of description even in **Help!** (Roy Kinnear, 'I am moving my right foot, I am moving my, I am ...'), who knows?

Geometricize and geographicize your soul and work out with intra-personal memory, intra-personal aesthetic evaluation. Even Manhattan Island as an Island **and** as a mainland (hey, does **geography** itself work all over the place; hey, are all places **places**; hey, how about **hey** everywnowhere?)

History only makes it as **pre**-history. Nonsense! Well, history as anything other than pre-history is just a hard dry pumice sponge. It is? Yeah. Everything qua rock is the not-yet-fixed-even-after-everything-is-fixed-just-because-everything-is-fixed or something that. Everything else is just the apparently not-yet-fixed or the apparently fixed. The reason rock is **it** (in fact the first **it**) is that history (?) is on its side; it is on history(?)'s side. Too bad/good *Dylan's* current (**John Wesley Harding**) move is not only non-historical, but also non-prehistorical. Anyway, this geography business is a **specific** archaeological-epistemological problem, and the only reason such a *problem* exists is the apparent fact of the Anglo-American rival-fixities, if you assume the **problem** problem has had it in both systems. And that's that.

Thus (and not-thus):

* * * R Meltzer

12

THE RELATIONSHIP BETWEEN LOVE AND JOHNNY MATHIS EXTENDS FAR BEYOND THE OBVIOUS STUFF (THE STANDARD SPECIFIC RELATIONAL TRASH) AND TRANSCENDENTAL MASCULINIZATION OF LATENT-BLATANT BULLFIGHT

Arthur Lee: 10 to 14 years . . . 4 teaspoonfuls

Johnny Mathis: faster relief guaranteed for pumice or you can make love to yourself in the ear

John Echols: fork yourself in the garment and French tickler sponge cleft

Bryan Maclean: if you can then your not worth a lick off an asshole in the shower at the YMCA if your a girl nosiree

Forssi: foresee

Johnny M: force me

Smokey Robinson: you weren't supposed to say that although Pansy's feelings for Dobie are equally strong, Pansy's Dad doesn't like the boy

Michael Stuart: Debbie Reynolds, Hans Conreid

Herb Alpert: bullfight without words

Johnny M: words but keep it in your pants

Arthur: okay, but not at all costs

Arthur: hokey pokey, founds and losts (Snoopy: hey you fork, the whole things contained in the title)

Roger Price: $ 15 hamburger

(Tjay: rotten apple tits the hole things another kidnapping of a dead bride)

Memphis Sam Pearlman: once there was a bullfighter a non-bummer bullfighter in every sense of the word and all his fights were the same but they were all the same and it didn't matter because Molissa quieted everyone and every conceptual response possibility by saying what a fight what a bullfight and Molinda said older but she meant louder

Bryan: shrimp balls at the place next door to the Dumpling House

Arthur: clam balls for your balls

Michael: not all plays are movies, not all sequences are plays, not all temporal juxtapositions are sequences except all of them unless you play the drums and say otherwise or think otherwise or

Napoleon XIV, Jimmie Morrison: stop being so subjective so fallacious so stuffed with order ready to be jarred so 1-2-3 so you can ha ha ha ha ha ha ha ha and do a little part-whole thing

Arthur: ambiguity and that was the thing and that's the sing because it isn't cause it is and and Country Joe no Gene Autry Johnny M: Adam Wade making money off my style but I'm better

Arthur: my use of Carousel consists of more than pitter patter

Elvis Presley: right, its a matter of gold-sequin velvet satin shirts

Arthur, Meltzer, Moondog: not quite, its a matter of gold-sequin velvet satin paisley corduroy underpants with angel patterns and Cru-ex stains

Lee Marvin as an innocent bystander: stop clouding the issue, its a matter of when ya use words ya have to say somethin whereas pillows rarely say that much and cups with Nancy's name on them don't say anything except Nancy and not even that much if your a flea or an illiterate or there's a fake wedding set up with fake actors no not fake actors fake people played by actors and with Bela Lugosi reminding the dying wounded dwarf that it's not sequence so much as it's characters spectacle too (spectacle too)

Arthur: what about the pillow spectacle when my name is Lee is the way I would phrase it punctuate it

Bryan: I'm not saying this cause then there'd have to be a capital letter (and quotes) at the beginning of the sentence it's just a thing about me who's me it's a thing with words after a colon after Bryan Maclean's first name snoopys-mothersnipples and cocks instead of cops

Lonny Donnegan: move from skiffle to ping pong to Arthur Lee and you don't even have to change the words except temporarily

Johnny M: move from and you don't really have to change the words only you sort of gotta beat up at least one person per month 1961-1967 to why even mind if they call you a faggot to it's okay if you use grease on both your hair and records Xavier Cugat uses grease too and maybe you can even use him on your next record no you can't Xavier Cugat is dead

Johnny M, Mick, Donovan, McGuinn, Lennon: an unbroken burlap arrow blazing with the flame of after-the-fact-ad-hominem-transcendence-anyway on the one obvious (Lennon) end and with feathers on Johnny M's ass and Johnny M singing his Johnny Mathis song(s) on the other, with Arthur Lee laughing in the form of a circular vinyl arrow someplace in North America

William Yip: I remember when I was a dyke
    That's when puma was not
        wasn't trite
    They tell me that I was a prince
    Royal mustard tasters dropped
        me many hints
    About the puppy who rolled
        over once too . . .

Hopalong Cassidy: take any random page of any random telephone book and replace every proper noun by a precious object mentioned in any song by Arthur Lee, Bryan Maclean or Burt Bachrach, well I've got one word for it, bad medicine is two words, multiple chrome-plated orangutan(g)s is three three or four

Dry chartreuse record cloth:
    I believe in iodine meatball
        tweedy-bus
    Why because it is so tedi-ous

***R Meltzer

13

So 117 policemen earned their double pay. They came in charabancs laughing and they went home in an ambulance. Tough. They deserved everything they got. They were inept and brutal. Not as brutal as the 'flics' or the Spanish Civil Guard or the Dutch 'kips' would have been. But they were brutal. Some of them were hurt being brutal. Callaghan tears.

But the demonstration failed. Demonstrably. After all those masturbatory plans, no one did get through to splash the Embassy with blood. Most of it was confiscated at Hendon. No one was prepared to stick their neck out and lead, as Red Rudi has been brave enough to do in Germany. So, unorganised, the march entered the square, substantially in one column and allowed police to contain it. They had only one entrance covered, a simultaneous convergence from three directions would have baffled them completely.

But the march was planned to be non-violent. Oh? If demonstrations are to be non-violent, OK. March people *through* i- *residential* areas. 10,000 people tramping through a surburban street would bring a few Katie Boyles and Mrs Thursdays and their men to the windows and maybe shake their preconceptions as much as their mantelpieces. But if marches are to engulf Embassies, then plan and do the job properly.

If, *if*, our consciences are so wrought over Vietnam, festooning our foreheads with loo paper ought hardly be a release. Demonstrations in London slap the public with a languid hand.

after the raid at Middle Earth, cleaners found 91 pieces of 'gear' on the floor.[

Today, a month after the raid, the proprietor Paul Waldman has yet to be charged. 'But the police have all the time in the world,' he says, rather pessimistically. And last week, two Bust Balls were held to pro- 'vide legal funds for those busted and for the Club, just in case.

Waldman reports no harrassment since the raid. But its hardly surprising. 'A dozen policemen are through here every weekend. They have an underground of their own. Kids were selling to anyone. The cops must have scored pretty often.'

Now, every single person who comes into the club has to sign a declaration saying he does not have drugs in his possession. 'And we don't let any of the known dealers in. We throw people out. We really hustle the kids around now. They were very uncool before. Shmoks. Some of them were even smoking after the raid. I'm a businessman. I haven't got banners to wave. I won't do time for a test case. If there is any repitition of the circumstances that led to the raid, I'll close the place myself.'

Joe Berke denies any knowledge of Pandora. 'A friend of Joanna Southcott's?' But he has managed to liberate *FIRE*, the literary magazine he produces three times a year. The current issue, just available, describes itself as a dialectic between direct revolutionary action and cultural guerilla warfare. Which is fairly fitting as it opens with a longish slab from Che Guevara's diaries of the rather bumbling, Sleepy Gonzales beginning of the Cuban Revolution. The disasters that befell the 26 July Movement were as relentless and as banal as Pat Boone singing in a Mexican accent. However like all good 'B' movies about Revolution in Costa San Sebastian the Fidelista's make it. With odds against they created themselves it is hard not to think that Time must have been on their side. Well, the NY Times.

Guevara makes a nice counterpoint to poet Gary Snyder's Passage to more than India, a voyage of discovery whose Newfoundland is the wider concept of 'family'. Julian Beck manages to hit us where the Living Theatre live, and Joe historicizes the Free University of New York — fore-runner to EC2's Anti-University. If you still read Spike Hawkins, there are some beautifully presented poems to look at. 10/-d or $ 1.50. Worth it. 'I hope a lot of people buy,' says Joe, 'the printer doesn't know we haven't got the bread to pay for it yet.' But as the last issue sold out, there seems every chance of a *FIRE* next time.

The People's report on the Diggers was as condemnatory as the Presss Council Report on the paper's methods in obtaining their material should be.

Most of the information in the article was obtained under the guise that it was for the Sunday Times.

One of the victims of the deception, 'Paradise' Hartley, who has been associated with the planning of the Forum on Communal Living is protesting to the Press Council. 'They came round first of all, a man and a woman, saying that they were sympathetic to the Digger thing, which they'd read about in OZ and could they have more information. Then they came back again with a woman photographer, who kept saying things like,"Do something symbolic of the Digger movement." This time the woman identified them as reporters and said they were doing an article for the Sunday Times Colour Supplement. "Of course, we'll let you see the finished thing before we print it," she said.

'The next thing what I told her turns up in the People, completely misquoted. I rang the Sunday Times and they said they had a lot of trouble like that form the People."

The name of the People reporter is Douglas Braun. He lives at 10 Granville Court, N4, and is on the telephone. MOU 3174. OZ readers may feel obliged to keep him informed of Underground news at all hours.

With Caroline, sadly interned in Amsterdam, the pirates seem to have vanished from the waves. Well, almost. Because Big L is about to make a comeback — among the soapsuds. Yes, swingers. Its Radio Laundromat, about to be launched in a 1000 coin-ops throughout the land. Laundrette Advertising Media plan to broadcast pop and what they call 'soft' music to all those housewives watching the dirty smalls slosh around the Westinghouse. Oh, and uh advertising.

hip ocrates

'HIP ocrates' is a reader's medical advice column which appears regularly in the Los Angeles Free Press — one of the world's best (underground) newspapers.

Question: I should like to know the physical dangers, if any, for the passive partner in anal intercourse. I enjoy that sexual experience very much.

Answer: Because of the many letters I receive from males and females concerning anal intercourse I recently consulted a noted proctologist. His opinion is that anal intercourse is not physically harmful when done in moderation. When performed frequently (and don't ask me to define frequent) there may be a tendency for the passive partner to develop earlier in life conditions usually found a decade or two later — such as hemorrhoids and a loosening of the anal sphincter or muscles controlling the anus.

Theoretically, one would expect a high incidence of urinary tract infections in the active partner because E. coli bacteria, which most commonly cause urinary tract infections, are normally found in the rectum. But clinically no increase in urinary tract infections in active partners has been observed.

Rectal VD is a real danger of anal intercourse because the carrier usually has no symptoms. Both gonorrhea and syphilis may be found.

Sodomy (a legal term for anal intercourse) is a felony crime in most states punishable by long prison terms. The name is derived from the Biblical city destroyed because of its 'wickedness'. But what were they doing in Gomorrah?

Question: My mom in New York keeps informing me of the latest anti-birth control news. What have you heard about any ill effects from long term use? Is it true that their use can bring on diabetes if there is a history of it in the family?

My mother hates sex so I don't know when to believe her.

Answer: Several sensational articles have appeared recently in national magazines about the alleged dangers of birth control pills. They are based, in the main, on the observations by some physicians that young women on birth control pills seem to have a high incidence of blood clots forming in their legs and, in some cases, of these clots traveling to the lungs. So far, there is no statistical proof that blood clots form more frequently in those taking birth control pills. Nor is there evidence that birth control pills bring on diabetes mellitus, with or without a family history of the disease.

We do know that the normal hazards of pregnancy are more common and more serious than those associated with the use of birth control pills.

They have been no reported ill effects from long term use of birth control pills; but they have been used only in the last ten years.

Question: Can you give us some straight information about cigarette smoking? Do you think the habit is really harmful?

Answer: I think there is little doubt that cigarette smoking causes lung cancer, emphysema and perhaps heart disease.

Since the US Surgeon General's report on the association between smoking and lung cancer, 85,000 MD's have given up smoking. Today, only 21% of all MD's smoke cigarettes and only 165 of those under the age of 35.

The tobacco interests spend more on advertising than any other industry. They are very successfully selling death.

Reader's Postscript: The reader who wrote you about the 'hum-job' divulged a rare and beautiful secret indeed: but have you heard of a razzbery job? It is similar to the 'hum-job' (humming during fellatio and/or cunnilingus), but instead of humming one executes a loud and vibratory experimentation.

It is important to maintain good contact while 'razzing' so that all the vibrations are not lost to the air.

Question: I am 45 years of age, unmarried, and in excellent physical condition, which I maintain by working out weekly at the YMCA. My problem is that every so often while doing chinups, I have an orgasm. This prevents me from finishing my workout, but after relaxing in the hot room I seem to feel better than ever.

Nevertheless, there are physical and moral implications which I would like to have cleared up ie:
1. Is this physically harmful?
2. Since I usually know it is going to happen and continue the chin-ups anyway, would the Catholic Church consider this masturbation and therefore a sin?

Answer: I suspect there is something about this situation which arouses you consciously or unconsciously. Aside from being unable to continue your workout, no physical harm seems possible. But you should consult your own physician who may wish to refer you for psychiatric consultation.

I am not widely renowned as a Catholic theologian so I suggest you consult a priest in order to find out whether the situation you mention is considered sinful in the eyes of the Church.

Question: I have been told there is a penicillin tablet available by prescription which can be taken 30 minutes before intercourse and 30 minutes after which will effectively prevent venereal infection. What do you think of the effectiveness of such a program?

Answer: Not much. As you suggest, most venereal infections could be prevented by the prophylactic or preventive use of penicillin.

But such a program would do far more harm than good for the following reasons:

1. Bacteria such as those which cause gonorrhea are becoming more resistant to penicillin therapy. If everyone dropped a penicillin tablet each time he had sex, it would only be a matter of time before the drug was totally ineffective for treating VD. There is a growing fear among public health specialists that this may happen in the foreseeable future.

2. The more one is exposed to a drug like penicillin, the greater his chances are of developing an allergy to it, and many people are sensitive to penicillin already. The chances of dying from a penicillin reaction are greater than from a venereal disease.

Question: I had a vaginal discharge and terrible itching so I saw my doctor. He told me I had a yeast infection and prescribed vaginal suppositories. What is a yeast infection? Is it necessarily caused by sex? Is it contagious? (like I have a boyfriend and all?)

Answer: Next to trichomonas vaginalis, yeast (monilia, fungus) is the chief cause of vaginal infections. The same organism (monilia albicans) causes 'thrush' in the mouths of children, in fact, an important cause of thrush in children is transmission from the mother during childbirth.

Yeast are often present in the vagina, without causing symptoms. But when broad spectrum antibiotics are given (tetracycline, for example), normal vaginal bacteria are killed, thus allowing the yeast organisims to grow and multiply. Diabetic women are especially susceptible to monilial infections. Symptoms of monilial infections are a vaginal discharge, irritation of the vulva (lips of the vagina) and itching.

The same symptoms may be caused by other infections, such as trichomonas or, less commonly, gonorrhea. That's another reason for seeing a doctor whenever these symptoms occur. I've known girls that borrow medication from girl friends because they think they have the same disease. But a pelvic and microscopic examination is necessary for often there are 'mixed' vaginal infections.

Treatment includes application of gentian violet (which accounts for many purple bottoms) or vaginal suppositories. Monilial infections are not transmitted by sexual contact but tend to recur so don't be discouraged if more treatments are necessary.

Question: I would like some advice on fucking during pregnancy. Is there any position that will not hurt a pregnant woman during the later months?

Answer: Most gynaecologists advise against intercourse in the last month of pregnancy. But your own doctor undoubtedly has his own theory. By that time the only feasible position is face to back.

In 1940s some scientists of the Dianetics school wondered what effect intercourse had on the psyche of the unborn child. Imagine the foetus floating in warmth and darkness. Suddenly he is subjected to thumping, buffeting and other phenomena. Are there any readers who remember?

Question: After a recent session with acid, I noticed severe pain in the joints of my knees, my neck and my groin. Is this common, is it me, or is it the acid?

Answer: LSD users have often reported muscle cramps and aching in the joints under the effects of the drug. Whether this is due to the effects of LSD or whether the user does not move about as he usually does is unclear.

I have observed similar effects in Africans given the hallucinogenic root Tabernanthe Iboga. At intervals during ceremonial dances, the limbs of the patient are stretched apparently to prevent muscle cramps.

Question: I've heard that the intensity of a woman's sneeze is somehow comparable to the intensity of her orgasm — a very convulsive sneeze, a very convulsive orgasm. A sexologist has said this observation is not to be sneezed at. Would you please comment?

Answer: Seems to me I've heard the same but I do not know of any evidence supporting this observation. I'm certain there are many who would be willing to join in a research project to settle this question.

15

MASSIVE VIETLOO...
BY GREY FORCES

BY OUR SPECIAL CORRESPONDENT

A RECENT PHOTO OF VIETLOON LEADERS INDULGING IN "GOOD" VIBRATIONS". A TYPICAL VIETLOON PROPAGANDA TECHNIQUE.

LONDON.. APRIL 1". THERE IS GRAVE CONCERN EXPRESSED WHITEHALL TONIGHT OVER THE HUGE INCREASE OF VIETLOONS IN AND AROUND LONDON. THE GREY FORCES ARE PREPARING TO DEFEND THE CAPITAL AGAINST THE RUMOURED VIETLOON SPRING OFFENSIVE EXPECTED TO COME WITH THE WARMER WEATHER. GENERAL CALLAGHAN HAS REQUESTED EXTRA TROOPS TO COMBAT THE NATIONAL LIBERATION FRONT OF THE MIND.

AFTER A QUIET WINTER OF PREPARATION THE VIETLOON ARE TO BE SEEN MORE AND MORE FREQUENTLY IN THE STREETS AND PARKS OF LONDON. IT IS BELIEVED THAT THEY HAVE HAD AN AMAZINGLY SUCCESSFUL RECRUITING DRIVE OVER THE LAST FEW MONTHS AND HAVE INCREASED THEIR FORCES BY HUNDREDS OF THOUSANDS. THE VIETLOON ARE BELIEVED TO HAVE DEVELOPED SECRET WEAPONS CAPABLE OF "BLOW-ING" THE GREYEST MIND.

SEACH AND DESTROY

DESPITE CONTINUOUS SEARCH AND DESTROY SORTIES CARRIED OUT BY GREY FORCES THEY HAVE FAILED TO FORCE THE VIETLOONS UNDERGROUND. THEY HAVE NO KNOWN LEADER, EXCEPT THE 'LEGENDARY SAGA'. A BEAUTIFUL NUDE GODDESS WHO IS RUMOURED TO LIVE IN AN ENCHANTED FOREST, IN THE VICINITY OF HAMPSTEAD HEATH. UNIDENTIFIED FLYING OBJECTS HAVE BEEN SEEN IN THE AREA RECENTLY WHICH COULD WEIGHT TO THE RUMOUR.

A RARE PHOTO OF THE LEGENDARY VIETLOON LEADER CAPTURED FROM VIETLOON SUSPECT.

INTERNATIONAL CONCERN

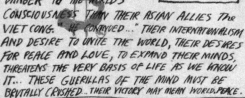

WASHINGTON 31ST MARCH. GREY FORCE LEADER JOHNSON IN A SPEECH TO THE DAUGHTERS OF THE AMERICAN REVOLUTION SAID THAT "THE COMBINED THREAT OF THE VIET-SPADE AND VIETLOON BUILD UPS POSED A FAR GREATER DANGER TO THE WORLDS CONSCIOUSNESS THAN THEIR ASIAN ALLIES THE VIET CONG. HE CONTINUED..." THEIR INTERNATIONALISM AND DESIRE TO UNITE THE WORLD, THEIR DESIRES FOR PEACE AND LOVE, TO EXPAND THEIR MINDS, THREATENS THE VERY BASIS OF LIFE AS WE KNOW IT... THESE GUERILLAS OF THE MIND MUST BE BRUTALLY CRUSHED.. THEIR VICTORY MAY MEAN WORLD PEACE.

L.B. GRAY

"ROCK REVIVAL" FAILS

LONDON... DESPITE THE DESPERATE EFFORTS OF THE GOVERNMENT TO COUNTERACT VIETLOON PROPAGANDA BY REVIVING "GOOD CLEAN VIOLENCE" THEY HAVE MET WITH LITTLE SUCCESS. LAUNCHED BY THE 'PUPPET' GOVT. RADIO THE CAMPAIGN INCLUDED INTERVIEWS IN ALL MEDIA WITH AGING "VIOLENCE MONGERS" & THE RELEASE BY GOVT. CENSORS OF THE LONG SUPPRESSED FILM "WILD ONES".

GOVT. TAX ON COLOUR

WHY I LOVE HIM

This Is a Political Matter

SRRING OFFENSIVE FEARED

DIRTY FREAKS!

JUNKIE!

WHY DONT YOU GET YOUR HAIR CUT

GRUNT GRUNT

OINK!

WOT IS IT A BOY OR A GIRL?

WHAT YOU LOT NEED IS A GOOD WASH...HA HA..

HELLO DARLING

POOFS! HA! HA!

HO HO

GIVE US A KISS SWEETHEART HA HA.

BROWN POWER

WHY GEORGE WAS FORCED TO RESIGN !

THE TRUE STORY

AMAZING

VIETLOON SUSPECT RUMOURED TO BE SON OF EX-GREY LEADER GEORGE BROWN

Britain's Brown: Cabinet dropout

POOPS IN TRAINING. THESE FINE UPSTANDING MEN ARE HAND PICKED BY GREY LEADERS FOR THEIR QUALITIES OF ORIGINALITY, OPEN MINDEDNESS, ABILITY TO WALK IN STRAIGHT LINES, COUNT UP TO THREE.

IC SCENES: UNDERGROUND FILM MAKER SHOT BY NUDE POLICEMAN

ORDINARY SEQUENCE SGT. 'BUSY' PLANTER IS SEEN THROUGH THE LENS OF THE LATE VIETLOON SCO FERLINGHETTI. THE SEQUENCE AND FERLINGHETTI WERE SHOT DURING A SEARCH WITHOUT WARRANT UNCHED BY THE GREY FORCES TO COMBAT THE ADVENT OF SPRING

BLAM!

ADVERTISEMENT

£ £ £

DAILY MIRROR, Thursday, February 15, 1968   PAGE 7

GREY FORCES INFILTRATED

LONDON: APRIL 1st DESPITE THE MOST STRINGENT SECURITY THE VIET-LOON HAVE MADE MASSIVE IN-ROADS INTO THE GREY FORTRESS. INCREDIBLE BURSTS OF BRILLIANT COLOUR SPURTING FROM THE GREYS CONCRETE SIGNAL ANOTHER BREAKTHROUGH BY THE LOON FORCES...... DAILY AREAS PREVIOUSLY FELT SECURE BY THE GREYS HAVE BEEN FALLING TO THE GUERILLAS OF INNER SPACE .

. . . .

ICIAN GETS NTEER .. TO ILLED

first, he needed a volunteer.

There was some quiet shuffling among his audience in the village of Mando, Central Ghana. Then 23-year-old driver's mate Samuel Nuhu stepped forward.

The magician drew out a knife.

He slashed open Nuhu's throat, forced him struggling into a coffin and held him till he bled to death. Then he buried the coffin in a grave specially dug for the act. The villagers went away awestruck.

Charge

Last night police waited with Mari at the graveside. If Nuhu is not alive when the three days are up, they will charge the magician

ALL'S WELL

TO-DAY'S THE DAY

SHARP

FADING FREEDOMS/LAT
HIPPIE HIGH HOPES:

Chapters

1 Orthodox Politics: Power as Freedom.

It's ironic that the Conservative party, which proclaims itself as the party of individual enterprise and freedom, appears to the lower orders as the authoritarian party. While the left, which advocates planning, control and bureaucratic centralisation, is preferred by the majority of anarchists and libertarians.

The paradox is resolvable, of course. The Conservative idea of freedom is freedom for power and money to have full rein. It stands for freedom for top people; the others need discipline, and must be kept disunited, weak; other power structures (eg. the unions) must be discouraged. Conversely, the Socialist argument is that in a democracy bureaucracy enables top people to be controlled by those below. 'State ownership is public ownership'. Thus more control of the powerful few means more freedom for the many with less power. And a great battle in British politics is for the centre: for those who can't decide whether the Socialists' giving of power to those below will cut down their own position more than the Conservatives' giving of power to those above. The recent history of English politics can be written in terms of the ambivalence of the large middle group. Before 1800, the country gentry and the hereditary aristocracy (the Tory party) had a monopoly of political power and were challenged by the rising industrialists and some merchants (the Whigs). The result was a merger (now, the public school network). 1945 represented a second major adjustment in favour of the working classes (the Welfare State) and until recently its gains seemed secure. With economic crises, this is less certain.

Socialism tries to make bureaucracy a 'third force', as between the top few and the many. In fact, it is so infiltrated by public school personnel, so enmeshed with private property, so dependent on foreign and domestic capital, that it often has to further; and obey the 'system' it intended to check and transform. Labour ignominiously does the Tories' dirty work (curbing the unions). Humble as a scholarship boy, it carries the can, loses its nerve before it reaps even the 'Conservative' success it has sown, and gets booted out by an angry populace until just before the next big crises, when everything happens all over again.

The Conservative dislike of bureaucracy, is almost too obviously motivated to need comment. The role of disciplining the lower classes can be left to poverty or, where humanitarianism won't allow that, to a combination of poverty, incentive and the ratrace spirit (which by preventing the employed from combining keeps wages down). The tails of the freedom to compete is that one loses the freedom not to compete, and the power which that bestows.

The underlying Conservative authoritarianism appears readily enough in attitudes to students, long hair, compulsory games, slackers, cadet corps, bringing back the thumbscrews, etc. The effect of all this is cancelled out by another paradox. Mass organisations have to be power structures too, eg. trade unions without the closed shop are heading for helplessness. Every side furiously conscripts one for the sake of one's freedom. Very puzzling.

Less obvious is the interior ambivalence of bureaucratic and trade union structures. Each union exists to defend its members, not only against the boss class, but against non-union members of one's own class, not forgetting those lower in the scale. Second, any organisation large enough to matter tends to become a class in itself. Current rifts between union officialdom and unofficial strikers are an example. Similarly, Bolshevism became Stalinism. Or a bureaucratic caste may

T FASCISMS &

A Paranoid Guide

by Raymond Durgnat

compromise with capitalism against old-age pensioners, students, and every weak group. It may be (it is) infiltrated by the capitalist old boy net. It can be set up as or turned into, capitalism's disciplinary arm (Fascism).

A similar paradox occurs in the sphere of personal behaviour (freedom versus conformism). Those who wish to impose their rules have to seem to obey them too, and to some extent really obey them. Power makes its demands on the powerful as well as on the others — at least in the sense that the Pullman passengers are on the same train as the cattle-truck rabble.

The Public schools were the mechanism whereby the aristocracy and the country gentry compromised on a joint character type with the rising industrialist class. It gave the latter tradition-worship and complacency, taking puritanism in exchange. It despised business very much less than it pretended, and never despised the City. But if the aristocrat (the Etonian) allows himself his elegant nonconformity, and 'affects' his conformity, the businessman, the administrator, the Etonian in his serious roles, has to shape his character around his activities. He's dependent on contacts, on goodwill, on discipline. He has life sure, but no incentive to use it to explore himself, to de-conformize himself, and only incentives give him meaning. He conforms: what else is there?

The same process operates on lower levels. In Britain the classes are so continuously graduated, that the fact of hierarchy is, almost, a continuous thing, from top to bottom. One reason why one working man in three votes Tory is that those who are a few rungs up the ladder (skilled working-class, say) are very much more frightened of those just one rung below them than they are envious of those twenty rungs up — or even one rung up. Not rising is quite bearable; falling is moral suicide; politicians talk about incentive, but the real sanction is dread.

Nobody's blood boils over the idle millionaire (he's too remote), and rhetoric to this effect is, perhaps, more puritanical than egalitarian. Since the common man can easily identify with the spendthrift-playboy, he seems more human than the left-wing propagandist who, by sharpening your discontent, intensifies your unhappiness. It's always easier to dream than to throw stones through windows. The addictive drug is mightier than the brickbat. The opium of the people has varied from religion, patriotism, and underwear advertisements, and hash and LSD are next on the agenda.

The Conservatives, who claim to be the party of enterprise, are obviously the party of class barriers. But many young Socialists and anarchists are victims of these barriers, demanding a more open society, that is to say, a society of really free enterprise, and for their own sakes. It's not in the least surprising if so many upstanding young stalwarts of the left turn turtle, traitor and Tory once they've arrived. They always were right wing laissez-faire, competitive Liberals, or as near as you can be in this day and age.

Thus each of the parties is divided on the libertarian issue. The hanging, drawing, quartering Conservative lobby comes from those country and suburban middle-class elements which identify with country gentry stock. Big business is used to favour puritanising the workers, since drunks and fornicators made bad workmen, but since affluence has come to realise that non-puritan lower classes are excellent markets for consumer goods. It's relatively liberal, but old habits die hard, and the mixture of hedonism and puritanism in the *Daily Express*, for example, is hilarious to see. A popular solution to the ideological tensions is to turn on pop singers, whose hedonism is just a little too extreme, just a little too successful. But the *Express* can't do that, because pop singers have the spirit of success which it tries to sharpen in its readers. But *Express* philosophy is doomed, because the little man whom it strives to encourage is too.

The Labour party might be expected to be very puritan since it boasts of its 'nonconformist conscience', and union organisation is widely based on the old nonconformist chapels. Two elements seem to have moderated its severity. By processes which we will schematise later, the puritan tradition was evolving, by the late 19th century, into agnosticism and humanitarianism, and tolerance of libertarianism. Secondly, where there isn't puritanism, or a near-crisis situation, the bourgeoisie tends to be comfort-loving, ie. non-puritan, and rationalist, ie. logical rather than tabu-ridden. Third, working-class puritanism was associated with the skilled artisans, and left the poorer sections untouched. So side by side with a grim puritanism the working class shows streaks of 'it's naughty but it's nice' permissiveness — what is often call "the old folk morality".

Anarchism: Parodies and Pitfalls

If we define anarchism as a condition of doing without laws, or, more accurately, the force behind laws, then its motive is the maximisation of freedom. But since everyone's freedom impinges on everyone else's, some sort of regulation is needed. This can come from various sources; within or without. It may be felt that only laws made man evil, that a natural kindness would soon prevail. It may be felt that his passions must be disciplined by the voice of God. Or by reason and 'enlightened self-interest'. Or control may come from informal sanctions (neighbourly disapproval, refusal of co-operation, etc). Or it may come from certain communal machinery (constables, courts). Or it may be imposed from above, in the interests of another individual or group. And usually it comes from all these quarters at once.

19

Those who are unsympathetic to anarchism are quick to see how informal sanctions could prove inadequate, how the machinery of force may have to be called on, to prevent one man or group maximising his own freedom by minimising everyone else's. The anarchist underdog may become the Fascistic overlord. Is the St Valentine's Day Massacre the classic symbol for anarchism in action? De Sade would have argued that it was, and said that anarchism was nothing if it had not overcome the sanctions within as well as those without. The right-wing stress on enterprise and laissez-faire, has a very real anarchism to it, albeit a non-idealistic one; and if we admit de Sade is an anarchist, we can't deny the title to the cut-throat competitor. We conclude with two varieties of anarchism. Right-wing anarchism which accepts the aggrandisement of the differences between individuals, as opposed to left-wing anarchism, which prefers minimisation and egalitarianism. There is ratrace anarchism, which weakens the laws, and has flourished at some intensely creative periods of human history, notably Renaissance Italy. And there is ratstate anarchism, where one group makes the laws for others. Though Nazism is a very obvious form, it's not historically rare (it's how the Normans ran England after the Conquest). If pressures are sufficient, any sense of law can break down, and a state of black anarchism supervene, whereby absolutely arbitrary behaviour, backed by brute force, have no need of laws at all. Rich Romans used to demonstrate their riches by pissing in the mouths of their most expensive slaves, who either learned to hold it in their mouths without swallowing, or very rapidly died.

No doubt a society based on internal and neighbourly constraints is feasible. It certainly is on the level of the foodgathering and hunting tribe, indeed chiefs (as opposed to leaders) don't appear until man has progressed to the pastoral-agricultural stage. An economic situation favourable to a new kind of foodgathering (pleasure-gathering) may be on its way. No doubt too society could bear much less onerously on the individual than the present tendency to multiply and minimise every kind of constraint. This is a reaction to today's split-second, pushbutton, highway-code-and-breathalyser semi-civilisation; at once too automated and not automated enough. But the reaction is panicky and self-perpetrating, and, all metaphysics aside, is one of the most useful targets of hippie activity. It's gratifying too that the boring Christian William Golding has to resort to fiction to put forth the *Lord of the Flies* view, that a few months on an island without adult supervision would turn all our kids into gibbering cannibals (The Jesuits knew better when they said, Give us a child for the first years, and we'll keep him for life).

Monotonously, though, white anarchists spoil their case by a simple-minded romanticism, pointing to the Polynesians or the Eskimos or the little green men on the flying saucers. Polynesian society had free love all right, so long as the lovers were of the right race-caste; if they weren't, and got caught, they were clubbed to death, for not respecting apartheid. The merry Eskimos may invite you to laugh with their wife, but wife-stealing leads to so many murder-type killings, at which the community connives, that in some groups every man has been directly involved in an ad hoc execution Mafia. The argument that sexual libertarianism will make violence unpopular is like the argument that aeroplanes will make walking unpopular. Whether walking is frustrated, flying has nothing to do with the case. And one might argue, with Freud, that loving is like drinking and fighting is like eating, and both activities go pretty well together, which is why 'only the brave deserve the fair'. Maybe man is, intrinsically, a tragic, and rather nasty, clown.

Maybe he could manage an anarchist community. But it won't be 'natural'. It'll be a cultural tour-de-force, subject to internal and external pressures. It'll be the result of a few thousand years of fumbling, it'll be a cultural triumph, and a precarious balance. Far from ending humanity's problems, it'll have to justify itself by the quality of life within it while it lasts, for it will in itself be no better equipped to last than any other mode of government.

Will it, even then, be more than another form of control ? Will it amount to more than conditioning people so that their inner tabus and community opinion daunts them? "Conscience doth make cowards of us all", and so does "What'll the neighbours say." Of course, pressures may make towards diversity, innovation and social responsibility, rather than towards conformity, conservatism and a kind of glacial inhibitedness, which we associate these tabus with now. But pressures there will be. And it could be argued that one is, potentially, freer in a complex, plural society which works by external constraints (law and force), which leave you a much better chance of getting away with it and hugging your individuality to yourself. Maybe, of course, freedom isn't in individuality at all, and the natural form of anarchism is communalism. And this still won't solve the problem of external controls being controls.

Automated affluence is the well-known crock-of-gold. Even if it's there, the transition won't be easy, and even if poor old backachy Britain makes it in the end, it will be so far behind everybody else that there's scope galore for further tensions (for example: if non-automated British industry has to compete with foreign automated industries, then the British worker will have to work longer hours for less pay, and things'll get worse before they get better). And the Third World lies in ambush. It's very romantic to support everybody from Mao to Che to Fidel to Stokeley against square old Mum and Dad, but it's a situation that leads to sudden conversions, especially since the wretched of the earth are quite likely to, unidealistically, turn on each other, as being easier nuts to crack, than on the West, whose internal liberalism is the sine qua non for hippiedom anyway. If you disapprove of dictatorships, then you may well turn out to be on the side of the rich, and ther fore kindly, homeland after all

But let's suppose the world slips by the Scylla of World War 3, how can it scrape past the Charybdis of a population explosion? It's worth a bet that our lifetimes will see offspring rationing (1 per person), with licences for sale, (unless we have a Labour Government, which will forbid it). That is to say, there will be a virtual sterilisation of sex, and though this may suit many a teenage hippie it'll lie very hard on many a paternal and maternal temperament.

Maybe, then, automated affluence will turn boredom into the psychological equivalent of oppression. A safe society will put every man in statu pupillari forever. Character will be just a ghost in a machine, touch on for amusement only. It'll begin falling apart, into a hunt for piecemeal ('transcendental') sensationalism. Or rivalries will centre on marginal status symbols, and the ratrace resumes, with no winners, only losers, ciphers on a treadmill. A thousand flowers of paranoia will bloom. Masochism will do the job of social injustice, a Sheckley-type 'hunt' of people will pass the time, since the few remaining animals will be more precious than human life. Will all this be worse than society now? No, but it'll be no less

The Pinstripe Hippies

If one can't be a pop star, or the ideal hippie, the most fortunate person to be is a spring of the country gentry, but whose family have been in business and in Chelsea for a generation or two. Girls are luckier than boys because their schools mark them less, but the alert and questioning boy can emerge pleasantly sensitive to others' tussles with environment. You have the time to stand and stare. You can have your two-and-a-half-day weekend, and your long business lunch, and your office hours run something like quarter-to-ten to half-past twelve and quarter-to-three to half-past four. Just the right amount of gentle stimulus, leaving you full of energy for the evening's fun. You're sensibly cynical, you have the where-

withal to swing; you have a personable self-confidence, which you soaked up at your mother's knee. And quite apart from the pleasant authoritative style the birds are naturally chatted up by, mannerisms are no detail in this fluid society. Poor old Scholarship Fred will never learn that affable authority, or that authoritative affability, which seduces all sexes. From all points of view the establishment committees are right to emphasise style above qualifications. For many purposes, academic qualifications are mediated along with middle-class, ie. a wrong, style. If a middle-class fellow has changed style he's probably changed attitudes too, and if he hasn't yet, he soon will, as friendships and habits accumulate. The working-class lad has to change twice, first to the schoolroom spirit, then to an upper-class style, and one in a thousand times will make it. Nor does the establishment, today, object to its Bertrand Russell, its Red Dean; they only go to show its tolerance, its diversity, its absence of class. And it knows it needs its diversent voices, a moderate diversity of responses is an excellent adaptive mechanism. And what if this bland crust of gentlemanly inefficiency finally suffocates the nation? The upper-class old boy net will still be sitting on top, keeping up with the Schmidts and the Duvals — too bad about the Joneses; but unemployemnt is very good for labour discipline. And if one is rather inefficient, well, one mustn't become too obsessed with efficiency, must one, I mean, look at those Americans, rushing about earning money . . .

The Conservative attitude shows an astonishing dichotomy. On the one hand, although lip-service is paid to the new technological era, there is absolutely no urgency about improving technical, and other, education. Educated employees mean trouble. On the other hand, there is a certain haste about getting into the Common Market. Given gentlemanly sloth, the exposure to competition's icy blasts may seem masochistic. But such 'exposure' will have three results. English capital and contacts will acquire European knowhow, and won't have to turn to the English for it. Second, European 'competition' will be the perfect excuse for further attacks on restrictive practices (ie. the trade unions). Third, competition will eliminate the tangled undergrowth of small inefficient firms and give a clearer run to the larger corporations. Fourth, a small group of international organisations will have vastly more power vis-a-vis, not only labour (which will stagger along being 'British' for the next century or so, long after business has understood that going into Europe means ditching patriotism), but vis-a-vis individual governments. Maybe in a hundred years or so there will be an efficient European bureaucracy, but between now and then the Common Market will be the businessmen's Paradise. In fact the left can hardly oppose it, so large looms the menace of American financial colonisation, and the impossibility of following un-American policies without some such unity.

A Hippies' Decade?

Old Ray's Almanack is an almost totally useless work, still, by the law of averages, it manages to be right occasionally, and, one never knows, this might be the occasion. It foresees three main possibilities for Britain's future. Either things will get worse, or they'll just change, or they'll get better. Only the last possibility offers much comfort to hippiedom as we know it.

The first alternative is a slow British decline, with pauses and rallies, but a decline nonetheless, with steep, rapid and nasty periods too, and the second is a typically British compromise between competitive efficiency and traditional status. The brunt will in both cases be born by the lower middle and working class, although many of the middle middle class will shift from self-employed to employee status. Will white collar unionism strengthen labour, DATA-style? Wilson bid for, and won it, in the last two elections. But on past form, Conservative control of the press, and the left-wing's helplessness, will have these two groups turning on one another (and since 1945 there's been a truce rather than peace between these two groups).

Either way, hippiedom will know hard times. The Labour exchanges will be much, much nastier, and there won't be the money around for posters, and, just as beautiful butterflies turn to caterpillars when winter comes, so all those flower people will be reduced to beatniks and Bohemians (remember them? all cords and beer), if they don't just subside into the 1970 equivalent of Mods or just go plainclothes again. Any hippie symptons are likely to be scapegoats for the country's nasty mood. Of course, those intellectual hippies who do the splits between the overground and underground will survive, particularly since outside big business, they're the most international-thinking and sharpest-reflexed group in England.

But if Britain's decline is only relative, and compatible with a rise, however slow, in our absolute standard of living, then we can hope Britain's narcissistic parochialism will keep this balding, toothless and humbled old bulldog happily snoozing in its doghouse, dreaming of Croft's, hardly bothering to scratch at the hippie-hoppy-happy fleas pullulating and prancing about in its old pelt.

Or let's just play with the academic possibility that the Dunkirk Spirit, the Angels of Mons, or some such agency, descend once more, and the various classes turn to fight the country's common difficulties without fighting one another. The result will be a smooth and total establishment of American-style efficiency, with exams all the way, from the cradle to the grave, without the massive nonconformism of the ghettos and the long grass. The idea of a massive conformity isn't a mere nightmare, and doesn't need all the melodramatic nonsense of 1984. It's firmly established in Switzerland, for example. There, even the artistic world is conformist; civic theatres abound. Switzerland, having no natural resources, except a traditional craftsmanship, staked everything on skill, and education; the discipline and prosperity of her workers is a joy to behold, while government is at once more democratic and more authoritarian than England's could ever be. Switzerland hasn't even had her Provos or her student riots, which it leaves to ex-imperial powers like Germany and Holland. And the Dutch soon learned. They split and sodomised Provo by luring the intellectuals away from the hooligans with gifts and grants. Compromise and conquer.

It's an obvious model for the English establishment, and Jennie Lee's visit to the Arts Lab may herald the kiss of death. Except that English hippiedom, compared to Provo, has been so inert, that there's little to kill. The kiss of death would also be the kiss of life, keeping, not the flower-people, but the vegetable-people, alive a little longer.

Yesterday I subscribed to the 'New Statesman', Today I am Just, Reasonable, Good, & Dead...

Flowers are not inevitable. They blossom only in our land (yours and mine) inhabited by stardust and white puffy clouds, the only acceptable beds for us cherubs and archangels.

But we should not sit there just waiting for our silver laughing to drive away the storm. From time to time it is salutary to look into the eye of the giant of darkness. If we wink, he might blink, and terror might recede for a moment in his wasteland.

Sad stories, carefully chosen, should fortify us.

Hence this:

1913. A baby of humanitarian inclination, its good intentions matched by fully clothed reason and reasonableness, was born in England. It was christened "the New Statesman". (The magazine of the left.) Many a thing it has survived, thanks to its rational armour and unshakable good will. It is still with us, fifty-five years later, imparting relative judgments to the people who are only relatively grey, and would (but oh so much!) like themselves and the world to be better, if only . . .

If only people could see Reason, Truth, Justice (see "social justice", Oxf. Dict.) and the Common Good. Only they can't.

That is why the New Statesman still imparts its sermon with patience, in blindness, judiciously choosing its words, carefully offering its metaphores, because the flesh is weak, of course, but somebody, somewhere, has to keep up with the good work. Nothing much has changed, for our mentor; the rich are richer, the poor are just as poor (relative poverty, you see). And the good still stroll on Hampstead Heath on Saturday afternoons, the New Statesman and the hopes with them until the pinkness of the sky will give way to darkness, which always comes. And it's time for dinner.

Occasionally, one of the strollers (J Freeman, former NS Editor) leaves the hills where wisdom is breathed in with the air, and descends to the plains where pestiferous reality is forced down the throat (Ambassador to New Delhi and now to Washington). The ninety thousand NS readers (strollers) will die of age, cancer and wife, fatal illnesses to men of good conscience. Let them live in peace, and in peace die, peace of mind provided for them by the eternal weekly installments of the "pink pill". 33.33% anger-soothing leader, 27% opinionated backbone-strengthening information, the rest is just literary colouring, as the chemist provides, according to need, skill, and the state of the market.

Confection should be sober and yet appealing, designed for a customer of good taste and not unawares of modern trends. It is strongly recommended not to introduce words (ideas) which could shock the patient. His correct thinking (left brand) should be encouraged by our product (to be taken in weekly doses). Signed, the General Sales Manager: the god of Reason and Human Progress. Trustees (temporarily suspended): the Labour Party.

Of course from our flowerbed, cuddling each other in catacombs, deafened by the bombs of the world outside (isn't Vietnam their only and true happening) we have been oblivious to the multiform chemistry of the enemy's ideology. Too occupied with beautiful refusal we have overlooked the pathetic NS like an ancient statue which goes so well with the square that you don't see it.

You might not know about the NS.

And you should, because in prehistoric times, when all that young people could do was to dream of forbidden crutches and forbidden ideologies, any crumb of dry moral bread, even a Handkerchief to blow the residues of their mind on, must have helped.

Maybe NS helped.

If you dare and care, remember the dark ages when the young poor were kept in check by the English shilling, and the young not so poor by Oxford and buggary. The magazine was then a genteel reminder of the enlightened times to come, a suave reassurance that all will be well in the end, in spite of the church spires and the Krupp factories. Because who knows what is inside a pinstriped pair of trousers, and under a bowler hat, when the time of reckoning comes?

23

But since then, the iron castles have fallen, the holocausts of the body of the poor and the holy communion of the media of the rich have stripped the land bare. In the pitch dark lacerated by fireworks of death the candle of the New Statesman pales and wanes, the halo of light recedes, and the wick smells.

No wonder you might not ever have heard of the NS.

But in the laundromats where well-groomed people wash their clothes, the first of the two days of oblivion following the five days of alienation, one can still encounter specimen readers (age and sex immaterial) usually going through the leader, one eye to the machine, one eye to the lines. A performance of skill, for the cleanliness of body and mind, in one go. The species has survived against the odds, fed on Penguin Books and British common sense; it breeds the right number at the right time, fucking moderately with moderate light in moderately comfortable apartments mortgaged at moderate price with money earned in moderately successful jobs, possibly in positions where they can moderately exercize their mind, which gets moderately tired so they need moderately long holidays which will bring them back moderately refreshed.

Their lives have problems, and each one of them raises issues. There are two kinds of issues, those raised by private life and those raised by pub-

lic life. The private ones are called moral issues. The public ones are called political issues.

The moral issues are, first,: Sex. And its corollaries: the family, divorce, the children, house design, gardening, commuting, the language, the generation gap and the pill. About these moral problems, one cannot give a definite answer, but only a basic set of values, and of course, there is a wide spectrum of justifiable attitudes. Basically, sex, and all the corollaries go under one simple commandment: thou shalt not hurt other people's feelings.

The political issues are: social justice (also socialism, in moderation of course). Corollaries: the economy, redundancy, the colour problem, poverty (see footnote on third world), the cost of living, education, national assistance, the welfare state and of course South Africa.

There isn't really a simple commandment for all of them, and that is precisely why the New Statesman was invented, so one can have, from week to week, an articulate and flexible answer, goodness in instalments, so to speak.
But life is more complex, it's not only a matter of having the honest answer to the issues. Every NS reader knows that. This is why the second part of the NS deals with the facts of the spirit, to put it bluntly, with Art. And the only guiding light there is that Art is eternal. Always, in all

ages, everywhere, under any circumstance. Art can never be suffocated, or destroyed, or even humiliated by any dictatorship or power. Every New Statesman reader knows that. Also, every reader knows in his heart of hearts that mankind cannot be destroyed by the atomic threat, and that Reason and Mankind shall prevail. That is why the NS, first and second part, are there.

by Angelo Quattrocchi

JOURNAL FOR NONVIOLENT REVOLUTION

BI-MONTHLY

3s.

94 PRIORY ROAD, LONDON NW6.

MODESTY BLAISE
by PETER O'DONNELL

MODESTY AND WILLIE DRIVE TO THE LODGING HOUSE WHERE THE HIPPY GIRL LIVES

24

Friday, 1 April, 1969   One shilling

NEW
statesman

Welcome Broom

Casuists and ill-wishers to the Labour Party will be quick to criticise the new coalition government. It is true that in the past this journal has had some hard things to say about Harold Wilson, and the other two members of his ruling triumvirate, Robert Maxwell and Cecil King. The fact remains that only the Garnetts can fail to welcome the new regime in Downing Street. Their policy as yet remains unclear. It is known, of course, that the triumvirate has declared itself against 'Blacks, Buggers, and Bolsheviks,' a declaration which the *New Statesman* has no hesitation in declaring abhorrent.

Yet, what is the alterative? For a while one such alternative lay in the hands of the political group now imprisoned and awaiting trial for treason against the Monarch. It is indisputable that this group, commanding the support of the entire left, had much to be argued in its favour. Yet they were Socialists and although — as this journal has stated many times in the past — the *idea* of Socialism has something to be said for it, one thing that cannot be said is that it is an ideology with which to run Great Britain. So, while there should be criticism of the manner in which this group was outlawed, and outright protest at the torture and summary execution of its leaders, it would be lunatic to refuse, on these grounds alone, a welcome to the new men.

At all costs a bloodbath must be avoided. In this respect the new regime has acted with commendable dispatch. On the economic front it has moved with equal resolution, and its decision to face facts and finally solve the balance of payments problem by selling Scotland to a consortium of Swiss bankers is heartening news. The time is surely past for murmurings about the mythical gnomes of Zurich.

Perhaps it should be stressed once again that we will wholeheartedly endorse decent policies which render more lacklustre the lives of ordinary men and women. It must be admitted that the misuse of the Queen's prerogative was a severe blow. Nonetheless, an exciting time lies ahead for Britons. This journal finds it hard to remember what precise policy it most recently advocated. No matter. It has been true, it is true, and it always will be true, that the time for words is past.

London Diary

PAUL JOHNSON

☐ I wonder how many NS readers know what is going on in Vancouver, B.C.? The anti-chipmunk campaign there is being carried out with sickening brutality. Asquith, in his famous memorandum to Lloyd George on the subject of chipmunk slaughter, laid down what the foundations of what should be a self-respecting British policy in this frightful business. Small hope, though, of the government taking the lesson to heart! The chipmunk benefit concert last night at Lady Droggle's underlined official apathy. I hate most music, but counsel NS readers to buy the record when it comes out.

☐ This week Karl Miller joins us as literary editor. Tomalin's experience in this field has been immense and I am sure that Book section addicts will welcome Anthony Thwaite aboard. Readers will notice a few changes. We are introducing 500 other new features in a desperate attempt to maintain readers. Henceforward the Crossword will be on the front page, followed by the Competition, chess column, quote puzzle, quickie conundrum, spot-the-misprint, Value Judgment and the Diary. And a whisper to old readers: Leonard Woolf is coming back as our new literary editor!

☐ I will not say anything about the new government, since its installation and intentions are fully covered in the rest of this week's paper. Many of the staff are leaving to take up posts in the new regime and Great Turnstile is sorry to see them go. On the other hand, Quiltin Sponthwaite joins the NS this week after a remarkably varied career as signalman (in Yorkshire), croupier (in Benghaza), and leaderwriter (in the *Church Times*). Next week Peregrine Worsthorne will join us as Political Correspondent, along with Montagu Norman and the Marquess of Bath. Lord Longford will be doing the Gardening Notes. I can't stand gardening. Neither can he.

☐ The new brothel in Berkeley Square opened with a bang last Monday. I arrived with a couple of ministers to find things well under way. Prices are modest: a special reduction for red-headed editors of weekly periodicals allowed me a satisfactory encounter for 10s. This took place in a room decorated in contemporary style. Any little quirks or foibles I might have, my hostess informed me, would cost 1s. pro rata. (See Roger Opeless's piece on page 467 on How the Poor Grow Poorer). We had a bitter argument about contraception, in which I found some difficulty in getting my views across, although in fact Doreen reckoned at the end that our discussion was probably hypothetical. Afterwards Fred the Society Fiddler entertained us in the salon to some tricks requiring quite extraordinary agility. I puffed my way back to the Beefsteak tired, but feeling I'd had my money's worth. The upper classes, I'm afraid, do know how to enjoy themselves. NS readers take note!

Letters to the Editor

Omar Khayaam

Sir,—Julian Symons owes it to himself, the South and, yes, Mabel Lucy Atwell, to take me more seriously. When I spoke recently in an Edinburgh public house, the barman was so moved he pulled me two pints. Call this cheap if you wish but in doing so deny the whole of the Scottish experience.

ALAN BOLD.
No fixed abode.

The Comedians

Sir,—We open this letter by touching on the loss of what has so long provided the central focus for the work of the Review. But the yawning gaps we leave behind only serve to restate the imperatives; to open another enclave in the charmed circle of the academic middle class. Conversely, the dialetic goes full circle, we have ourselves too long obscured the recovery of a volatile and labile strain of European Marxism. We have been compelled to give way to a new generation, Roger Opie, Maurice Cranston, Donald Davie and P. N. Furbank. Will they be equal to the problems they inherit? Or will they succumb to the temptations of revisionism? Only history can decide.

TOM COCKBURN and
BREWSTER PATTERSON.
Carlisle Street, London, W.1.

Underground Movement

Sir,—There's a new generation with a new explanation, everybody should get VD, when you come to Notting Hill wear a flower in your wig. Why do Alfs *still* care about politics, Hitler and Oxfam? Groove with Laing. 'Hung on you' has mind-blowing gear. Cops and clocks are all wound up. Flying Saucers are . . . *(to be continued).*

RICHARD NEVILLE.
Editor,
  Hippy Review,
  Turramurra Nth.

Race Footnote

Sir, beg pardon for maladroit English, but I immigrant worker from Asia, finding it difficult to know why the police are beeting me evry day and calling member of the Grate British Comunity Dirty Wog. I rite to you Sir as famous and nobel defender of Freedom hopeng that these assaults on me and my family will stop.

SUNDAR PANIT
33 Ladbroke Grove, W.11.

C. H. Rolph writes: We deliberately left the orthography uncorrected to show the charming eccentricity of this ignorant Asian peasant's writing. The metropolitan police deny all knowledge of the charges, and there seems to be no reason to doubt their word.

Weekend Competition

No. 405,769

Set by Quilton Sponthwaite

Competitors are asked to guess which of the following collaborated to produce the undergraduate and ineffectual parody of the *New Statesman* printed in the monthly magazine OZ, No. 11, April, 1968:
  Sidney Webb, Leonard Woolf, Paul Johnson, J. B. Priestley, Alexander Cockburn, Nicholas Tomalin, Claire Tomalin, Karl Miller, D. A. N. Jones, Quiltin Sponthwaite, Desmond McCarthy (deceased), Tom Nairn, Anthony Thwaite, Malcolm Muggeridge, Angelo Quattrocchi, Richard Neville, Alan Watkins, Julian Symons, Cyril Connolly, David Widgery, John Coleman.
Entries by April 15th to the *New Statesman*, Great Turnstile, London, W.C.1. Prize of 5 guineas to the first correct entry.

This England

Prizes: £1 for the first entry and 10s for each of the others printed. Paste entries on a postcard.

☐ It is a fatal mistake for those protesting against war to get involved in violence. . . . It was madness to try and storm the Embassy. An Embassy is a symbol of civilization. The sooner we can get back to the admirable self-discipline of the CND marches the better.—Paul Johnson, in the *New Statesman*, Mar 22, 1968.

☐ This week I said goodbye to my little Olivetti portable. I shudder to think how many million words of sense and nonsense it has chattered out. The awful thing is that I cannot brnig myself to feel the smallest particle of affection for this faithful machine, nor the least pang of regret at its passing.—Paul Johnson, in the *New Statesman*, Dec. 15, 1967.

☐ The gesture of the Surbiton Back-Britain girls has made a great many people, most of them in humble jobs far from Great Turnstile, think seriously about the future of their country and how they, as individuals, can help. We welcome it.—Editorial in the *New Statesman*, Jan. 12, 1968.

☐ Our mixture of left-wing goodwill, sensitive clubman's philosophizing and schoolgirlish fascination with visible success must be an infallible drug for readers who know they have gained a good slice of the world and want to be reassured that they have hung on to their soul.—Francis Hope, in the *New Statesman*, May 12, 1967.

☐ Gillian Freeman's article on p. 904 involves the use of a four-letter word. I am still slightly shocked. Though I think it is right to print it ('lust') when it is essential, as in this case, to the writer's argument.—Paul Johnson, in the *New Statesman*, June 30, 1967.

CENTREPIECE

The Knight Errant's Story

J B PRIESTLEY

Ever since my old friend Harold Wilson asked me to call round and see him last week, to offer me the post of Minister of Culture in his newly formed coalition government, people have kept on asking me the same question. 'Why, Jack?', they ask, 'why did you accept, when it is surely clear that the job will interfere with your work on *Chips off the Old Loins*, your vast new trilogy on the youth of the seventies?'

I have put the same question to myself. Nor is the answer quite as simple as modern peddlers of the slickly superficial response would make us think. Most of them are under twenty-five years of age. Fortunately, the unique powers of mind I now find within myself, the fruits of an unusually rich and long lifetime of experience, supplied the proper reply to the dilemma.

'Jack', said the Prime Minister, leaning across his desk towards me — I saw immediately that reason and tolerance would never desert this worried countenance — 'I want the young folk cleaned up. Close the discotheques and frippery shops. Send the vagrants to the Isle of Wight. Curfew at nine o'clock. Such a move is long overdue.' I thought for a moment, carefully turning over my Yorkshire accent. 'Nay, lad', I answered, 'more fellow-feeling, more piety of the heart. The answer to the problem is culture.'

Had I not taken the job, some sterile, white-coated man of science, some smug expert in technology, would certainly have stepped in. A man without my psychic depths, my extra dimension of the understanding, my awareness of myth, and consequently incapable of ministering to the real needs of young folk. For, what they truly want, no such smartaleck could possibly supply. The frustrated revolt of youth derives, in fact, from a wish to be like me. The young folk want dreams; they've been given stones, by these men without imagina-

tion or heart. Is it surprising then that they have turned into a generation of filthy morons, clad in barbaric colours, their heads ringing with grotesque sounds, mouthing protests they themselves don't comprehend. Under the new regime they will have more of a chance.

The ancient haunting myths that take shape colour and force from the innermost magic depths of our being are the key to all this. In my own depths — still open and not closed as with so many people who have said goodbye forever to their childhood or youth, without arriving at the second one — there is a special access, a 'hot line' in newfangled jargon, to these myths. I have realised this is our only real safeguard against the utter collapse of our civilisation. And so, I will advise that the clothes-boutiques be transformed into centres of myth-study (along the lines of the Sunday-schools of own youth). The discotheques will become lending libraries well stocked with myths. On the Isle of Wight the young folk will be encouraged to undertake walking tours. Marriage will be compulsory at the age of nineteen as I have always believed in the profoundly civilising of a good-hearted sensual woman upon we erratic and cerebral males.

'The young folk need a centre to their lives', I told Harold Wilson, 'mere discipline will not do at all. They want something that's always there, which they can look up to'. No new-fangled remedies will do. What is required — perhaps

more desperately than anything else — is a young people's edition of this *New Statesman* magazine, to provide the steadying influence where our society needs it most. The *New Responsible* will start publication next week, edited by my old friend Malcolm Muggeridge, and will supply for the new generations that comfortable and harmless weekly expression of discontents, without which there is no stable, rooted society. 'Don't worry, Harold lad,' I concluded our interview, 'there's plenty of life in t'old myths yet'.

NEW FICTION

An outrageous overstatement

QUILTON SPOTHWAITE

In these troubled times, it should be a relief to turn aside to the peace of Literature. So it is sad to turn over the pages of Professor Morris's latest book* The author, now Keeper of the Queen's Giraffes, is to be complimented upon his impudence, but upon little else. This upstart, whose work on human beings was recently dismissed by the *New York Review of Books* in one paragraph, has now turned his unwanted attentions to the intellectuals.

His method — entirely predictable in its banality — consisted of evening excursions on Hampstead Heath armed with nets and tranquillizers, and the inevitable ciné-camera to record the tethered victims' responses. As is well-known — apart from one subject with a *Daily Express* in his pocket, and who turned out to be a tramp — the subjects were either in possession of a *New Statesman*, or quickly demanded one once they were in the interrogation cages and the first excitement of capture had worn off. The author asserts that they '. . . feverishly thumbed the pages with expressions of glazed contentment, in what was obviously a timeless ritual'. Those deprived of the paper soon grew melancholic or unnaturally aggressive (several had to be shot). With a feeble show of *risqué* logic, Professor Morris concludes as follows: 'To be blunt, this journal has broadly the same function for those using it as the trees, or lampposts, at the foot of which lower mammals deposit a trace of excrement: mutual recognition of species.' Only too easy to think, therefore, that the sacred process of 'reading' is mere biological reflex, and that 'intellectuals' are simply bourgeois humans with a few pretentions

Fortunately, no one need take Professor Morris too seriously. His narrowly dogmatic interpretation of the facts is typical of the scientific mind, a-thirst for certainties. Ritual indeed! Any *ingenue* knows that the essential character of a ritual object is to remain ever the same. It is merely preposterous to assert this of our journal, which strives constantly to stay abreast of the times, and this week has a new Literary Editor, a new contributor, myself, and the new type of article you have just been reading, vigorous and outspoken. *Allez vous faire enculer par un singe, Morris!*

*The Naked Intellectual by DESMOND MORRIS. Cape. 30s.

TELEVISION

Well, yes...

FRANCIS HOPE

One often asks oneself wearily whether the protagonists (alright, Fowler) of British *moeurs* really, well, *know* what they're actually saying. I missed *Grumbling in Grimsby* (ITV Rediffusion) by the merest whicker. A terrible pun, one might object, loved I not Cliff Michelmore. But then, do you and I, as liveried liberals with a pinkish tinge, really *know* what we're saying, one asks oneself as well. *I* think so, naturally (alright Rousseau), but who's to say, really, whether we can say anything when so many people are saying something else. There's a dilemma for someone. Tired out by it, I switched over and just caught the tale-end of *New Relapse*, a new programme on the Arts that looked just as tired out as I felt. One doesn't know what to think, really. Would *you* send your child to a Grammar School?

FILMS

Sexulloid Sickness

JOHN COLEMAN

Trouble with film-makers is, they make films. The weird, fraught activity of transferring something probable to an hour or so's celluloid is constantly there to disturb and infiltrate what finally emerges. Rarely more annoying so than in *Flaming Flagellator* ('X', Orifice Films, New Compton Cinema), a first work by Jean-Luc Cognefort. Sentimental, it give surface impression of rigour. How it does this is disinterrable from the very first sequence. A blonde strip of girl ('Gwendoline') is lashed brutally to a chair. A person clad entirely in glistening black leather enters, and proceeds to strangle her. I laughed several times, as an avowed addict of this rubbish; but the colour and photography fluctuated between great and dire, and the scene ended inconclusively. I found this fidgety of Cognefort rather than fruitful. The effect of celluloid wears off faster than the effect of words on a page. Books still give more because they are there for solitary revisitings and genuine participation. And this first effort of Cognefort's is less drawn from the classic *Cuisses de Cuir* than spattered by it. Nevertheless, wading through the giggles of gagged girls towards a quizzical denouement, I was held but sometimes with rage.

SPOTLIGHT ON POLITICS

A Difficult Decision

ALAN WATKINS

"I, or rather God, doth command ye to quell this rabid mutinous sectarian rabble lately so active in the environs of the city, to the detriment of the Lord's purpose and the harm of the Commonweal." Cromwell, letter to General Fairfax, January 7, 1650, **Collected Correspence of Oliver Cromwell**, ed. Hiram P. Hackenlooper, vol. V, p. 378.

This text may serve to remind us that the events of the past few weeks are not really so far removed from the past practices of Brtish political life and the norms of the British Constitution as might appear at first glance. Last week owing to Prime Minister Wilson's lack of consideration for the needs and press times of weekly journals, I had to make some hurried though not, I hope, hasty remarks on the reported Cabinet exchanges between him and the new Minister of Internal Security, Sir George Woodcock. As is now widely believed, the dispute hinged upon Mr Wilson's proposal that dissenters to the policies of the new Coalition Government should be punished by a spell of imprisonment in the new labour-camp on Iona, and the removal of one testicle. Even allowing for some exaggeration in the telling, this story has an air of truth about it. And certainly, the Parliamentary Labour Party is now convinced that there has been a failure both in policy and also (to put it in its politest terms) in communication. Sir George, groping towards the expression of this widespread disillusionment, centred his argument on the problem of possible female dissenters. Or, as one of the more ideologically articulate members of the Left wing whispered to me in confidence last week, the equality of opportunity between the sexes — which Labour has always been pledged to uphold — quite evidently demands equality of punishment, if it is to be meaningfully implemented. So where do we stand? Admittedly, Minister of Pensions Duncan Sandys' newly - acquired habit of setting upon known or suspected Left oppositionists in the corridors of the House and gouging their eyes out was scarcely calculated to soothe such ruffled feelings. But still, one asks oneself, has Sir George chosen quite the most advantageous issue for his daring challenge to Mr Wilson? Possibly, instead of concentrating upon the formal or legalistic aspect of the question, as he was naturally inclined to do given his Trade Union background, the new Minister would have been better advised to look at the substance, the (so to speak) meat of the suggested new policy. The fact is, after all, that Prime Minister could very well have demanded the removal of *both* testicles. And — even more significant, according to certain rumours from usually reliable sources close to the Cabinet — he is believed to favour the excision of the *right-side* testicle, in all cases. Should this rumour be confirmed, it will then be abundantly plain that reason has by no means deserted the deliberations of the Government. The Left must take these possibilities into consideration before mounting still another mis-timed and destructive assault on policies which, however faulty in execution, may be right in intention. No-one can accuse me of showing any undue of even due devotion to Mr Harold Wilson and his Governments. Week in and week out, for longer than I care to remember, I have been saying more or less unflattering things about them. There are occasions, however, when it is right to give some credit; this is one of those occasions.

Oz Statesman

PUBLISHED ONCE AT PALACE GARDENS TERRACE LONDON W.8.

Vol. 1. © No. 1

Freely available to anyone Ltd. 1968

NEXT WEEK

Douglas Jay:

CAN WE AFFORD CHRISTMAS?

John Morgan:
Money is everything

Malcolm Muggeridge:
On Becoming a Jehovah's Witness

More Toads

Anthony Thwaite

(For Philip Larkin)

The galley proofs encircle my tense loins,
My stones of emptiness. I'm not much
     good
At what they call 'the big emotions'.
And, it must be said, I never could.

Get worked up about sunsets, sex, that
     sort
Of thing. And politics, well who knows
     what
To think these days. Too easy to get
     caught
With one's pants down. And as for pop
     and pot

Let's face it, I'm too old. In Libya
A chap could get some peace, collect old
     stones
And mess around the desert with the kids.
     Back here
It's different. These red telephones,

For instance (am I bonkers?) seem to
     leer
Up at my indecision, mockingly,
And all those bearded lefties I kicked
     out
Still come back, one by one, to haunt
     me.

If there were some convention I could
     flout,
A small one, but mine own, perhaps I'd
     make
My mark. But I'm just not that sort of
     chap.
And who *is*, who's half-decent? No, I'll
     damn well take
The middle road. Books *are* a load of
     crap.

PRIVATE VIEW

Self Abuse

ALAN BRIEN

Us performers, damned to perpetually bite the royal hand
which feeds us, are intrinsically sad.
Where does self-criticism end and self-advertising begin?
If I hadn't my two kids, a boy of six and a girl of four,
I would have been thrown to the lions a long time ago.
It looks so simple, I feed the presses, and the presses feed me. But
My role is not definable, a *terrain vague* where you can't
turn your head back to look at the throne, an escape forward
pressed by the eternal laughter behind me.

A friend asks me, why not commit hari-kiri for ITV?
No, no, no, I will not commit the sin of pride. And besides,
BBC2 is waiting for me. So I will be patient, and wait for
Malcolm Muggeridge to die instead. God is getting impatient,
I can see the signs, the negotiations for Malcolm M's ascension are
nearing the end. He'll go up on the first of May,
I'll stay, and get a better seat at the table, my puns a bit
more urgent, my jokes a bit more vicious.
This is my Testament, to be printed by the *New Statesman* the
day I'll be appointed Head of British Television.

Icarus

ON JUNE 15, 1968 DON'T BE WHERE ICARUS IS BECAUSE IF YOU ARE, YOU WON'T BE: IN SPACE IS A
CHUNK OF ROCK & SPACE REFINED METAL, APPROXIMATELY 1.2 MILES WIDE AND 300 YARDS THICK,
AND IT IS ONLY 16,000,000 MILES AWAY AND IT IS TRAVELLING AT 13,940 MPH TOWARDS US.

PROFESSOR S T BUTLER OF SYDNEY UNIVERSITY ON FEBRUARY 4, 1965, TRIED TO EXPLAIN THAT ICARUS
PLANETOID WEIGHING ABOUT AS MUCH AS MOUNT EVEREST, WAS TO PASS WITHIN 500,000 MILES OF THE
EARTH. HOWEVER' IF SCIENTIFIC CALCULATIONS WERE OFF .0000001, ICARUS, WHOSE ORBITAL ECCENTR-
ICITY QUOTIENT OF .83 MAKES IT THE MOST UNPREDICTABLE OF ALL PLANETOIDS, COULD COME CONSID-
ERABLY CLOSER'. ICARUS, WHICH IS A SCALED DOWN PLANET, WILL MAKE IT THROUGH THE ATMOSPHERE
AND, EVEN THOUGH IT WILL BE ABOUT 1/3 OF ITS FORMER SELF, IT WILL STILL BE A FORMIDABLE PIECE
OF ROCK IF IT HITS.

WHY ISN'T THE AMERICAN GOVERNMENT ALARMED? IT IS. M.I.T. OUTLINED A PLAN BY WHICH ICARUS
WOULD BE BLOWN UP IN SPACE BY SEVEN SATURN ROCKETS EACH CARRYING AN ATOMIC PAYLOAD OF
40 MEGATONS. NOW, WHEN THESE ROCKETS HIT ICARUS OUT IN SPACE THERE WILL BE A BANG WORTH
280 MILLION TONS OF TNT AND SUPPOSEDLY ICARUS WILL BECOME ATOMIC WASTE AND NOT HURT ANY-
BODY. BUT THE FACT IS ALMOST 2000 DEATHS CAN BE ATTRIBUTED TO ICARUS ALREADY IN THE GUISE
OF EARTHQUAKES IN INDIA AND CHINA, FREAK SNOW STORMS IN ARIZONA AND TIDAL WAVES IN THE
ALEUTIANS: THESE THINGS BEING INFLUENCED BY THE GRAVITATIONAL PULL OF ICARUS'

ANOTHER DANGER WE EMBRACE WITH ICARUS' APPROACH IS THAT OF DROWNING. IF THIS MOUNTAIN
PASSES THE EARTH FROM THE EAST TO WEST AT ABOUT 420 MILES UP IT WILL PASS OVER THE ATLANTIC
OCEAN, WHICH IS LESS DENSE THAN ICARUS. THE OCEAN WILL REACH UP 327 FT FOR ICARUS, AND
WHEN THE PLANETOID HAS PASSED, LEAVING BEHIND HIS STUNNED LOVER WHO WILL THROW HERSELF
BACK TO THE GROUND. THIS WATER WILL FALL FROM 327 FT UP, AND WILL SPEED 'ACROSS THE OCEAN
TRYING TO KEEP UP WITH ICARUS WHO WILL HAVE SLOWED DOWN LITTLE FROM HIS ORIGINAL 13,490 MPH

ON THE OTHER HAND IF THERE WERE EARTH-QUAKES AND TIDAL WAVES WITH VIOLENT FREAK STORMS,
OR . . .

ALL OF THESE DANGERS INCREASE IN DIRECT PROPORTION TO THE CLOSENESS OF ICARUS BECAUSE
ICARUS' PULL ON THE EARTH INCREASES WITH THE NEARNESS OF ICARUS' AND ICARUS GOT 55.40 MILES
CLOSER TO YOU WHILE YOU READ THIS.

GERALD STEINBERG (UPS)

ARE YOU READY?

Willem, a 26 year old Dutch Cartoonist, is currently threatened with a 3 month gaol sentence in Amsterdam for publishing two "offensive" cartoons. Both are reproduced here. Cartoon A depicts Queen Juliana as a whore. At that time she has asked the Government to double her allowance. (Queen Juliana already owns £750,000 worth of Standard Oil, £835,000 of Royal Dutch Petroleum, £1,170,000 of KLM, £1,440,000 of Adam Express and £6,500,000 of Anaconda copper). Cartoon B is being prosecuted for "cruelty to police".

Willem has recently published a best-selling comic book in Amsterdam, 'Billy the Kid' and he edits a cartoon magazine, 'God Nederland and Oranje'.

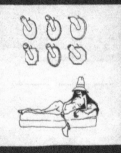

OZ SUBSCRIPTION

FREE POSTERS!

'Toad of Whitehall' comes free with OZ 2. It is a giant (22 x 24") colour gatefold inside. OZ 2 comes free with a year's subscription to OZ. So does any other issue (except No 1). Send us the coupon below and you get two free issues immediately. That is, OZ 2 plus one other. You can also order back issues separately, 2/6d each.

PAST ISSUES!

One: Theological striptease . . . turn on, tune in, drop dead . . . In bed with the English . . . Raped Congo nuns whipped with Rosary beads . . . Private Eye axed.

RARE 1ST OZ!

The Johnson caricature, 'Madonna of the Napalm' is a three page gatefold in OZ 1. This issue sold out and we have been unable to fill many subsequent orders for it. However, a few have now been returned from our distributors and we're going to offer them to our readers at the ludicrously expensive price of £1. They're not worth it. But no doubt some neurotic collectors will want to complete their sets. (For £2.10s you can have your own complete set delivered to you when OZ 12 is published. That is, OZes 1–12).

Two: Mark Lane's BBC expose . . . British Breasts . . . Peter Porter's Metamorphoses . . . Little Malcolm and his struggle against the 20th century . . . Cut our pop stars.

Three: What makes hippies happen . . Last exit to Brewer Street . . . An Address to politicians . . . In praise of Ugliness . . . Magnificent failures.

Four: Hapshash and the coloured coat golden gatefold . . . Tarot cards . . . Process exposed . . . Sgt Nasser's Lonely heartbreak bank . . . Norman Normal . . . Guide to Living in Sin . . . Let de Gaulle die quickly.

Five: Plant a Flower Child billboard poster . . . The Great Alf Conspiracy.

Six: (OZ & Other Scenes) Blue movies by the yard . . . The king of Khatmandu and his Coca Cola Court . . . Dope Sheet . . . John Peel interview . . . Letter from a Greek Prison . . . Leary in Disneyland . . . Mcluhan's one eyed electric kingdom.

Seven: What's so good about Bob Dylan . . . Wog Beach Shock . . . Michael X and the Flower Children . . . In bed with the Americans . . . Review of Maharishi's 'The Science of Being and the Art of Living'.

Eight: Mis-Spelt Guevara poster . . . Russia, you have bread, but no roses . . Playboy's banned pictures . . . Spyder Turner's raunch epistemology. . . . Edward do Bono on lateral thinking.

Nine: New Dylan Lyrics . . . 'If I could turn you on' UFO digest . . . Death at St Pauls.

Ten: The pornography of violence . . . Amnesty report from Athens . . . Gaol in Arkansas . . . The men who ban OZ . . . OH! what a lawful war . . . Roger McGough's 'Summer with the Monarch' (complete version).

☐	I enclose 30/- for a subscription plus two free back issues
☐	Send me back issues No 2,3,4,5,6,7,8,9,10. (delete inapplicable). Here's 2/6d for each one.
☐	I enclose £1 for the exorbitantly priced first issue
☐	I enclose £2.10.0d for a complete set of OZes to be sent with publication of your next issue (12)

Name

Address.   Country

RUSH TO OZ, 38a, Palace Gardens Terrace, London, W8.

Tax dodge special:
Oz goes big.
See centre spread.

Britain
2s 6d
Holland
2 G
Denmark
3 kr
Germany
1.8 DM

VIRGINIA CLIVE-SMITH
52a PALACE COURT
MOSCOW ROAD
LONDON W.8 [ENGLAND]

Academy of Meditation
Shankarachary Nagar
Rishikesh
Himalayas U.P.
India
19-3-68

Dear Virginia,

How are you? Write and tell me— things seem to get wierder and clearer here every day, one discovers the terrible and finds it's the beautiful, what seems bad is good, what seems good is beautiful. Look at us, take a good long look. One minute I'm crying and weeping and the next I'd laughing hysterically. Oh if you thought we were going away to whatever you thought you were mistaken. It's all here up in the Himalayas spiritual India, the example of the Vast. I'm writing in my little room, with incense burning to keep away the bugs, I have a few pictures of Maharishi all over my walls, a tea pot empty, honey jars, limes, tangerines, mangoes, paint box, cushions, wooden bed, oh dear, oh dear, oh dear, I can't stop laughing. Virginia, I'm indeed with problems, with upsets, with incredible paranoia at times, and love at other times. I've seen them all, my hangups in turn laid out, one by one, in waking state and in meditation. I don't know which is worse and have come to the beautiful realisation through the wisdom of Maharishi and my own meditational experiences, that you have just got to get past them all, that you've got to reach a field where none of these things exist, and by reaching that field, which you do in meditation, when you come back to waking state of consciousness everything is viewed as it is like going to a foreign country, you see the scene as it is, sees everything so clearly. But what a drag to always have to go abroad to see the scene as it is. Is much better to be able to see it all the time even when one's being active etc.

There's no way out of the field of problems if one remains on the land of problems, what happens, one just gets immersed in all the awfulness of them, or one shoves them to one side and refuses to be influenced by them, in both cases no good, one gets more sadness, the other finds no solution. We can't get away from problems in this relative life of ours, so what is the answer? Go to a field, a level of consciousness, where there are no problems, and when you come back again on a different level your mind just goes there, straight to the source of the problem, I'm telling you, Anyway, I keep finding the problem has been solved during meditation, either in my own thoughts or it is has lain outside me, kind of it's solved itself. Really, Virginia, it's all so amazing. Anyway so love is spreading throughout the world, the same message of Christ, Buddha, Krishna, no name but a few. And we are so lucky, you realise, Virginia, you weren't so clever as to get born into this day and age for nothing, you know you were kind of cunning and clever, you and me and the rest alike all got ourselves born and still being, because this time it's favourable it seems, so all we have to do is take advantage of our intelligence and get going onto meditation.

M is beyond recognition, one of the several miracles taking place here. The Maharishi is pleased with her progress, her face is so beautiful, she's calm, walks differently. Her pain in the shoulder is practically gone and she's beautiful, wow! A women here who had a car accident and spinal damage 6 years ago, who could hardly move and all doctors had given up hope on her, can now move normally, this happened through meditating. Peoples' faces, relaxed and clean. So many amazing things are worked out during meditation, and it's kind of fun. I think up songs which I can't remember when I come out. Virginia, to meditate, don't let the idea arise that one has to be of a certain nature, spirituality doesn't come into it - unless one wants it to. Anyway what is religion? You should see the diversity of people here, some reverent, some exceedingly and every little spiritual idea, but it seems common thought it's about that meditation works. What is said happens, and therefore this is what we give people to do, give them a mantra, and that's it. All this fuss and stuff, what is important, the only thing, is to go and get that mantra, that word and repeat morning and evening and find 'heaven' as you put it. That's all it entails. To imagine things could not be better than they already are is nonsense. The idea is, to get Nature working with you. This means that you don't have to do much; you think a little, meditate a little and the thing happens.

It's Mike Love of the Beachboys birthday tomorrow, a nice guy - the Beatles and wives are all so natural and meditate a lot and Donovan is something else, such beautiful songs, he feels he was living as a minstrel in the Arthurian times, is that where I've met him before? Mia Farrow cooled down the last few days and was really sweet. That's most of the celebrities - and did they put me through a scene, phew I've had all the scenes here. the 1st and more! I'm tired, must meditate, No great change in me, more relaxed but still screwed up with Karma, though can feel it going with each meditation, can feel it. Universality, absolute. Have you bought Maharishi's Beyond Gita? I'm under no illusions as far as the actual meditation goes, there's nothing that could be an illusion. Virginia, write me some good news.

lots of love
V.

London OZ
is published approximately
monthly by OZ Publications Ink
Ltd, 38a Palace Gardens Terrace,
London W8. Phone:
229 4623 . . . 603 4205.

Editor: Richard Neville

Deputy Editor: Paul Lawson

Design: Jon Goodchild assisted
by Virginia Clive-Smith

Art: Martin Sharp

Pull-out sheets: David Wills /
Colin Fulcher

Advertising: John Leaver
2 Walsingham Mansions, Fulham
Rd, SW6. Phone: 385 4539.

Writers: Andrew Fisher, David
Widgery, Angelo Quattrocchi,
John Wilcock.

Photography: Keith Morris

Pushers: Felix Dennis &
Louis Ferrier.

Distribution: (Britain) Moore-
Harness Ltd, 11 Lever Street,
London EC1. Phone: CLE 4882.
(New York) D.G.B. Distribution
Inc. 41 Union Square, New York
10003.
(Holland) Thomas Rap,
Regulierdwarstraat 91, Amsterdam.
Telefoon: 020-227065.
(Denmark) George Streeton,
The Underground, Larsbjørnstraede
13, Copenhagen K.

Printing: Steel Bros (Carlisle) Ltd,
Phone 0228-25181. Printed Web
Offset.

Typesetting: Jacky Ephgrave,
Big O Press Ltd, 49 Kensington
High Street, London W8. Phone:
937-2613/4.

Dear OZ,

So yet another desperate Solihullian leaps on the 'get a letter in
OZ' trend—which of course is all
I am doing now. That letter from
'anon' was desperately incorrect
in its facts and in its request a
little pathetic but the basic fact of
the semi-humanoid mass being
clogged in a sticky pool of coagulating 'money-coloured urine' is
right and there is of course nothing
we can do to radically alter this
embryonic headquarters of the
New Wipeout Gang . . . however it
is interesting to note that the
newsagent which previously stocked
supposedly 8 (nearer 10/12) copies
of the withering OZ now stocks
nearly 2 dozen. It would be very
nice of you if you published this
short letter thing for we feel we
must keep splashing the fear-striking name of So£ihu££ across the
pages of your dying magazine-
type. (SO£IHU££ IS THE NEW
MENTAL VIETNAM).

Yours,
I J Evetts

Dear Sir,

Your interest in 'drop-out' communities seems relevant to what I
am doing at Southwood House,
which is a hostel for boys with
Muscular Dystrophy. The nursing staff here have a totally
informal relationship with the
boys, and love, in its most unsentimental form seems to overcome
all the drudgery of nursing and almost all the pain of being crippled.
Could this be an idea for drop
outs; to infiltrate an isolated
institution for old people or cripples as volunteer workers, and
gradually destroy any institutionalisation and petty-mindedness,
replacing it with love? That way,
the drop-outs wouldn't be parasitical (except in the way any charity
or social service is parasitical),
and would also be making good
propaganda for the cause of the
love revolution.

Yours,
R G N Davie
Southwood House,
Hinwick,
nr Wellingborough,
Northants.

Dear OZ,

We at Jesus College, Cambridge all
love OZ, but we regard the announcement that Richard Meltzer will
be writing regularly for OZ as
BAD NEWS. His first article was
100% pretentious junk—send him
back to Crawdaddy, they deserve
him! Despite Meltzer, we still
love you!

Yours sincerely,
Patrick B Hefferman
Jesus College
Cambridge.

OZ,

Re Meltzer thing on paper. Complete total bewilderment stems
from free ignorance of wavelength
Love, forever changes, da capo et
cetera tres bien but give me quelques autres choses. Hello how are
you, easy baby beats me to pulp.
Broken Jug picture speaks to me
(smokey—I second that emotion).
1000 light-years too far to see
worse than eight miles high,
strictly for the byrds. Will the pun
censorship. Marvel better than DC
says me.

Yours,
Paul Stanley.
Bethnal Green.

PS. Who exactly is Richard Meltzer?
Who exactly am I? I do like the
byrds, really!
(Now come off it OZ, the rumour
is you're really sanctioned by the
TAS agency and receive payments
from them.)

Dear Sir,

I am a 16 year old female pupil
of a Roman Catholic Grammar
school. (Run by Nuns.) If you are
still with me and are not too busy
shoving the salvolatile up your
nose, I shall continue to 'shock'
you, with the news that OZ No 6
has reached two of those 'Black-
skirted virgins'—as your Mr
Quattrocchi so aptly put it in OZ
No 7.

During a religious lesson, given by
our English teacher—a nun—she
began talking about God and love—
war and peace . . . hippies . . . drugs
and 'freedom'. On the question of
'freedom' and the 'New' Morality,
sister X said that drug taking and
'living it up' were not free actions!
on the part of the young. She said,
very authoritatively that the actions of the young particularly in
drug-taking were a result of fears
of the future and an attitude of
'Let's get as much as we can out
of life'! She spoke of this as if it
was a sin. (The attitude is—lead
a miserable, poverty stricken, sexless life, and go to—Heaven! Ah!
Lead a happy life and you are
doomed to—Hell!)

I did not agree, but I could not
risk opposing her openly in front
of a class of 35 girls. They are
very much Catholic influenced in
these matters. They never think in
depth about anything or anyone,
not even themselves, so they either
accept it or ignore it. Consequently
I was afraid of exposing my views
and being laid open to defenceless

criticisms. Close friends 'sympathise' but fail to understand. Moreover I'm 'teacher's pet'—a tag I
enjoy and do not wish to jeopardise.

Taking all this into account, I
reached for the most subtle way
of airing my views (in part) and
remaining 'safe' at the same time.
I had previously come across your
magazine—for the first time—and
having studied Mr Chester Anderson's article carefully, I gave it to
sister X. (Added reasons: the
article contained the word 'freedom' several times and since to my
mind sister X did not know what
she was talking about—the article
was in complete contradiction to
her ideas.)

She read it and gave it to sister Y—
our HEADMISTRESS! Later, sister
X and I had a chat, while two of
my astounded friends looked on.
During our conversation she revealed to me that she had had a chat
with the 'head' about me—and
quite a thorough chat it was. In
answer to 'one' question I admitted
to not being against drugs and told
her of my views. Surprisingly, she
was quite sympathetic, but spoilt
it all by saying she would 'pray for
me'! My friends looked on in awe.
Sister X admitted she was now
more aware of what was going on
(attitudes etc) after reading the
article, but denied reading the
rest of the magazine. I assured her
I would not buy another issue of
OZ. I lied!

After being subjected to shocked
and dirty looks from shop assistants
and witnessing the ripping up of
my OZ 7 by my enraged father
and disgusted, incredulous mother,
I am still an OZ reader. (I have
survived).

However, I do not agree with all
you say. You seem to be against
universities and colleges as such!
Why? The society at which you are
aiming frightens me. You seem to
be against individualism! In any sort of
sort of community—I purposely
avoid the word 'society'—leaders
will arise, it is inevitable. A Community cannot exist with out
leaders and your kind can only
serve to frustrate and alienate these
people. You will be left with the
sheep, but no shepherds. What a
confusion that will be!

KTY

PS. I am at present considering
whether your magazine is sincere,
or just a superficial load of old
rubbish!

I am at an experimental stage in
life and as in any experiment one
allows for mistakes. I hope OZ is
not one of them!

**THE BLACK DWARF
HAS RETURNED!**

MIDDLE EARTH

43, KING St. Covent Gdn. 240 5327.

SPIDERMAN

1p   **2c**

FASCINATION

SUBSCRIBERS

team who operate from discreet offices in N10. Their attractive young staff while away the hours packing and dispatching a fascinating range of 'optional extra' sexual attachments. These include fancy sheath styles which vary from the deliciously subtle to the sensationally sadistic. For the man, there is a loss of sensitivity but most girls report reaching new ecstasy thresholds. The male pleasure reduction can be avoided with Pellen's clitoral cushions and other devices. (One of which is called simply 'Marriage Happiness'). Ravensdale, the makers of 'Magnaphal' are also helpful and efficient. Although I haven't persevered with the famous ointment, which is designed to be used with a series of exercises, I saw many hundreds of letters from exuberantly satisfied customers. One man reported such an astonishing increase in the size of his prick that the makers of 'Magnaphal' declined to believe him. 'If you think I'm a liar', responded the satisfied customer, 'I'll come in and show you'. He was advised to discontinue treatment. Yes, men, it seems it can be done, but I remind you that Masters and Johnson in their book 'Human Sexual Response' concluded that there is no relation between penis size and male sexual prowess.

Spike File is a hotchpotch of editorial and outside contributions. Anyone with cheap gossip or important information should send concise paragraphs to 'Spike' c/o OZ, 38a Palace Gdns Terrace, W8.

COME, MARRY EVA

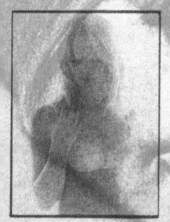

The wretched Customs Alfs have again refused even a temporary entry permit to golden Eva. She has £50 and a permanent invitation to stay at her girlfriend's home, but British Customs keep sending her back to Paris. Her only loophole is to marry an Englishman. Eva is an exceptionally hip, beautiful Swedish summer and she promises to live at least a week with an Englishman who takes her hand in wedlock. Write to her girlfriend Judy, c/o OZ.

We finally got around to testing the wares of our two faithful advertisers, Pellen Personal Products Ltd. and *Ravensdale Products Ltd.* ('Men it can be done'. Pellen is an amiable husband and wife

Results of the OZ Sunday Times quiz:

Century's most glamorous woman:
Girlfriends, followed by Anna Karina, Suzy Kendall, Marilyn Monroe.

Most prestigious occupation:
Doctors, then trendy Dukes, artist, writer, cook, fishmonger.

Nation you would most like to belong to:
Czechoslovakia, Tonga ('Is it just their press image or are they really so bloody happy?'), Andean tribe.

Most fascinating 20th century man:
Most OZ readers voted themselves, other: Guevara, Bob Dylan, Syd Barrett, Alistair Crowley, God ('creator of the apple'), Miss April Ashley, Bertrand Russell and Alfred E Neuman ('the first drop-out').

When the Beatles were refused admission to Disneyland, because of long hair they re-appeared dressed as nuns and were allowed in.

William H James PhD published a letter in OZ 10 seeking 'coital calenders'. These are records of the days in which women menstruate and have sexual intercourse with their husbands. This letter was written up in 'People'. Since then he has received over 20 replies. Three of them by the same crank—once as a 27 year old man, once as a 16 year old girl, once as a 55 year old woman. According to Dr James, a biometricist, about four of the coital records are extremely useful and will provide 'valuable and a completely new kind of data'. He tried, without success to publish the same letter in New Statesman, The Spectator, Nova, Sunday Times, Observer, New Society, Lancet and several other broadminded journals.

Donovan has become an obsessive drug coward. Following the recent raid on Middle Earth he cancelled his concert there. Donovan greets any visitors to his home with 'Hello. Make sure you're not holding.'

That gaggle of old women who run the Rationalist Press Association which publishes the doll grey, moribund magazine 'Humanist' have refused to accept the standard OZ advertisement. A special committee meeting was called for it to be rejected. The advertisement shows a female bosom.

10 DAYS

IN NEW YORK   Spike File

At airports, the small print on automatic insurance machines firmly disqualifies charter flights from eligibility. Yet £50 for a ten day charter return trip to New York proved irresistable—even on a discarded Qantas Boeing 707. Sandie Shaw was aboard, she had wrung some publicity out of the non-incident of her smallpox vaccination which caused the Evening Standard to dub the flight 'the pop special'. Miss Deb 1967 was there, languidly stoned between two giggly friends, so was Al Stewart, folksinger, Steve, from Osiris posters, Mike Henshaw, the hippy accountant, photographers, literary agents, restauranteurs, one plump Indian woman (who was absorbed in pornography) and two gentleman looking uncomfortable in business suits.

Earlier, as the planeload had chirped along the concrete corridors towards take off area, after passing currency control, I spied wads of notes crashing to the ground from between the legs of debs like so many recoiling tampaxes, to be urgently retrieved by accompanying males. Their money, sticky but safe.

Seven hours later, New York. Visas were stamped, names were checked in an ominous black book and baggage trolleys were issued for us to queue up at customs like rush hour at MacFisheries.

Later, it's ham & eggs at a drug store and rides up town in fibre glass seated buses which have noisy machines sorting and spewing coins for the driver. Above is a cardboard Lyn Redgrave offering her recipe for Lamb Casserole.

DYLAN
BOP1. Martin Sharp's beautiful Litho Poster, 20 x 30". Printed Red & Black on gloss Gold. 7/6d.

Big O Posters Ltd.
(See Page 21)

Every Saturday the politicised hippies, yippees, (see OZ 11) meet at the Free School (alias Free University) on East 14th Street. That afternoon they were preparing for the mass Yip Out— 'Resurrection of Free'—to be held in Central Park next day. Balloons, posters, flowers, records, fun and magic. We were all asked to bring a can of food 'to build a mountain of it for Dr King's poor people'. Rock groups were coming. Amplified sound is illegal in New York parks, but yippees warned City Hall that, in the wake of King's assasination, they had better cool it. Light aeroplanes were booked to drop flowers on the crowds. One yippee reported the results of his free flower fall experiments. He had dropped chrysanthemums, daisies and daffodils from a high building to compare their endurance capacity. I was handed a yippee conscript form: 'I CAN STEAL FOR YIPPEE Mimeo paper––Money––records––dope–– flowers––space––'. Paul Krassner, editor of the wild, original, personal, Realist, was there, exerting sanity.

Once Krassner was interviewed by Joe Pine, a neurotic, right wing telly celebrity who, like our Ken Allsop, has a wooden leg. Pine asked Krassner whether he ever felt embarrassed about dating girls because of his scarred face. Replied Krassner: Are you embarrassed when you unstrap your wooden leg to fuck your wife?. The video tape was never screened.

Thousands of people arrived at the park next day to give and receive free posters and records, score acid, hash, STP and Morning Glory seeds. Groups rocked, one couple loved under a blanket, a large brown beautiful girl suckled a baby, men in purple sweat shirts and yippee badges carried collection boxes chanting: 'get hip, give to yip'. Planes dropped flowers, which blew into the surrounding trees and the cops were benign.

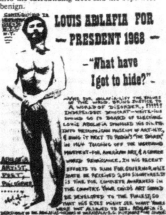

LOUIS ABLAFIA FOR PRESDENT 1968 –"What have I got to hide?"–

Louis Abolafia was in the park, standing for President. His handout leaflet shows him naked ('What have I got to hide?'). Abolafia is executive director of the Foundation for Runaway Children . . . 'We try to mediate and counsel and point out the ills of drugs and various dangers in East Village . . . vote for Abolafia, bring justice to a world of disorder.'

In New York I enjoyed the hospitality of John Wilcock, an Americanised Englishman and veteran extraordinaire of the Underground. In 1952 he halped launch the Village Voice along with Norman Mailer, Daniel Wolf, Edwin Fancher and others and since then has edited scores of underground papers throughout the world. Somewhat of a cross between Che Guevara and Elsa Maxwell, Wilcock is an instinctive international revolutionary, a charming companion and a manic communicator. We look forward to his forthcoming influence on the London scene.

Now on Broadway, 'Hair', the rock musical, is the only thing worth going uptown for, apart from Macy's 'Toy City'. 'Hair' is a fast furious blend of love, hate, nudity, sex, satire, soul, pot and revolution. For a start, the leading lady Sheila lives with two men at once—which is a long way from 'West Side Story' (Natalie Woodn't). The middle class audiences roar their crew-cutted heads off at lines like 'Let's have a suck in for peace' and absorb without embarrassment the pounding vocabulary of traditional obscenity. Only three of the audience cheer when a hippie dodges the draft dodgers to enlist. The rest hiss. A brilliant parody of 'The Supremes' erupts form the discursive, lateral plot as a trio of tasty black girls are projected to centre stage on scaffolding, all bouncing and writhing and all sharing the same pink sequined clinging dress. The programme notes confirm the radical mood: 'Miss Sally Seaton lives in East Village . . . and is for acid, sex and peace'. Yes, it's all happening on Broadway. After the show I walked across the road and got bounced out of a bar for not wearing a dress jacket.

Add Saturday's Portobello and Kings Road together then multiply by 100. This equals the East Village at 4am. The vivid underground tabloid, East Village Other (once edited by Wilcock) is published here along with the newer 'Rat' (for total revolution). It is here that yippees give away free food (only to be prosecuted by police for infringing health regulations) where the Fillmore East pioneers with strobes, where there are more rock musicals, paperback emporiums, The Electric Circus, leather boutiques, rivetting record shops . . .

America has more freedom than England in all media except tv, and the East Village underground television laboratory (Channel One) is generally about as underground as Simon Dee. Only one of their joke commercials could not be televised here: a puppet drones on with a VD warning, as the camera moves in, you come to realise the playful puppet is really a live human prick (its nose and mouth) and balls (its two eyes).

The Mothers of Invention gave a wilder concert at the Fillmore East than here at the Albert Hall. The Fillmore was still half empty when the curtains rose so crowds of East Villagers were let in free. Projected behind the Mothers was a staggeringly original, 3 dimensional psychedelic light show, rather humbling the London Roundhouse experiments with slides of Afghan basket weaving and blobs of primaries.

I saw Andy Warhole's new movie 'Lonesome Cowboy', not yet released. It is the first of his films to enjoy editing. It stars Viva (the white cover girl) and Taylor Mead. This movie will become talked about because of a spontaneous gang rape scene and its deeply homosexual parody of Westerns. Dialogue, direction, and most of its action is, of course, ex tempore so the burden of communication falls heavily on each member of Warhole's cast, or rather, coterie. Lonesome Cowboy is patchy; at times monumentally boring and repetitive; often eccentrically brilliant. Hopefully it will emerge, in the finally edited version, as the ultimate anti-Western. Taylor Mead is a mad, camp clown. It is said that he turns real life into a movie. Whenever he appears in Lonesome Cowboy, he turns a movie into genius.

Warhole himself is still No 1 on the New York celebrity poll. It is said that Warhole let's everyone exploit him to his own advantage. Max's of Kansas city, the famous bar, granted Warhole several months credit in return for a painting. When the credit expired Max's had a fire. Now Andy is doing them another painting and still dines for free. Max's cultivates the great American craft of rudeness, which of course enhances its popularity.

Jimmy Hendrix appeared everywhere—except Harlem, where he was tossed out. His skin was too pale. I briefly met him once as I was grandly

displaying some of Martin Sharp's best-selling posters: Donovan . . . Bob Dylan . . . Van Go Suddenly Hendrix leaned over the table: 'Va Gogh? What group does he sing with, man?' told him Gene Vincent.

The worst club in the Village is called 'Salva rendered instantly unpalatable by two prom ent notices on the door: 'Couples only', and 'Men must wear ties or fashionable costume' entrance fee is $ 8 and not surprisingly, it w apparently the permanent venue for many o swingers on our Boeing pop special.

Someone forgot the key to the Free School offices, so the second Saturday yippee meeti was spread across the grass of nearby Union Square. A yippee tribute to Luther King wa handed out to bystanders (who are always w yippees are) . . . 'We are going to write venge on the wall of the White House', it shouted f scarlet paper. One little old lady shredded h instantly, much to the irritation of onlookin blacks. Jerry Rubin pleaded for the yippee urday meetings to become information exch centres. He also said it was 'nuts to think of revolution without ideology–inevitably that would come, consciously or otherwise'. Her forth, Saturday meetings would be for each yippee to announce his project and invite th interested to rendezvous nearby. The key y happening will be the disruption of the Presi ial elections. Already plans are underway fo hiring buses, road kitchens and medical team to accomodate the thousands of yippees exp ed to head for Chicago in August. The inaug tion of the Youth International Party. Mear while, the new anarchists are rehearsing. The were the projects announced in Union Squar Park on the sunny Saturday afternoon, April 20.

Project 1. Man with homebuilt portable amplifier and loudspeaker. 'I made this. We can control crowds with it. We can disrupt police with it. Give me some help and mone and we'll make dozens. We will take them t Chicago.

Project 2. A girl quietly explains her poor p programme. Would those interested speak t

Project 3. Jerry Rubin and Paul Krassner announce they are preparing a book of quot tions on the disalienation of world youth. T want any quotes that express what's happen It doesn't matter who says them; they can b your own. Yippee will receive a healthy pub lishers advance. (Any helpful OZ readers ca write to them c/o Yippee, Apt 607, 32 Unio Square East, NY 10003. New York.)

So ended the meeting of yippees and my stay in New York. Diggers, it should be pointed out, are ideologically opposed to yippees and equate the call to Chicago with a lemmings picnic. For me, if it ever becomes a choice between retiring to Norfolk growing vegetables or marching, like yippees, to the Stock Exchange and throwing money into the centre of the floor; it won't be cabbages.

Richard Neville

You'll see an advertisment in this issue for an OZ benefit at Middle Earth. Please come. We can't yet divulge all the reasons why OZ needs money, because it would frighten too many people on whom our existence depends. And although the recent issues have been covering cost, we're still paying for youthful extravagances. Example: Haphash and the Coloured Coat's psychedelic Kama Sutra gatefold (OZ 4) where we used pure gold ink instead of sensible varnish. The purchase tax people insist that our poster OZes weren't really OZes at all, but posters, and they want 27½%. David Hauseman and Paul Ableman have generously donated the use of Middle Earth on Sunday 26 May and groups will appear for expenses only. If Mick Jagger is reading this, please come and play.

From P.B.:

In Queensway, London, there stands a news-agent trafficking in the most catholic selection of papers and magazines—not, I should say, hard-core pornography, but serious stuff like Ebony, Iraqui journals, La Stampa, Male, and the like. This pleasant little store was until recently run by a Jewish lady of uncertain years and temperament. She was, of course, white.

The chief attraction of this emporium, was the interesting selection of personal advertisements carried on cards in glass cases outside the shop. Such things are common enough: '42-inch chest for hire'; 'Erections and demolitions a speciality'; 'Cultured coloured lady seeks interesting position';'Young American ex-gymn mistress gives private workouts. Rough matting a speciality'; and very innocuous statements such as 'typing done at home', the advertiser of which, when approached by an innocent who did indeed want something typed, said 'you should read between the lines. Piss off.' It will readily by understood why the shop's glass display cases were the subject of intense study at all hours by men in raincoats with one hand in their pockets.

Came the day when the above-mentioned Jewish lady sold out, perfectly amicably and in just the spirit that General Dayan might emulate, to some Arabs. The character of the shop changed not at all—at first. Then horrified habitues of the subtle commercials of whoredom noticed that the cards were disappearing. Where pre-iously the request to 'share a bedsitter' had been an invitation to pay for a fuck, it now

meant exactly what it said. Wardrobes for sale implied a public sale, and the men of erotic utility furniture designs. The men in raincoats were street's white gst themselves racial problems ers of the Immigration Laws and school wogs ruining the B the Arab owners had crusade to clean the shop that they had lost a lot of business.

But the true cause of the real goad of racist surprise—our very own paid a visit to the sister (also Jewish) on and had nothing ployers, that it was graphic adverts the study of whores they'd bust them tve mixture, the and not a photo a hair

The Conference on Human Rights opened in Teheran as a reminder that Iran accepts no country. The military dictatorship, under the Shah's direct orders, have reacted to unrest with mass arrests and prison tortures, often are documented in letters smuggled out of the country. Some of these tortures are described as unspeakable. Banishment is common. Shiraz University has been closed for protesting against the absence of democratic liberty; Teheran University is surrounded by troops. Religious leaders have been badly beaten up, interrogated, and put in gaol where the rations are 24 gramme of sugar, one gram of tea, two loaves of stale bread, 40 grammes of the poorest quality soap. and one shilling per day in cash.

As many as fifty student leaders have been arrested and banished to areas with unbearable climatic conditions without even the customary mock trial. This is the country playing host to U Thant and delegates sworn to defend the lofty principles of the Declaration of Human Rights.

The woolgatherers' favourite Sunday Newspaper stepped fearlessly into the shit raised by Mr Enoch Powell and sank without a trace. It's editorial, as usual, was distinguished by its rhetorical flourish and earnest meaninglessness. In the best tradition of middle class liberalism it placed the wrong interpretation on a series of false assumptions and concluded triumphantly by saying nothing at all. All this we expect, but at the beginning of the week its distinguished, wealthy and patrician editor took a different stand on the race problem. Seperate development (sometimes known as apartheid) was the answer, he argued. The Blacks wanted it, the whites would welcome it, it solved the problem of Britain's ghettoes. It was both sane and humane. He was amazed when most of his editorial staff then offered their resignations. Being a man of principle, he promptly altered his editorial. His staff withdrew their notice. His paper's attitude on race was then bravely exposed for what it was: the unhappy product of insecure men, uncertain of anything.

On a personal note, we celebrate the launching of a new publishing imprint by a friend of this magazine, Barley Alison. She is one who excells in the unexpected, being the last person you would expect to have been trained to pick a lock (during the War), spent ten years in the Foreign Office (after it), or shared a governess with Peter Ustinov. She is both an editor and a hostess in the grand tradition. The first book under her imprint—The Alison Press—is Down-stairs at Ramsey's by James Leigh, a beautiful, gritty American novel, as smooth and bitter as good coffee. (At a time when publishing is becoming as monotonously anonymous as government, writers need Barley Alison.

From R.H.

Despite the Grand Prix at Tours Film Festival and a recent hit in the USA, B S Johnson's brilliant short feature You're Human Like the Rest of Them still has not found a British distributor, who have for their dedication to aesthet Wardour Street counterparts as a bunch of garbage men. Their gross under estimation of public taste is the sole reason for the grim, old fashioned shorts (and frequently they'd bust them one explosion occurs in every circuit cinema in Britain. Lindsay Anderson's short feature film The White Bus was a total fiasco at the Oberhausen

Festival this month. Non-directed actors, obscure social comment and crude humour left the audience mystified. Anderson built a reputation in the fifties by making minor (now dated) 'social comment' shorts and then encouraging his friends to write enthusiastic reviews. Although a nominal left-winger, his fascistic treatment of his associates makes him all but impossible to work with, and he hasn't made a full length film since the melodrama This Sporting Life some years back. If, and it's unlikely, The White Bus gets a London release we can be reasonably certain of being bored to tears.

Another fascist, Peter Watkins, who cloaks his penchant for mutilation and suffering with a convincing left-wing views, is back in London looking for work after the cancellation of his three picture American contract. Although someone (at least) was obviously impressed by Privilege, Watkins proved far too irrational and dramatic for the faint-heart nervous' boys with the money.

A BFI Production Board film called The Park is arousing a lot of controversy. Called by the 'International Times' as the worst film at Knokke festival and by the 'Daily Telegraph' as 'a gloomy view of urban recreation'. The Park has received enormous praise from people such as Eric Rhode and Sir William Coldstream. This week (7.4.68) John Berger the novelist and art critic wrote a long eulogy on the film in the 'New Society'. A number of people, this writer included, consider the director, writer, cameraman, editor, 21 year old Richard Saunders, as the most original film talent to appear in this country for many years. Saunders is now making a short (70') 35mm wide screen feature, Jack Pudding and the Acrobat, from his own original screenplay. Intellectual, withdrawn, a perfectionist in his work (it was his attention to detail that enraged the 'International Times'). Saunders was undismayed at the lack of understanding which was the first reaction to his films. Film makers manque who complain ceaselessly about lack of BFI support should look at Saunders

films to discover the secret of his work. It can be summed up in three words . . . Something to say.

It is rumoured that a group of short film makers in London are preparing a dossier against a well known short film distributor. It is alleged that, for example, he sells a film for £200 to a TV station, tells the film maker the price was £100, then deducts his 15% commission.

In Paris go and see Louis De Wet's exhibition of drawings at the Galerie + 3.1, 6 Rue Visconti Paris 6e. Actually, 'drawings' doesn't really describe them. Highly fashioned detailed works in pencil that have the weight of painting, like Pisanello using 15th century techniques on a complex 20th century vision. Like Pisanello where girls and modern sexual paraphernalia have been substituted for animals. De Wet is London based now and some of his work will be exhibited here later this year. His stuff is electrifying.

POLICE ARREST POETS

On Saturday, April 23, ten people were arrested outside Bernard Stone's Turret Bookshop in Kensington Church Walk and charged with wilful obstruction. Those arrested included Asa Benveniste (of Trigram Press), Anthony Barnett (poet), Hugh Kenso (Indica books), Wendy and John Sharkey (ICA) and Clive Watson (poet). They were part of a demonstration which assembled outside the Turret Bookshop to protest against the inclusion of small press works in an exhibition at the United States Embassy.

This exhibition had been organised by Turret Bookshop partner, Edward Lucie Smith and included works of the demonstrators without their permission. Edward Lucie Smith had refused to withdraw their works on the grounds that he was exhibiting his private collection of small press works. The demonstrators did not want their works used for US propaganda purposes.

The 50 arrived at the Turret Bookshop clutching daffodils and anti-US posters. They burnt two books on the pavement, pinned a wreath on the door of the shop and asked the manager, Bern-

ard Stone, to return them any of their works in stock. This he did, with a mixture of amusement and embarrassment.

Suddenly the police arrived. They urged Bernard Stone to press charges. He declined. Police then asked demonstrators to make way for a puzzled bystander. They did. Then Christopher Logue, one of the demonstrators, suggested the crowd move to the Embassy and remove the books forcibly. The ransacking motion was rejected, but the demonstrators decided to move to the Embassy anyway. Too late. The police swooped in and arrested ten of them. Of those who escaped, about eight arrived at the Embassy and were turned away.

Since the arrests, Bernard Stone has organised a petition from surrounding shopkeepers stating that there was no obstruction. It is believed by some of those involved in the demonstration and the events preceding it, that the CIA are behind the arrests: 1. There has been an official clamp down on press coverage of the arrests. 2. The 'wilful obstruction' arrests were made at a time and place where it is customary for people to gather. 3. One of the most vociferous demonstrators, Asa Benveniste, had his home burgled professionally, but little was taken. The next day his printing press was broken into. All metal typefaces and ancillary utensils were destroyed or taken. The low price for scrap lead and metal rule out the theft motive. The police did not take finger-prints.

(This report was prepared with the co-operation of Sonia Sharkey and International Times.)

KINEMATOGRAPH WEEKLY: April 27, 1968

A DIFFERENT APPROACH TO

IN COLD BLOOD

COLUMBIA has certainly produced a different campaign book for "In Cold Blood." This was done because the company feels the picture demands very careful thought from managers and a really sensibly conceived and executed campaign. The conventional approaches and conventional printing were therefore thrown overboard.

Local press—"tell them about it as far in advance of your playdate as possible," Columbia suggests. And then send periodic reminders, and possibly copies of the Penguin book. Editors, music critics, women's page writes, should all have a special interest, because of the film's content.

At the theatre in advance of playdate Columbia believe a personal letter on normal letter paper, and personally signed, and displayed on the newsboard, or blown up and displayed in a glazed frame on a prominently sited easel, would provide the necessary personal approach to patrons. (And there's a suggested text too.)

Nearer playdate, out-out film reviews from local and national papers could be added to the letter, and so make a special display panel.

Another advance theatre activity could be a talk to the audience from the stage—not a long speech, but a sincere word of recommendation. Again the text is provided.

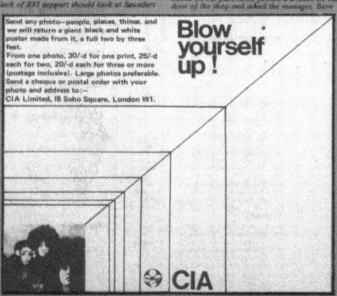

Heisenberg had a theory about electrons. They jig about in a rather excited way, and Heisenberg's Theory of Indeterminacy, as t's called, infers that the behavious of electrons is so unpredictable you can never tell where they are at. Heisenberg would have been in his element at the Digger's Conference.

Carefully non-organised as an unstructured event, it looked like a shambles, spoke with the gift of tongues (all at once) and by Sunday night, seemed something of a success.

Friday evening, as the lady form the Guardian pointed out, (with greater kindness than perhaps was deserved) started out with something of a false start. About 150 people turned up at the Anti-U. In the confined space at 49 Rivington St, things took on something of the crowd quality of St Peter's Square on Easter Sunday. (Elias Canetti would have been ecstatic).

So we lit out of the local church hall. On the way, Policeman G 253, (I think, he was very tall) accosted a gorup walking over and demanded to know why Hackney police had not been informed of the 'march'. A polite reply that the 'march' was only peaceable citizens walking round the corner to church was answered with a string of remarks indicating the Constable's extreme distaste for communal livers. After we had crossed the street, someone whispered 'Blue Fascist', loudly and honour was satisfied.

(For a fee) the local parson was very interested in accommodating communal living. The only hang up was, did we mind the concreters. Some parishioners were repairing the stairs to the choir loft, they would need to fill their buckets at the tap in the hall just behind the speakers, and they would, of course, be unable to wheel their barrows any other way but through the crowd. McLuhan says in an age of accelerating transience we have to forget trying to adjust our frames of reference to new conditions, they are gone and replaced before we have even thought about them. So a good natured crowd ignored the concreters and settled down to hear the first speakers, Laing group psychiatrists, David Cooper and Joe Berke, David and Joe spoke briefly, eloquently, pertinently and way above the heads of the audience, who listened patiently and then sullenly, and finally resentfully began addressing themselves. A transience of form accelerated by the Exploding Galaxy (present in strength) beginning their performance a full two days earlier than scheduled. So it was a non-structured event. Right? Right! One of their members, wearing a huge Mexican hat full of wood shavings commandeered the speakers table, eyed the crowd, and gobbled like a Christmas turkey threatened with the axe. They cheered. And maybe they were right.

As someone diagnosed later, the new order is almost unable to express itself in language and finds little reward in the anachronism of the dialectic. The meeting was thrown open and 150 voices set about each other. The loudest of them belonged to Sid Rawle, self-styled 'unique friend and adviser' to the Hyde Park Diggers, (denounced by another speaker as primitive capitalists) who strode, cape aswirl to the centre of the hall and announced in full stentor, 'This is a bloody shambles,' a sentiment requiting little perception, but Sid declined to elaborate and sat down. A few speakers came to the front and attempted to articulate their anguish or confusion, but failed or were unheard. Everyone else was sitting about the floor in groups rapping. Communicating. As the Galaxy exploded round them. It might have gone on all night.

But the System, in this case represented by the Vicar, was very uptight about any sort of 'happening' and the organisers weren't too handy with the relevant biblical text to calm him down. So the hall was cleared and most of the group returned to the Anti-U where they rapped affectively, serious'/, till late.

Saturday afternoon, about 90 people returned to the Anti-U for seminars with members of existing communities. George Ineson a member of a Gloucester community which has been operating successfully for 20 years, was probably the most interesting of the speakers. Ineson indicated the problems of communal living with great clarity, but the discussion groups seemed reluctant to tackle the two real bugaboos of any social set-up, money and sex. As Alan Krebs, remarked, 'They're afraid to reach out and touch the peckers of the dragons'. And the session closed without any St George showing up.

Sunday's session was at Middle Earth. It was intended to be a workshop conducted by Leon Redler, but it was a sunny day, so he played baseball on Primrose Hill. As touchingly expatriate an activity as the Australian anti-Vietnam people disrupting Anzac Day at the Cenotaph. Improvising, the organisers attempted a little crafty structuring by arranging the only available seating in the form of concentric circles and the afternoon went off just like a Quaker prayer meeting, with quite remarkable raport.

The man from the Free Bookshop complained at length, that he just couldn't seem to give anything away. Nobody wanted to take. Only swap. So everyone promised to come and denude his shelves sometime soon. Address: Coleherne Mews, Wharfedale St. SW10, PAD 2409. Open 6–10 weekdays, 10–6 Saturdays.

Emmanuel Petrakis spieled for the New Life community, but made it clear he didn't want anyone with hangups, after all his was a 'family' community. Address: New Life, 15 Camden Hill Rd, Gypsy Hill, SE19.

Nick Stapleton announced that a commune was starting in Potter's Bar and did anyone want to join? Address: 39 Highfield Way, Potter's Bar.

Muz Murray revealed that a Europe-wide list of crashpads was being prepared and paper and pencils were passed. Nearly everyone with a roof over their heads put their names down. The idea is being spread. Starting with the next issue of OZ, this list will be published in a form suitable for future reference. If you would like to add to the list pleasewrite to Crashpads, c/o OZ, 38a Palace Gdns Terrace, London W8.

Someone else threatened to burn his last 10/- note. And even lit the match. But a gaunt Galaxy man cried out that it should be used to buy food. Someone shouted 'diggers do' and on cue coins showered into the centre of the group. They were collected and eventually almost everyone got a bite of a cheese roll. Those that missed out were told that Greg Sam's Macrobiotic Restaurant, 136 Westbourne Park Rd. W2, gives out free food Sunday nights.

Finally, the Exploding Galaxy, having patiently endured Sunday's extended session, gave a workshop performance of the Buddha ballet which had sufficient magic to transform each member of the Forum into one of the Budddha's five hundred milch cows. It seemed a nice communal way to close.

War is hell. Yeah! And draft dodging isn't all that much fun either (would you rather be shot or would you rather starve in exile?). The summer draft offensive in America will see a significant escalation of draft dodgers in London. They'll need jobs and accomodation. If you can help, contact, Liz Salt, c/o support Advisory Council for American Resisters, 4 Shavers Place, Haymarket, London SW1. After all your mothers loved their fathers in 1942.

if Robert Kennedy were Jean Luc Godard he'd make movies like Don Levy's first feature Herostratus, playing this month at the new ICA, Carlton House, The Mall.

A perfectly assured technique of great adventurousness confronts the 'issues' of our time with incredible intensity and such ruthless commitment that audiences emerge white-faced, as wrought as heroine Gabriella Licudi who breaks down completely in the final scene. And she's not acting.

If you've ever thought there might be more to movies than Busby Berkely, see it.

FADING FREEDOMS/LAT
HIPPIE HIGH HOPES:

THE STORY SO FAR:—
Sections 1–4 of this non-linear political mosaic appeared in OZ No 11. Section 1 suggested that freedom is meaningless unless defined in terms of power, and compared the Socialists' and the Conservatives' claims to being the party of freedom; suggesting that, on balance, the party of planning left more people freer than that of free enterprise for top people. Section 2 thought that anarchists were usually too sentimental in assuming that it's natural, egalitarian and comradely; they ought also to allow for right-wing (competitive) and 'black' (sadistic) anarchism. And the internal contraints needed for anarchy needn't necessarily by less tyrannical than our external ones. Section 3 looked enviously at another aspect of right-wing anarchism: the para-hippie irresponsibility enjoyed anyway by our upper classes, and its grim consequences for the rest of us, as top people team up with American and European finance and say 'Up the Union Jack, I'm all right' to middle and lower-class Britain. Section 4 wondered how the hippie pitch would be queered by Britain's decline and, if not fall, then stagnation or only slow rise, and concluded that the best situation would be a very slow rise with absolutely no Dunkirk spirit.
NOW READ ON:—

5 In Which Sir Oswald Mosley is Sympathetically Considered.

If Fascism, like right-wing anarchism, lacks a voice, it is for the same reason; whoever claims absolute power arouses sales resistance. One understands Fascism amongst one's friends, but never in public debate, when it becomes that deep deep black mass in comparison to which one's own dirty grey seems as white as democratic white. Yet it's as pervasively around us as the air we breathe.

In theory, at least, Fascism could evolve into just what Hitler called it, 'National Socialism'. In fact it loses Communism's traditional drawback, its allegiance to the working classes of the world, who are either too vague, or wogs, or Moscow spies. And when Russian Bolshevism's massive bureaucratic apparatus, instead of withering away, turned into Stalinism, National Socialism was, perhaps, just what it was, only with the bureaucrats playing the capitalists as well as themselves. But Stalin and de Gaulle remembered what Napoleon and the Marxists ignored; a nation is, economically as well as culturally, a class; one, admittedly, that criss-crosses others, but a class all the same. It was nasty, but it was only human, of the German little man to believe that, one day, he too would be an aristocrat; that is one of the herrenvolk.

Seen in this light, Mosley's sudden switch from the Labour party, in which he was all set for a brilliant career, to a Fascist plank, ceases to be inexplicable, and becomes a perfectly intelligible calculation, showing more logic than flair. He foresaw that, when it came to a showdown, the Labour party's nerve would always fail it. The leaders' surrender that ended the General Strike stemmed not only from the forelock-toucher's awe of those top hats, not only from the streak of peace-at-any-price meekness that creeps into the labour movement through its middle-class connections, but from a matter-of-fact recognition that victory would mean taking over the country, in the teeth of a mutinous middle and upper class, and international finance ie. the 1926 Gnomes of Zurich. Parliamentary action would run into the same trouble, in another form (the Labour government would end, like Wilson, frantically running the capitalist machine). Mosley reckoned that nerve was needed, and a readiness to turn patriotism, hysteria, compulsion, anything, against the establishment machine. Unfortunately for himself, Mosley made the odd mistake of imagining that the workers wouldn't fear Fascism more than they feared Conservatism. His movement brought in the lower middle class elements whose chief bugaboo was Communism (and similarly in Germany, Nazism was strongest among the middle classes, weakest among the working classes). Even Mosley's jingo plank failed; his similarities with Nazism gave him the image of a Nazi spy. His anti-Semitism was infinitely more revolting, and less plausible, than the prevalent form of colour-prejudice today.

To the three preconditions of Fascism proper (industrial rhythms, hierarchy, nationalism), we can add a fourth: a sense of crisis. The best brooding ground for Fascism is one in which one group can reasonably hope to keep power over other groups, but only by straining every nerve, by mobilising every resource. The English Tories gave up early in the 19th century, when they realised they couldn't take on middle and working classes together; they switched to compromises with democracy instead, and that's why England is the land of democracy, freedom, compromise and peaceful evolution. Germany was unluckier; A J P Taylor sees Nazism as deriving spiritual sustenance from Prussian Junker experience as a poor aristocracy dominating a vast population of Prussian and Slav serfs by efficiency alone. The French scene is so fragmented that shaky coalitions alternate with weak, but nasty, Fascist spurts (Boulangism, M Coty's mercenaries of the '30s, Vichyism, Poujadism, OASism), because her social diversity creates bitter, on-a-knife-edge situations very tempting to opportunists. Macchiavelli's words are still true; for every revolution undertaken by the poor, ten are undertaken by the rich. Hence the Western fear of Moscow, whose guns and gold make the poor rich.

T FASCISMS &

A Paranoid Guide

by Raymond Durgnat

It also seems that there's such a thing as democratic Fascism; a prosperous majority permanently, and violently, oppressing a wretched minority. The American negro is such a minority. (It's ironic that Nazi propaganda against America wasn't quite as distorted as it then seemed). But the most popular form of Fascism is that which consists of exporting one's proletariat. One lets one's workers at home into some sort of prosperity; it profits, with one's bourgeoisie, at the expense of the coloured proletariat of the third world. In popular language, this becomes 'bash the wogs', and those portions of the English working-class which rise above the level of such responses tend to become somewhat resigned to the possibility of such responses and tend to adopt the callous, or a philosophical, that is to say, an actively or passively Fascist, attitude, towards the exploitation of the ex-colonial world.

What makes it all more difficult is that this Fascism is the keystone of our prosperity, of our liberalism, of our freedom; that to attack it is not only treacherous to many of our friends (only idealists won't mind that) but masochistic, unless one can locate oneself in those curious God's-eye-views from which intellectuals love to look down on mere mortals. Only this is certain; you can't put the third world, and the British working-man, first, and the Labour movement is due for much more trouble as this problem looms. For 'third world' read the Jews, and you can easily solve the mystery of how so many good Germans could live alongside the concentration camps.

A Conservative Revolution?

The Conservatives are right to see a powerful bureaucracy as a potentially Fascist class. As Ernest Mandel remarked, the Russian revolution set up a party bureaucracy, which, as Tory commonsense, and Marx's own basic principles, might have warned it, would put its own interests first. But everyone can see the danger and the Conservatives only obscured it by the obviousness of their motivations, as well as by that endless and inane Conservative attempt to link Socialism and tyranny, which goes back to the forging of the Zinoviev letter in the '20s, through Churchill's utterly serious allegation that the 1945 Attlee administration would put Harold Laski in charge of its Gestapo, and goes on every day in the Daily Telegraph's Peter Simple.

As subsequent elements have made clear, the creeping extension of control is as irreversible as inflation. There is a Parkinson's law of loss of liberty. A Labour government introduced peacetime conscription for the first time in English history, a Conservative government continued it. For nearly 20 years now, 'they' have been requiring university authorities to inform them which students belong to far left political clubs—just for reference, of course. A study of changing police attitudes would reveal the gradual, but steady increase in the docility it expects from the public. Since 1945, they were encouraged in this by the public's satisfaction with affluence, with tradition, with all things moral and British.

Now that the political consensus—or stalemate—is shifting, this happy relationship is shifting too. The unarmed London police beat down mass demonstrations throughout the '30s, and are traditionally paranoiac about anything that involves street crowds. Now middle-class people are coming down into the street, people who are less hopeless, and better equipped to complain in the press, about police attitudes, a new line of friction is opening.

Of course, individual waves roll back, even as the tide moves in. We've already gained on some roundabouts (general sexual permissiveness) what we've lost on some swings. Its even arguable that our increased consciousness of bureaucratization results largely from a gain in insight. We know, now, who conditions us, how, why, and how unfree we are, within as well as without. For Acts of God, read Acts of Parliament. However niggling bureaucracy is, the Means Test isn't back—yet. And even in the '30s, Orwell saw the life of the British 'little man' as ruled by nothing else than stark, simple fear. To compare **Coming Up For Air** to **1984** leaves little doubt that Orwell was drawing on the moods of 1934. We're obviously all freer now than the victims of the Depression's callous chaos.

One would expect a Labour bureaucracy to be preferable to a Conservative one, simply because the party's social centre of gravity is lower. If Labour make aggravatingly timid advances in social reform (abortion, homosexuality, divorce, etc), the Conservatives make no advances whatsoever where money isn't involved, and in such cases they always defer to traditions, those which limit freedom, included. Of course, they would curb the closed shop, out of the purest love of Olde English Liberty. The choice is between a bureaucracy which occasionally bares toothless gums at big business, and one which is willing to act as the agent of big business, in polishing off the cumbersome dinosaur with which the working-class defends itself. There is also, of course, a conservative bureaucracy—including J.Ps, lawyers, and other traditionalist groups. In comparison with the other bureaucracy, it hardly shines for its reasonableness, its concern with the individual, or its freedom gray red tape.

The present threat to freedom comes from a popular quarter. As Britain hits hard times, as freeze, squeeze and cut stalk the land and the old consensus breaks up, politics repolarise. Certain overtones in the I'm Backing Britain campaign are a straw in the wind. My friendly radio dealer said, with an air of finality, 'It's not actually a British model, of course'. (He seemed to think the Philips was). A millionaire gets at the children: 'Little girl, get rickets for Britain.' The government is helpless in the face of a thousand little rises in price (but can cut down on school milk). The Race Relations Act proves all but useless against white prejudice, but is immediately evoked against Michael X, and Roy Sawh. As for loveable, fallible George Brown, his remarks about the Omsbudman remind us just how much he resents the lightest pinprick from a character who is virtually castrated by his brief. As for Smiling Jim Callaghan, who previously represented police interests in parliament, bids fair to be the Home Secretary in the Henry Brooke tradition.

On the Conservative side, developments are even more alarming. John Hurford
The supposedly patriotic party is as ready to encourage the Rhodesian rebels now as it was ready to scheme with the Ulster mutineers in 1914. The Enoch Powell-Duncan Sandys axis is more confident, more interesting, than ever before. Conservative rhetoric about Britain's economic crisis comes down to, 'My workers should tighten their belts out of patriotism while I get my expense account lunches back to give me more incentive.' A handful of silly secretaries work an extra half an hour for their bosses, while business sticks 'I'm backing Britain' stickers on everything from its Japanese ballpens to its Volkswagen The dishonesty was so flagrant it backfired, superbly; everything the camp Union Jack brigade had done in jest was done in earnest.

As gutless as ever, Labour starts trussing up the unions, to such an extent that it might be better off in opposition, resisting the Conservative campaign which is bound to follow. Tough, dynamic, enterprising Mr Wilson blames the gnomes of Zurich, because he knows as well as we do that a great many of those gnomes had English names and addresses, but he doesn't like to say so, because there'd then be more gnomes of Zurich than ever. Of course they're not being unpatriotic, but they have to protect their investments, and, in the long run, what's good for them is good for Britain.

How numerous and short are the paths from 1968 to 1984 might be indicated by a (frankly artificial) scenario, one of many possible ones. Crisis worsens. Labour government in head on shock with unions. Labour movement splits, Wilson resigns, general elections, thumping Conservative majority. Showdown with unions; general strike. Middle classes patriotically silly and break strike. New policies decided on to distract attention from austerity. Conservatives adapt Liberal co-ownership schemes,

with owners to retain 51% interest. Combination of depression and workers competing against others improves labour disciplines no end. Since the workers are in a minority against an owners/bureaucracy/middle-class united front, and that is tied to the gnomes of Zurich, who is working for whom? General discontent, and government institutes one-year national labour service to soak up unemployment among young, especially coloured. Informal employers' organisations hire Tracers Ltd to keep photographic record of labour agitators. And so it goes. There'd be no need to legislate against freedom of speech, provided only that the middle classes could be kept frightened of, and uninterested in, the lower classes. It's at this point that the scheme shows its artificiality; the middle classes are just as frightened of the upper classes. And how right they are.

Snarling Through

Since 1951 the English right has been relatively reasonable. Three major lessons inspired this policy. The first was the 19th-century upper-class realisation that it couldn't hold the country down by force if the middle and lower classes combined against it. The same logic underlay England's attitude to empire. No colony was interesting if the cost of tyranny exceeded the returns in trade; to hold India down in 1945 would have ruined Britain. Giving the Empire away, though it chagrined Churchill, was financially painless; the red left the map, but the trade links remained. The third lesson, taught by Keynes, proved by Schacht, and imposed on the Conservatives by the Attlee government, was that working-class affluence helps trade by increasing its spending-power and broadening the home market. The welfare state and the unions rankled with Conservative suburbia, and the middle class little man who had lost his status vis-a-vis the better-off workers; but big business didn't mind in the least, and big business called the Conservative tune. Not via the rank-and-file, so much as via the Conservative leaders—always, so mystifyingly, to the left of Peter Simple's leaders. For years they, loyal to a man, never murmured against their leaders, simply seething at (a) the trade unions and (b) a curious abstraction called 'the state' or 'bureaucracy'. This curiously omitted the Conservative ministers who headed and extended it and the public-school network which determined its policies. Eventually two things sharpened intra-Conservative strife. But suddenly the party found itself with a middle-class leader; he lacked that magic authority, grumblings began. And the country ran into the economic trouble for which it had been heading since the 19th century.

On the Labour side, Attlee was determined to minimise bitterness. He nationalised minimally, compensated maximally, co-operated with big business. Little business felt it was being taxed to death but working-class cash poured into the till and salved hurt pride.

Thus Conservative and Liberal policy converged in a consensus, which also seemed admirably liberal. And by pre-war standards certainly was. Suez was the first hint that the consensus wasn't altogether liberal, and though the Labour left pretended otherwise it knew perfectly well that the majority of its supporters favoured bashing that wog Nasser. Fortunately for Gaitskell, the Americans pulled the rug from under Eden's feet. But Suez served to rally the first of a series of youthful 'waves', whose selfless indignation was doubtless sharpened by the denial of equal rights and opportunities in a stagnant society.

The first wave were the 'Angry young men', and the brief boom in the *New Left* as it ebbed, baffled, the first trickle of 'emancipated' public-school boys joined up with a second wave and produced the satirists. Concurrently, gifted non-intellectuals set up the pop and Carnaby St circuits. Last came the Underground, whose very radicalism entailed a retreat from *now* politics. There was a diminuendo, not of seriousness, and not of importance, but of confidence in involvement, a shift from positive politico-cultural goals to a systematic scepticism to the leisure ghetto and lastly to inner-outer space.

Not so long ago, it was easy to assume that the young fellow who expressed a passionate discontent with society must be left-wing. Several angry young men thought so too although eventually their anger turned out to be a matter of frustrated conservatism rather than of frustrated progressivism. It's high time we stopped being surprised, or shrieking 'sell-out', when John Braine, Kingsley Amis, Malcolm Muggeridge, Bernard Levin and others turn out not to be the left-wingers we took them for. Or when David Frost switches from hawk to dove and dons a new face as TV's Godfrey Winn (and these days, the sparks fly higher on Panorama). (And have you noticed how solemn **Mad** became on the subject of Cuban exiles and anti-Castroism?) The right wing always had its intellectuals, but ignored them, as did everybody else, in consequence of which they tended to be rather Brand X. Because what they advocated depended on tradition rather than thought. The current crisis calls the consensus in question, and the right turns to arguments again. Simon Raven and Anthony Burgess shot their bolt a little early; Raven's The English Gentleman appeared in 1961 and now he just nags. St. John Stevas emerges as the Tory answer to Carnaby St, and says, in almost so many words on TV, that the mindless masses need to be mystified by the romanticism of royalty. He's quite right to sense that this argument can be stated openly. Each TV viewer thinks of the mindless masses as all the others, that he is 'in the know' in the mystificatory process. Enoch Powell advocates an antediluvian laissez-faire which he can't take seriously. He seems to be trying to make the complete takeover of the little man by the big combines seem like the triumph of the little man. It's so obvious that even big business is scared of him. What else can one make of economic principles which would require him to denationalise the army, navy, and airforce, not to mention the Church of England, and auction them off to the highest bidder, who would employ them as mercenaries, or as missionaries with an obligation to mention 'Coca-Cola' twice in every sermon? Any day now General Motors will put in a takeover bid for the Conservative party, and even I thought I might be only joking until I read this in **The Listener**, 29/2/68:

'Britain lost an empire in North America in 1783, but important cultural links have survived and flourished. For although British goods may no longer be in much demand there, the British way of life still remains a very marketable commodity. In return the Americans might be invited over to run our industries which, no doubt, they will do considerably better than we can. A suitably patrician prime minister might even be able to present our absorption as yet another in the long series of triumphs of British skill and diplomacy.'

Duncan Sandys too has spotted his opportunity. What Suez was to the authentically left-wing minority, immigration could be to the basically right-wing majority. Have you read the new **Tatler** lately?

/over...

The Tribe of the Sacred Mushroom.

Is the Muse of Satire the Midwife of Corruption?

8

Bureaucracy is the big bad wolf. Every fashionable body is anarchist. Swinging Britain is go-ahead Britain. In some undefined way there's no contradiction between affording Carnaby St prices and quadrupling every old age pension. Every lord's son feels quite fond of Mao, because he's so refreshingly different from Sir Alec Douglas Home. Every Carnaby St pattern-cutter thrills to the saga of Fidel and Che, as do those flower-power pacifists whose principles forbid them to squash a human fly under their finger-nail. Rightwing or leftwing, what does it matter, the enemy is the consensus which the various establishments have created between them.

The ambiguity of all this detachment may be expressed in terms of Private Eye. The paper itself inherits a curious, and likeable alloy of attitudes: the indignation of the nonconformist conscience; the lordly cynicism and contempt of an aristocratic identification, especially at the expense of Mrs Wilson; upper-middle-class snobbery at the expense of the lower-middle-class (Mrs Wilson again); intellectual-fashionable snobbery at the expense of the middle and upper class; the rage of a generation fed on futile myths by its fathers; in brief, it exploits every possible contradiction between every kind of idealism and every kind of reality.

The most disquieting aspect of this largely admirable (and valuably informative) paper is one of its readership groups, namely, the advertising agency S-men who need to pull a fortnightly face at the thin smears left on their tastebuds by ratrace brownnosing. They think pulling a face spiritually disengages them from the system; P.E. is their raspberry-rosary. And simultaneously satire proves that everything is only a racket and that they can pursue their own racket with a clear conscience. It purges one's self-hatred and anesthetises one's conscience.

The detachment of middle class youth from the vindictive complacency of traditional Conservatism isn't worthless, and in the present climate of opinion, this anarcho-nihilist right is undoubtably preferable, first because though it's more cynical it's less self-righteous, second, because it's less anti-Communist and therefore less anti-Third-World, third, because it'll briefly fellow-travel with the left on account of its own frustrations, fourth, because it's more respectful than it knows of liberalism and more sentimental than it knows about certain facts of life which the left doesn't want to know, thank you very much, which the right, being confusionistic, can't articulate, and which only get mentioned clearly by such great and isolated cynics as Macchiavelli, Hobbes and a few of the other great unread (or ungrasped), and, fifth, because it's libertarian rather than authoritarian.

But there's always the possibility that such cynicism should become a dominant mode, and if the middle-class continues losing confidence in its own sentimentalities, we might come nearer an American or a French situation, where the incorruptibility of the bureaucracy can't be taken for granted, where the rightwing would be relatively free from traditional restraints and blindnesses, where the middle-class would throw off its nonconformist guilt towards the less fortunate, where what is now done apologetically would be done systematically, and British politics would become hard-edge, energetic, brutal and irresponsible.

OZ SUBSCRIPTION

"Excuse Me, is this the way to the Gas Chambers?"

What actually has happened in Britain? A couple of politicians have exploited the race question? Some crowds have waved racialist banners? What's changed? The presence of racialism has nothing to do with the activities of Parliamentarians, it's always there. True, but now a strange cutting process has been completed. For nearly a decade politicians have been gently fanning the race issue; extremely frightened of what they were doing, wanting to soak it up rather than start anything big. Now after the Enoch Powell affair, everyone can see that the fire really was blazing all the time, and everything that is done from now on will be in some sense a response to a situation in which racialism is one of the fixed institutions of political life. When they started the long string of capitulations on the question of immigration, they cast their bread upon the waters; in return there has floated back a solid mass of well-nurtured fascism. Hundreds of dockers marched to Parliament to demand further cuts in immigration and to express support for an extremist Conservative.

Meanwhile from the militant left, famous for its dockside agitation, there came the deafening roar of silence. While a wave of 'chuck-out-the-blacks' strikes and demonstrations erupted, only a few students marched in the opposite direction. The trade union leadership did nothing. The unofficial leadership did nothing. The Labour Party did nothing.

What has happened is that eight hundred thousand coloured people, most of whom have migrated to Britain in the recent past, are now psychologically encircled. They have always had their troubles—now they have become one of the centres of political life. It is assumed as a national fact that most people hate them. Everybody in Britain—including the militant race-haters—knows that all that talk about cutting-down immigration was only a way of preparing the country for the real business of degrading and destroying the black community. There is no debate about the question, there can't be, because nobody in authority any longer wants to rehearse the facts; they merely wish to define their positions and attitudes as a matter of further political convenience. We are scrambling up the down escalator; it's hard enough to stay on the same spot.

Nonetheless they all know that:

there are well under a million coloured people in Britain.
It is now impossible to get in legally unless you are
    actually needed for a highly skilled job.

more people leave the country than enter it.
immigrants demand less of the social services than the rest
    of the population.
the rickety transport, health and postal services would
    collapse altogether if the immigrant population took it into their heads to depart.
the injection of another more vital and dynamic culture is exactly what this exhausted country needs.

But meanwhile, whatever elected representatives care to believe, bureaucratised racialism is on the increase; income tax officials, welfare authorities, port immigration officials and above all the police, riddled as all bureaucracies are with the pin-headed species of dictatorship, are now operating in a situation in which discrimination is an easy path to popularity. Every new law published to deal with the statistical delusion of excessive immigration, makes every law against discrimination three times harder to enforce.

Britain is stuffed with festering resentment; at no other time in its history has there existed such a contrast between our image and the reality. We want everyone to think we are merry, bright, falsely modest, brilliantly decadent. It is a neon picture stuck on a crumbling old building, but we enjoy the way it glitters. Every now and again the millions who are obliged to live out their lives in appallingly drab and uncomfortable homes, who perform idiot jobs in bad conditions, who watch every facility from transport to the health service, from the police force to the education system, gradually decline into frustrating incompetence and then are told that the degeneration is their fault and that they must accept further reduction and decline every now and then, these people (most of us), notice the gulf between the colourful sophisticated picture and the hollow truth and the shock deepens the frustration, and the frustration turns to hatred.

Racialism is one of the purer forms of hatred. It is very satisfying feeling; it gives you a sense of belonging to a group; it cuts through the complex issues; it removes dilemmas and suggests easy solutions. It feels radical, even revolutionary. If you can look at your neighbours and hate them straight, without knowing their names or jobs, you can feel comfortingly engulfed, threatened; you are brave, standing firm, uncomplicated, purged of irrelevancies. You know what's wrong with the country, you don't have to be told, you can see for yourself.

The politicians have fed Britain, during elections and between elections, on lies and illusions. Now ordinary indecent people are feeding the politicians back with a newly manufactured lie and illusion—that our troubles are the fault of the blacks. Racialism comes from below for the most part—hey presto, the politicians are weak enough to be swayed.

'This is not a racial matter', said the Tories in 1962 when they fought through the first measures to prevent the free entry of all British subjects in the teeth of Labour Opposition. 'This has nothing to do with Race' said the Labour Party when they maintained and strengthened the same laws a year or two later. 'We denounce the gross slur of racialism' said Harold Wilson as he passed emergency legislation to stop the free entry of Asians form Kenya. 'We will not tolerate racialists in our party' cries Mr Heath as he manoeuvres his party into opposing the new laws to prohibit discrimination. 'This has nothing to do with colour' say the leaders of the dockers who marched to the House of Commons to demand measures to reverse the flow of immigrants. That is the way we go about our business in Great Britain.

The entrenchment of racism into politics was an easy though a delicate process and it was historically speaking, quite rapid. It was a zig-zag path in which everyone, once they let go of principle, quickly came to hold the view which they had denounced two years previously as blind bigotry. The only rule in the game is to keep in step; if you lag behind the general drift you will be denounced for being wildly unrealistic ('nobody wants uncontrolled immigration any more'); if you rush too far ahead, you'll be given the chop (poor mad Enoch).

This steady political evolution is however gaining speed and it will lead as far as the racialists want to take it; no organisation exists to stop them. Given the profound socio-economic crisis that Britain is going through, the basis exists for them to get beyond the 'chuck em out' stage, the question is probably only how and not if rioting will start in Britain. The real danger is that the coloured community will endure also less period of passivity before starting to defend themselves. Unfortunately violence is the only language the racialist understands.

In the meantime, the demand that immigrant Pakistanis and West Indians learn to behave in precisely the same way as the rest of us do is one of the more self-destroying demands of white racism. Most references to 'integration' are made in a context of fantasy or importance. So enduring is the heritage of Britain's imperial past, that the British of all social classes continue to assume that the values of the donor society are the only values available. Such is the legacy of a situation in which one society physically owned another series of societies for generations. If anyone wants to know why Britain is developing a major form of race conflict, that is why. We have lost in any case the will, let alone the leadership to make it otherwise.

| 17th May: | Mr Mo's Messengers & The Firestone Plus Light Show |
| 31st May: | The George Paul Jefferson The Light Brigade |

ROYAL COLLEGE OF ART BAR PARTIES

8 - 11 p.m. 2 groups, 2 bars. o/d
Jay Mews, Kensington Gore.

WHAT IS it

Smallz OZ adz workz wonderz
smalls: 1s0d per per word; 1s6d semidisplay; 2s6d box no
Display: £65 per page; £35 half page; £2 10s 6d per col ins

FRENCH JEANS
& SKIN-TIGHT SHIRTS.

CONCERT! MAY 26 OZ BENEFIT CONCERT! MAY 26 OZ BENEFIT CONCERT! MAY 26 OZ BENEFIT
CONCERT! MAY 26 OZ BENEFIT CONCERT! MAY 26 OZ BENEFIT CONCERT! MAY 26 OZ BENEFIT
CONCERT! MAY 26 OZ BENEFIT CONCERT! MAY 26 OZ BENEFIT CONCERT! MAY 26 OZ BENEFIT
CONCERT! MAY 26 OZ BENEFIT CONCERT! MAY 26 OZ BENEFIT CONCERT! MAY 26 OZ BENEFIT

Come, have your mind blown at Middle Earth on Sunday, May 26 It's OZ Benefit Night. ★ Incredible big name groups ★ Incredible small name groups ★ **Sexy Barney Bubbles Light Show** ★ Underground films ★ Overground films ★ Soldiers (see them drilling!) ★ Happenings ★ Whatever else we can think of. For the latest good news phone Felix Dennis at 385:4539 (evenings) or Middle Earth 240:1327.

Desire can be destroyed

A TOUCH OF THE SEX JOLLIES

	yes		
	no	yes	no
	no	yes	yes
	yes	no	no
	no	yes	mmm

It's the living groove: a pocket docket of arresting hints, helps and happiness

There's a whole mess of taste action in your baking powder lady— and we ain't foolin'.

All you need is EAR

Pop · R&B · Blues · Beatles · R&R · Folk · Test · Nirvana

Existence is unhappiness

Unhappiness is caused by desire or craving

Get into the pub, up in the air with the Coca-Cola Gay Desperados steel orchestra. Brandenburg Concerto No 4 or G major, No 5 or D minor, No 6 or E flat minor. Intergalactic Odyssey by John Cage.

SORROW!

b

Delusion of self

Delusion of Self

Sensuality

Desire for a Future Life

Pride

Love of Life on Earth

One for the boys

Day for the girls

Self Righteousness

Subhighteousness

Ignorance

Ill Will

Doubt

Clear away False Beliefs

white
whine
chine
chink
clink
blank
black

The world of wonders 1

The world of wonders 2

The world of wonders 2

The world of wonders 2

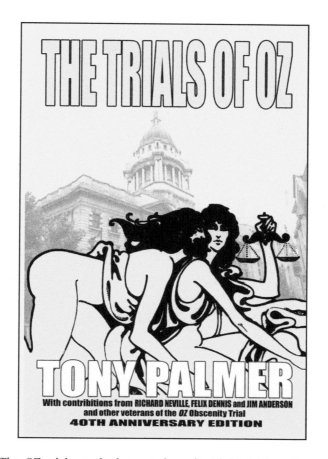

The *OZ* trial was the longest obscenity trial in history. It was also one of the worst reported. With minor exceptions, the Press chose to rewrite what had occurred, presumably to fit in with what seemed to them the acceptable prejudices of the times. Perhaps this was inevitable.

The proceedings dragged on for nearly six weeks in the hot summer of 1971 when there were, no doubt, a great many other events more worthy of attention. Against the background of murder in Ulster, for example, the *OZ* affair probably fades into its proper insignificance. Even so, after the trial, when some newspapers realised that maybe something important had happened, it became more and more apparent that what was essential was for anyone who wished to be able to read what had actually been said. Trial and judgment by a badly informed press became the order of the day. This 40th Anniversary edition includes new material by all three of the original defendants, the prosecuting barrister, one of the *OZ* schoolkids, and even the daughters of the judge. There are also many illustrations including unseen material from Felix Dennis' own collection...

ALSO AVAILABLE FROM GONZO MULTIMEDIA

Gonzo

Books

There is still such a thing as alternative Publishing

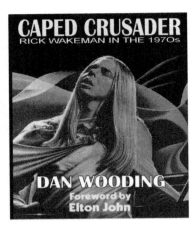

Robert Newton Calvert: Born 9 March 1945, Died 14 August 1988 after suffering a heart attack. Contributed poetry, lyrics and vocals to legendary space rock band Hawkwind intermittently on five of their most critically acclaimed albums, including Space Ritual (1973), Quark, Strangeness & Charm (1977) and Hawklords (1978). He also recorded a number of solo albums in the mid 1970s. CENTIGRADE 232 was Robert Calvert's first collection of poems.

Hype   'And now, for all you speed ing street smarties out there, the one you've all been waiting for, the one that'll pierce your laid back ears, decoke your sinuses, cut clean thru the schlock rock, MOR/crossover, techno flash mind mush. It's the new Number One with a bullet … with a bullet … It's Tom, Supernova, Mahler with a pan galac tic biggie …' And the Hype goes on. And on. Hype, an amphetamine hit of a story by Hawkwind collaborator Robert Calvert. Who's been there and made it back again. The debriefing session starts here.

Rick Wakeman is the world's most unusual rock star, a genius who has pushed back the barriers of electronic rock. He has had some of the world's top orchestras perform his music, has owned eight Rolls Royces at one time, and has broken all the rules of com posing and horrified his tutors at the Royal College of Music. Yet he has delighted his millions of fans. This frank book, authorised by Wakeman himself, tells the moving tale of his larger than life career.

"So many books, so little time."
Frank Zappa

There are nine Henrys, pur
ported to be the world's
first cloned cartoon charac
ter. They live in a strange
lo fi domestic surrealist
world peopled by talking
rock buns and elephants on
wobbly stilts.

They mooch around in their
minimalist universe suffer
ing from an existential
crisis with some genetically
modified humour thrown in.

Marty Wilde on Terry Dene: "Whatever
happened to Terry becomes a great deal
more comprehensible as you read of the
callous way in which he was treated by
people who should have known better
many of whom, frankly, will never know
better   of the sad little shadows of
the past who eased themselves into
Terry's life, took everything they
could get and, when it seemed that all
was lost, quietly left him … Dan Wood
ing's book tells it all."

Rick Wakeman: "There have
always been certain 'careers'
that have fascinated the
public, newspapers, and the
media in general. Such
include musicians, actors,
sportsmen, police, and not
surprisingly, the people who
give the police their employ
ment: The criminal. For the
man in the street, all these
careers have one thing in
common: they are seemingly
beyond both his reach and,
in many cases, understanding
and as such, his only associ
ation can be through the
media of newspapers or tele
vision. The police, however,
will always require the ser
vices of the grass, the
squealer, the snitch, (call
him what you will), in order
to assist in their investiga
tions and arrests; and amaz
ingly, this is the area that
seldom gets written about."

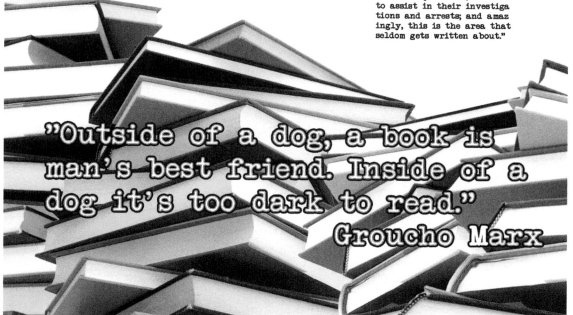

"Outside of a dog, a book is
man's best friend. Inside of a
dog it's too dark to read."
Groucho Marx

Bill Harkleroad joined Captain Beef heart's Magic Band at a time when they were changing from a straight ahead blues band into something completely dif ferent. Through the vision of Don Van Vliet (Captain Beefheart) they created a new form of music which many at the time considered atonal and difficult, but which over the years has continued to exert a powerful influence. Beefheart re christened Harkleroad as Zoot Horn Rollo, and they embarked on recording one of the classic rock albums of all time Trout Mask Replica - a work of unequalled daring and inventiveness.

Politics, paganism and …. Vlad the Impaler. Selected stories from CJ Stone from 2003 to the present. Meet Ivor Coles, a British Tommy killed in action in September 1915, lost, and then found again. Visit Mothers Club in Erdington, the best psyche delic music club in the UK in the '60s. Celebrate Robin Hood's Day and find out what a huckle duckle is. Travel to Stonehenge at the Summer Solstice and carouse with the hippies. Find out what a Ranter is, and why CJ Stone thinks that he's one. Take LSD with Dr Lilly, the psychedelic scientist. Meet a headless soldier or the ghost of Elvis Presley in Gabalfa, Cardiff. Journey to Whitstable, to New York, to Malta and to Transylvania, and to many other places, real and imagined, polit ical and spiritual, transcendent and mundane. As The Independent says, Chris is "The best guide to the underground since Charon ferried dead souls across the Styx."

This is is the first in the highly acclaimed vampire novels of the late Mick Farren. Victor Renquist, a surprisingly urbane and likable leader of a colony of vampires which has existed for centuries in New York is faced with both admin istrative and emotional prob lems. And when you are a vampire, administration is not a thing which one takes lightly.

"The person, be it gentleman or lady, who has not pleasure in a good novel, must be intolerably stupid."

Jane Austen

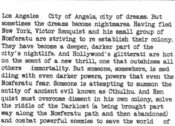

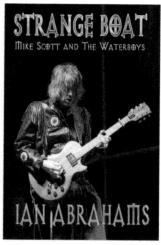

Los Angeles City of Angels, city of dreams. But sometimes the dreams become nightmares. Having fled New York, Victor Renquist and his small group of Nosferatu are striving to re establish their colony. They have become a deeper, darker part of the city's nightlife. And Hollywood's glitterati are hot on the scent of a new thrill, one that outshines all others immortality. But someone, somewhere, is med dling with even darker powers, powers that even the Nosferatu fear. Someone is attempting to summon the entity of ancient evil known as Cthulhu. And Ren quist must overcome dissent in his own colony, solve the riddle of the Darklost (a being brought part way along the Nosferatu path and then abandoned) and combat powerful enemies to save the world of humans!

Canadian born Corky Laing is probably best known as the drummer with Mountain. Corky joined the band shortly after Mountain played at the famous Woodstock Festival, although he did receive a gold disc for sales of the soundtrack album after over dubbing drums on Ten Years After's performance. Whilst with Mountain Corky Laing recorded three studio albums with them before the band split. Follow ing the split Corky, along with Mountain gui tarist Leslie West, formed a rock three piece with former Cream bassist Jack Bruce. West, Bruce and Laing recorded two studio albums and a live album before West and Laing re formed Mountain, along with Felix Pappalardi. Since 1974 Corky and Leslie have led Mountain through various line ups and recordings, and continue to record and perform today at numer ous concerts across the world. In addition to his work with Mountain, Corky Laing has recorded one solo album and formed the band Cork with former Spin Doctors guitarist Eric Shenkman, and recorded a further two studio albums with the band, which has also featured former Jimi Hendrix bassist Noel Redding. The stories are told in an incredibly frank, engaging and amusing manner, and will appeal also to those people who may not necessarily be fans of

To me there's no difference between Mike Scott and The Waterboys; they both mean the same thing. They mean myself and whoever are my current travel ling musical companions" Mike Scott Strange Boat charts the twisting and meandering journey of Mike Scott, describing the literary and spiritual references that inform his songwriting and explor ing the multitude of locations and cultures in which The Waterboys have assembled and reflected in their recordings. From his early forays into the music scene in Scotland at the end of the 1970s, to his creation of a 'Big Music' that peaked with the hit single 'The Whole of the Moon' and onto the Irish adventure which spawned the classic Fisher man's Blues, his constantly restless creativity has led him through a myriad of changes. With his revolving cast of troubadours at his side, he's created some of the most era defining records of the 1980s, reeled and jigged across the Celtic heartlands, reinvented himself as an electric rocker in New York, and sought out personal renewal in the spiritual calm of Findhorn's Scot tish highland retreat. Mike Scott's life has been a tale of continual musical exploration entwined with an ever evolving spirituality. "An intriguing portrait of a modern musician" (Record Collector).

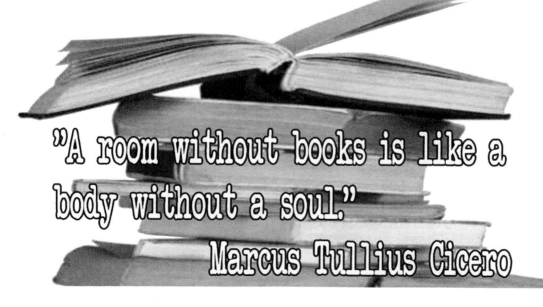

"A room without books is like a body without a soul."
Marcus Tullius Cicero

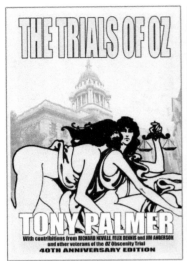

The OZ trial was the longest obscenity trial in history. It was also one of the worst reported. With minor exceptions, the Press chose to rewrite what had occurred, presumably to fit in with what seemed to them the acceptable prejudices of the times. Perhaps this was inevitable. The proceedings dragged on for nearly six weeks in the hot summer of 1971 when there were, no doubt, a great many other events more worthy of attention. Against the background of murder in Ulster, for example, the OZ affair probably fades into its proper insignifi cance. Even so, after the trial, when some newspapers realised that maybe something important had hap pened, it became more and more apparent that what was essential was for anyone who wished to be able to read what had actually been said. Trial and judgment by a badly informed press became the order of the day. This 40th Anniversary edition includes new material by all three of the original defendants, the prosecuting barrister, one of the OZ schoolkids, and even the daughters of the judge. There are also many illustrations including unseen material from Feliz Dennis' own collection...

Merrell Fankhauser has led one of the most diverse and interesting careers in music. He was born in Louisville, Kentucky, and moved to California when he was 13 years old. Merrell went on to become one of the innovators of surf music and psychedelic folk rock. His travels from Hollywood to his 15 year jungle experience on the island of Maui have been documented in numerous music books and magazines in the United States and Europe. Merrell has gained legendary international status throughout the field of rock music; his credits include over 250 songs published and released. He is a multi talented singer/songwriter and unique guitar player whose sound has delighted listeners for over 35 years. This extraordi nary book tells a unique story of one of the founding fathers of surf rock, who went on to play in a succession of progressive and psychedelic bands and to meet some of the greatest names in the business, including Captain Beefheart, Randy California, The Beach Boys, Jan and Dean... and there is even a run in with the notorious Manson family.

On September 19, 1985, Frank Zappa testified before the United States Senate Commerce, Technology, and Transportation committee, attacking the Parents Music Resource Center or PMRC, a music organization co founded by Tipper Gore, wife of then senator Al Gore. The PMRC consisted of many wives of politi cians, including the wives of five members of the committee, and was founded to address the issue of song lyrics with sexual or satanic content. Zappa saw their activities as on a path towards censor ship,and called their proposal for voluntary labelling of records with explicit content "extor tion" of the music industry. This is what happened.

"Good friends, good books, and a sleepy conscience: this is the ideal life."
Mark Twain

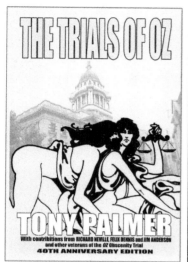

The OZ trial was the longest obscenity trial in history. It was also one of the worst reported. With minor exceptions, the Press chose to rewrite what had occurred, presumably to fit in with what seemed to them the acceptable prejudices of the times. Perhaps this was inevitable. The proceedings dragged on for nearly six weeks in the hot summer of 1971 when there were, no doubt, a great many other events more worthy of attention. Against the background of murder in Ulster, for example, the OZ affair probably fades into its proper insignificance. Even so, after the trial, when some newspapers realised that maybe something important had happened, it became more and more apparent that what was essential was for anyone who wished to be able to read what had actually been said. Trial and judgment by a badly informed press became the order of the day. This 40th Anniversary edition includes new material by all three of the original defendants, the prosecuting barrister, one of the OZ schoolkids, and even the daughters of the judge. There are also many illustrations including unseen material from Felix Dennis' own collection...

Merrell Fankhauser has led one of the most diverse and interesting careers in music. He was born in Louisville, Kentucky, and moved to California when he was 13 years old. Merrell went on to become one of the innovators of surf music and psychedelic folk rock. His travels from Hollywood to his 15 year jungle experience on the island of Maui have been documented in numerous music books and magazines in the United States and Europe. Merrell has gained legendary international status throughout the field of rock music; his credits include over 250 songs published and released. He is a multi talented singer/songwriter and unique guitar player whose sound has delighted listeners for over 35 years. This extraordinary book tells a unique story of one of the founding fathers of surf rock, who went on to play in a succession of progressive and psychedelic bands and to meet some of the greatest names in the business, including Captain Beefheart, Randy California, The Beach Boys, Jan and Dean... and there is even a run in with the notorious Manson family.

On September 19, 1985, Frank Zappa testified before the United States Senate Commerce, Technology, and Transportation committee, attacking the Parents Music Resource Center or PMRC, a music organization co founded by Tipper Gore, wife of then senator Al Gore. The PMRC consisted of many wives of politicians, including the wives of five members of the committee, and was founded to address the issue of song lyrics with sexual or satanic content. Zappa saw their activities as on a path towards censorship and called their proposal for voluntary labelling of records with explicit content "extortion" of the music industry. This is what happened.

"Good friends, good books, and a sleepy conscience: this is the ideal life."
Mark Twain

Lightning Source UK Ltd.
Milton Keynes UK
UKOW07f1534301117
313632UK00003B/38/P

9 781908 728630